D1460254

media studies for GCSE

PETER WALL
SEG CHIEF
EXAMINER

and

PAUL WALKER

Collins Educational
An Imprint of HarperCollinsPublishers

Published by Collins Educational, 77-85 Fulham Palace Road, London W6 8JB

An imprint of HarperCollins*Publishers*

© Copyright 1997 text Peter Wall and Paul Walker

First published 1997

ISBN 000 323065 1

Peter Wall and Paul Walker assert the moral right to be identified as the authors of the text.

All rights reserved. No part of this book may be reproduced or transmitted, in any form or by any means, without prior permission of the publisher.

Acknowledgements

Dedications

For my family – Paul

With grateful thanks to all who have helped in the making of this book – Pete

The following permissions to reproduce material are gratefully acknowledged. Numbers refer to pages.

Illustrations Parfums Yves Saint Laurent Ltd (3); cover of *Esquire* magazine courtesy of The National Magazine Company Ltd (5); cover of *GQ* magazine courtesy of *GQ*, Condé Nast Publications Ltd (5); Clinton Banbury (7, 31, 63, 65, 178 bottom, 181, 191, 197, 201, 214, 226, 229, 236, 239); Gay Galsworthy (9, 36, 58); Telegraph Colour Library (10, 135, 223); Rex Features Ltd (11 top left, 162); models Sarah Maltravers & Jason Bailey, MOT Model Agency, photograph by John Wallace (11 top right); Scottish Widows (11 bottom left); Steve Pyke/Katz Pictures Ltd (11 bottom right); *Daily Mail* (13); Debbie Clark (15, 33, 215, 219, 227); Tony Stone, Bruce Ayres (17 top); Tony Stone, Zigy Kaluzny (17 middle); Tony Stone, David S. Robbins (17 bottom); Corbis-Bettman (20); Steadicam is a registered trademark of Cinema Products Corporation, Los Angeles, CA, USA (21 top); David Hoffman (21 bottom); Tony Stone, Nicholas Parfitt (22); photo © AKG London (24); Corbis/Everett Collection (25); Capespan UK Ltd (28); Central Broadcasting (30); Famous (34 left, 35 top left, 167 left); Monitor Syndication (34 right, 35 top middle); Famous, Fred Duval (35 top right, 46 right, 124 bottom right); Famous, Rob Howard (35 bottom, 167 middle and right, 175 left); Guy Smith, Mainline Design (40); *When Saturday Comes* (41); Mike Moran (45, 57); Famous, Kurt Krieger (46 left, 166); Famous, Hubert Boesl (46 middle, 175 right); National Viewers' and Listeners' Association (59 middle); *Sugar* (59 bottom); British Board of Film Classification (60); HarperCollins*Publishers* (43 left, 61 top, 127, 159, 205 bottom left); Independent Television Commission (61 bottom); Advertising Standards Authority (62, 206); Harry Venning (64, 74, 128, 149); Broadcasters' Audience Research Board Ltd (67); Radio Joint Audience Research Ltd (68 top); National Readership Surveys Ltd (68 bottom); Mark Doman (p78, 80, 81, 82, 85, 86, 88, 91, 93, 95, 98, 99, 100, 103, 106, 139, 142, 170, 171, 172, 176); Sky News (89); Calendar (104); Tom Cross (109, 222); BFI Stills, Posters and Designs, (110, 111, 117, 158); Blockbusters (114); Comet (116 top left); Cinemania (116 top right); Musical Images (116 bottom right); Moviestore Collection (119, 121, 124 left); courtesy of W. Steenbeck & Co. (122); BFI Stills, Posters and Designs and Yves Coatsaliou (124 top right); *Sight and Sound* (126 top left); *Film Review* (126 top right); Innes Photographers (130); *Evening Standard* (131 top left); *Daily Record* (131 top right); *West Wales Mercury* (131 bottom left); *Brighton and Hove Leader* (131 bottom right); © Times Newspapers Ltd, 1959 (133); *Daily Mirror* (143); Courtesy of Sheffield Newspapers Ltd (145, 198, 199, 200); *Flashing Blade* (148); D. C. Thomson & Co. Ltd (153 top and middle); William Tucci and *Shi* (154); Martin Salisbury (156 top left); Peter Dennis (156 top right); Terry McKenna (156 bottom left and right); Hulton Getty (160, 187, 189 bottom); Sony Music Entertainment (UK) Ltd (164); Popperfoto (165); Concrete Recordings, Ian Watson, Piers Allardyce, Martin James and *Melody Maker* (169); Chart Information Network and *Melody Maker* (174); *Melody Maker* (177); *New Musical Express* (177); *Mojo* (177); *Blah* (177); Smash Hits (177); *Line Dance UK!* (178); Sony UK Ltd (180); Future Publishing (cover of *Classic CD*) (178); Argos Distributors Ltd (182); Swansea Sound (184); Scot FM (184); Cool FM (184); Sanyo (184 bottom, 187); Adrian Cook (189 top); Radio Authority (190); Classic FM (191); Virgin Radio (191); Talk Radio (191); Cheshire Building Society (198); NCH Action for Children (203); Niall McInerney (205 top); Storm advertisement December 1996 (designer Anita Darke, company Sun 99 Ltd) (205 bottom middle); Studio Massimo (205 bottom right); Ocean (208 top); Jamaica Tourist Board (208 bottom left); City Ballet of London (208 bottom middle); Fila UK Ltd (208 bottom right); House of *Viz*/John Brown Publishing 1996 (212); *Time Out* (213); Panasonic Business Systems UK (218); Sony UK Ltd (220); MCA and BFI Stills, Posters & Designs (245)

Text extracts *Evening Standard* (38); *The Big Issue* (42 left); Highbury House Communications (42 middle); *TV Quick* (42 right, 52); ITN (43 right); Rex Features Ltd (50); Press Complaints Commission (54-55); Broadcasters Audience Research Board (67); Today, Nicki Pope (70); *Daily Mirror*, Jack Bell (76); Calendar (92, 93, 94); Columbia (96); Greenpeace (97); © *The Guardian*, Kevin Berry (113); *The News of the World*, Rex Features Ltd and Dave Hogan (123); *Marie Claire* November 1996 issue (126 bottom left); *What's On TV?* (163); *Satellite Times* (185, 186); Radio Authority (193, 194); Southern Examining Group (240, 243, 246)

We wish to acknowledge the help of Fujifilm with this book.

Whilst every effort has been made to contact the copyright holders, this has not proved possible in every case.

Design by Wendi Watson
Cover design by Nigel Wright, XAB
Commissioning editor: Domenica de Rosa
Editors: Helen Clark, Kim Richardson

Production: Susan Cashin
Picture research: Katie Anderson
Printed and bound by Scotprint Ltd, Musselburgh

CONTENTS

1. WHY MEDIA STUDIES?

The media: monster or angel?

There is a powerful force sending its messages to virtually everyone on earth. It is using every form of communication tool available. It is in your sitting room, your bedroom, maybe even your bathroom. It is in shops, cinemas, libraries and churches. It travels in cars, on buses, trains, planes and ships. Even if you blast off into space it is out there waiting for you. No matter how hard you try, you cannot escape it.

The name of this force is 'the media' and, whether you like it or not, to a large extent it defines your life and the way you think. 'The media' is the name given to the channels of communication a society uses speak to itself. It includes television, cinema, video, radio, newspapers, magazines, books and computers. Really, it is a mass of individual contact points between communication tools and human beings.

It is difficult to visualize this, however, and most people speak about the media as if it were a single being with a personality of its own. It has been portrayed more as a monster than as an angel. Television has been criticized for luring schoolchildren away from their homework. Videos have been accused of encouraging violence and drug abuse; newspapers and magazines of filling our heads with gossip; and computer games of turning us into goggle-eyed morons. Whatever the problem, it seems the media is in part to blame.

However, television has brought information and learning to millions of people, with satellite broadcasting allowing us to experience history as it happens. Videos are widely used as teaching aids in schools and colleges. Radio supplies a lifeline for those cut off from the outside world. Magazines and newspapers provide knowledge as well as entertainment, while computers present us with an information superhighway that makes worldwide communication possible.

Is the media a good or bad thing? As we have seen, the media is not one 'thing', but a large number of interactions between individual receivers and specific media products, or texts; so really, the question is meaningless. Also, judgements about what is 'good' or 'bad' tend to differ between individuals, groups and societies over time. A more

PRESS CLIPPINGS

Collect stories from the press that focus on the positive and negative roles that the media is seen to play in our society. What views of the media can be seen in the clippings? Do you agree with the views put forward in the stories?

helpful approach is to examine media products and ask how they are made, what they contain and what receivers make of them. In doing this, we can begin to understand the massive part media products play in modern life.

Stop press...
Stop press...
Stop press...

Group discussion
Do videos encourage violence?

Media focus

Look at the advertisement for men's perfume, taken from a glossy lifestyle magazine. It is made up of a black-and-white photograph of two men in sharp suits. One of them has his arm around a woman in a chic outfit. They are walking along a street between skyscrapers. A picture of the perfume bottle, which resembles the skyscrapers in its shape, is positioned over the main photograph. Nearly all the writing in the advert is in French.

C'EST SI BON D'ÊTRE JAZZ

JAZZ

EAU DE TOILETTE

YVESSAINTLAURENT

YVESSAINTLAURENT

COMMENT

Group discussion
What does this advertisement tell us about the media and about society?

Think about:
• The appearance of the people
• The words (NB it is an English-language magazine)
• The context of the advert (in a men's magazine)
• What the perfume might be like.

Analysis

The advert was taken from a men's lifestyle magazine. Such magazines only started to become successful in the early 1990s. The rise of men's magazines could reflect a change in the habits of men, who are now paying more attention to their appearance, health and relationships. On the other hand, it could be an attempt made by magazine publishers to exploit a new sector of the market.

GROUP DISCUSSION

■ What is 'lifestyle'?

■ What is a 'lifestyle magazine'?

■ Why are men's magazines unusual?

■ Look at the cover of a men's lifestyle magazine such as the ones on the page opposite. How does it tie in with what we have learnt about the advert?

The men in the advertisement are obviously successful. The setting suggests that they work in the city and have enough money to buy smart clothes. The fact that one of them has his arm around a woman also implies that their success makes them attractive to the opposite sex. The message of the advert is that the perfume is part of these men's prosperous lifestyle. The use of French in an English-language magazine adds an air of sophistication that marks out the perfume. The advertisement uses images to convey a message, in order to sell the product to the readers of the magazine. We can see that the media plays an important role in the economy of our society through its ability to persuade people to buy goods and services. The advertisement tells us that success in our society is measured in terms of a well-paid job, good clothes and sexual attractiveness. The magazine's readers receive the message that to be successful, today's man needs to be well-groomed.

Think about what the advertisers are trying to sell – a smell. There is no description at all of how the perfume actually smells. In fact, a smell is simply a smell. All the images in the advert and the meanings they aim to create have been linked with the perfume by the advertisers.

In pairs

• Do you think men will buy Jazz?
• Is the advert effective, or will readers see straight through the hype?
• Can a smell give you all the things that the advertisement appears to promise?

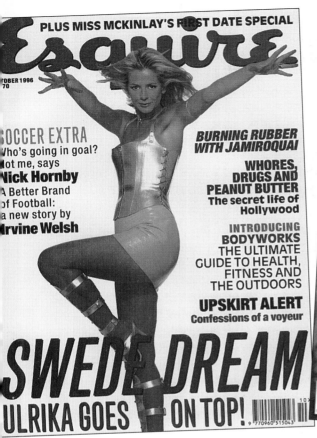

Key concepts

In a brief examination of one advertisement, we have drawn out themes and issues that are important to an understanding of the media and the society that it reflects and creates. In GCSE we are concerned with the key concepts of **language**, **representation**, **institutions** and **audience**. Looking at these ideas can help us to understand the media and the part it plays in our lives.

In looking at **language**, we explore the words and images that the media uses to communicate with its users. In adverts, these are chosen with a great deal of thought. Think about the words used in the advert for Jazz. To start with, there are very few of them and most of them are French. The magazine the advertisement appears in is in English. In the United Kingdom, French is often seen as the language of romance, sophistication and mystery. By using French, the advertisers are saying to the potential buyer 'our perfume has these qualities. You too can have them by wearing it.' In this way, French is used as a kind of code to convey a 'secret' message to the reader. Throughout this book, we will be helping you to develop the skills necessary to understand or decode media language and describe its use.

Representation is the way the media portrays individuals, groups, events and issues. In the perfume advert we see three people: two clean-shaven men with stylish haircuts, wearing expensive-looking clothes, and a perfectly made-up woman in a designer suit. The way they are shown has been designed to give a message about the product. The advertisement suggests that the type of person who wears Jazz is successful and happy, with money to spend on looking and smelling 'good'. The producers of the advert have chosen to present this image. They did not use a picture of someone in worn-out clothes, begging for money on the street. This is because in our society this would not be a 'good' image for the product.

In GCSE we look at the **institutions**, or organizations, that produce media products. The Jazz advertisement did not appear in the magazine by chance. It was produced by someone on behalf of the company that makes the perfume. The advert appeared in a magazine published by a large company that produces many other periodicals. The magazine market is dominated by a few big publishers. In GCSE we ask what effects this has on the range of magazines on the shelves of our newsagents, and how difficult it is to produce new ones presenting alternative views. We look at who owns media organizations, how they make their money, how they produce their products, what laws they have to obey and how they go about selling their products to an audience.

The media cannot survive without an **audience** – the people who watch, listen or read. This should be taken into account when studying its products. The advert would be useless if no one actually saw it, and to see it, people have to read the magazine.

ADVERT

Using a computer or art materials, produce an advertisement for a perfume to be used by both men and women. What sort of person are you trying to sell the perfume to? How will you persuade them to buy it?

CLASS DISCUSSION

■ How can the perfume makers be sure that the people they think will buy their perfume will actually see their advertisement?

■ How can the publishers of the magazine judge what their readers want? Or do they assume the readers will want what they give them?

■ Who might be interested in reading a men's lifestyle magazine, and why?

You and the media
Now you can look at your own involvement with the media by having a go at the tasks on the opposite page.

1 Media journal

So how big a part does the media play in your life? Over the next week keep a diary of when, where and for how long you come into contact with media products.
Note down:
* What you watch on television or video
* Radio stations you listen to
* Tapes and CDs you play
* Newspapers and magazines you read
* Computer packages you use.

Record not only the media products that you choose to use, but also those that you see and hear around you, for example:
* Adverts on billboards, buses and trains
* Music in shops
* Videos in shopping centres
* Magazines in waiting rooms.

How much time in total have you spent in contact with the media during the week?

2 Analysis

After completing your diary, compare it with those of other students and note the differences.
* What is your reaction to the amount of time you spend in contact with the media?
* Why do you use the media in the way you do?

3 Who does what?

'Mam, I'm bored!'

Make a note of the electrical media products you have at home, for example:
* Televisions
* Video recorders
* Radios
* CD and tape players
* Computers.

In pairs, discuss the following questions:
* Who are the main users of each product?
* Who controls their use?
* Do conflicts arise over their use?

2. LANGUAGE

Aspects of language

Visual language

When you hear the word 'language', you will probably automatically think of words, either spoken or written. Words are an important means of communication between human beings. But the media does not communicate with words alone. It also uses pictures and sounds to convey meaning. Indeed, some media work mainly in a visual language, through pictures that you look at and understand in the same way that you hear or look at words and try to make sense of them.

You sometimes hear people say we live in a media-saturated society. They mean that everywhere you look, words and images are fighting for your attention and bombarding you with messages. But with so much information overload, how much do you really take in?

Photography is an example of a visual medium, or one that relies for its impact on images. Film and television are also visual media, although both use words and sounds as well to communicate information. Print-based media, such as newspapers, magazines and comics, employ a combination of printed words and pictures, such as photographs, drawings and graphics, to give you information. Radio, on the other hand, is obviously a medium that relies on sound, or an aural medium, which relies on words and other sounds to communicate. However, pop music, which makes up a large part of many radio stations' output, carries with it a lot of visual images in the form of pictures of the bands and CD cover designs, for example.

As small children you learn how to use language. For one thing, it helps you let other people know what you want. Of course, the vocabulary that you learn will depend on the culture in which you grow up. The words learnt by French children for describing the world are different from those learnt by children in the UK. As you grow up, you also learn to understand visual signs. No one sits down with you and explains how to watch television. Simply by repeatedly watching TV, you learn how to make sense of the two-dimensional pictures on the screen in relation to the three-dimensional world in which you live. Of course, you also learn to make sense of the various short cuts that a visual medium, such as TV, uses to tell you a story more quickly. For example, if a character is shown leaving a room and is seen in the next shot driving a car, the viewer fills in the missing sequence in their imagination and understands that the character has left the house, got into the car and set off.

You learn to fill in the missing information needed to make sense of the narrative.

In the same way that you learn to read words on a page, so you learn to read visual language. The idea of 'reading' is important in Media Studies. When you read a book, you use your imagination to create pictures in your head; you bring something of yourself to the book by working on it in your mind. Similarly, if you apply the idea of reading to television, it suggests that you are active in bringing something of yourself to it. Just as you use your imagination to fill in the missing parts of a visual narrative to make sense of what has happened, you learn to read other elements of visual language. However, the way in which you read an image or set of images may well be decided by your upbringing and previous experiences.

Not everyone who watches a set of images on the television will take from them the same meaning. For example, an advertisement that uses an attractive young woman to sell a product may well have a positive impact on many men in the audience. Female viewers with strong opinions about the way in which women's bodies are exploited by the media are likely to read the advertisement very differently.

Similarly, a cookery programme featuring recipes for cooking pork chops would have little appeal to vegetarians or members of certain religious groups. In fact, many of them will turn off such a programme on the grounds that it is offensive.

GROUP DISCUSSION
Are men offended if their bodies are used to sell products?

In most media, words and pictures work together to create meaning. Very often words can be used to limit or anchor the meaning of a visual image. In newspapers, photographs have captions that tell the reader how to read or interpret the images. On news bulletins, newsreaders or reporters talk over images to explain what is happening, which guides the viewers' interpretation of the meaning of the images they see. This process is called 'anchorage'. Just as the anchor of a ship is used to hold it in one place, so the words in a caption or commentary are used to hold or limit the meaning of an image.

CAPTION COMPETITION

Choose some images from newspapers and magazines, complete with their original captions. Think up new captions for these images, which will change their meaning as much as possible.

• Is it more difficult to change the meaning of some images than of others?
• If so, why is this?

Denotation and connotation

Both words and images, it is argued, work on at least two levels:

Denotation: The common-sense or everyday meaning of a sign. A red rose is a garden plant. That is its denotational meaning.

Connotation: The additional or associated meaning that an image or word carries with it over and above its ordinary, everyday meaning. A red rose is a symbol of love. If you give someone a red rose, they are unlikely to think you are simply handing over a garden plant. For someone who lives in Lancashire, it is also the symbol that represents their county.

When you read a TV programme, magazine or film, your understanding of these texts relies on your ability to respond to both these layers of meaning at the same time.

Models Sarah Maltravers and Jason Bailey, MOT Model Agency.
Photograph by John Wallace.

MEANINGS

Working in pairs, look carefully at each image. What is its:
•Denotational meaning
•Connotational meaning?

Use each pair's work as the basis of a class discussion on the meanings of the images. Does everyone think they mean the same thing?

Texts

The term 'media text' refers to any product of the media, for example, a magazine article or quiz show. The word 'text' has important connotations when it is used in an educational context. Because English Literature has been such an important part of the curriculum for many years, the word 'text' is often associated with literary texts. Texts are the books that you may study as part of your English course. Often these will be the classics of English literature, which represent high levels of achievement by great writers. *Hamlet*, *Pride and Prejudice*, *Wuthering Heights* and *Great Expectations* are texts in this sense. Because of this connotation of the word 'text', calling a quiz show a text may seem a little strange. Some people would argue that a quiz show is trivial compared to the great classics of English literature. But this concept of a media text is important. Just as the classics of English literature are studied, so you study and analyse a soap opera in order to learn about the society in which you live. If that idea seems a little silly, then remember that in his lifetime, Shakespeare's plays may have been performed in pubs, with people of all social classes crowding in to watch them. It is now a common idea that Shakespeare is of interest only to an élite, but this was certainly not true when the plays were first written. This is not to suggest that *Coronation Street* or *Neighbours* will one day have the importance of *Othello* or *Silas Marner*. The argument is that by studying these texts we can learn a lot about the lives and culture of the people who consume them.

CLASS DISCUSSION

Imagine you are in a Media Studies class in your school or college in the year 2500. Your teacher brings in an episode of *Neighbours* and the front page of *The Sun* newspaper from 1997.

- What do you think the class would make of it?
- What impression would the class get of life at the end of the 20th century?
- Do you think it would be an accurate impression?

The argument can be taken one step further: that the more texts you study, the better you become at reading them. For example, if you were to go to the ballet for the first time, you might find it hard to understand what it was all about. People who go to the ballet regularly would have learned the codes and conventions that ballet uses and, in most cases, would easily follow what was going on. The same is true of people who go to the cinema regularly; they are likely to be very good at reading films. They may spot jokes, for instance, in the references one film makes to another, that those who go to the cinema less often would probably miss.

As you can see, the words 'read' and 'text' themselves have important connotations. In the chapter on audience (see pages 58–75), the way the media affects people is discussed. The word 'read' implies a reader who is actively involved with the text. Just like the reader of a book, readers of other media texts are contributing to the meaning that the text makes, by means of their involvement with it. This is obviously a very different idea from the common picture of the passive TV viewer, who mindlessly consumes whatever images are displayed on the screen.

Codes

To most people, the word 'code' stands for a secret method of communicating, which must be cracked or decoded so that the hidden message can be understood. For example, numbers or symbols may be used instead of the letters of the alphabet; until you work out how to decipher the code, the message will have no meaning. Language itself is a code; words have meanings because everyone who speaks the same language uses them in roughly the same way, to mean roughly the same thing.

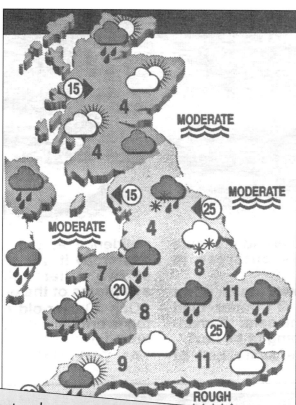

Weather charts, such as you see in a newspaper or on TV, are good examples of a code. If you don't understand how to read the symbols, the chart makes little sense.

CLASS DISCUSSION
- What codes are used on radio?
- When you switch on your radio, can you tell what sort of programme you are listening to?
- Is it easy to tell what sort of station you have switched on?
- If so, what is it that gives you this information?

Each medium has its own code. Once you have learned the code, you can understand the meaning. For example, the music that is played at the beginning of a news bulletin is part of a code. It is serious music that sounds important and calls the viewer to the TV set, in just the same way that a town crier used to ring a bell and shout 'Oyez' to summon an audience to hear an important announcement. There are other codes at work in a news bulletin. Well-spoken, well-dressed people sit behind a desk in a studio and tell the viewers about the world. They introduce other people, tell the viewers what is happening and show them pictures of events that have taken place. Sometimes the viewer can hear only their voices and at other times they talk directly to the viewer. All these are codes that TV news uses to communicate with the viewers. These codes come together to form a convention, or an accepted way of doing things that people are used to and have learned to recognize. There is a convention that the news appears at fixed times every day and that certain people will present it in a specific way. Because of these conventions, if you switch on your TV set half-way through the news, you don't think you are watching a quiz show. We will look further at these concepts later in this chapter under the heading of genre (see pages 27–29).

Image analysis

Making an image

The study of how images are put together, and how the audience takes meaning from them, is called image analysis. The factors that affect still photographs also apply to moving images on film or television. Imagine that a friend has asked you to take their photograph. Before you take the photo, there are a number of decisions you will have to make.

Shots One important decision is how large you want the subject to be relative to the frame. The size of an image within the frame has various technical names according to how close the camera is to the subject:

The long shot (LS) shows the subject in their environment or context. The subject takes up only a small amount of the frame. In film and TV this is sometimes called an establishing shot, because it establishes where a character is. An establishing shot is often used at the beginning of a sequence to give the audience an idea of the setting or context the character is in.

The medium shot (MS) usually shows the top half of someone's body. A roughly equal amount of the frame is given to the subject and the setting. This shot is commonly used when TV reporters are speaking to the camera, for example, outside 10 Downing Street, so that both the reporter and the setting are noticeable.

The close-up shot (CU) shows head and shoulders. The subject fills most of the screen and you can see a great deal of detail on his or her face. This is a good shot for showing emotion and creating a strong feeling of intimacy with the subject.

The big close-up (BCU) shows the face of the subject filling the whole of the frame. This is a powerful shot for showing strong feelings, such as someone in tears.

Point-of-view shot – see the section on point of view (pages 20–21).

| LS | MS | CU | BCU |

On storyboards, the names of these shots are usually abbreviated.

On your own

Collect some examples of photographs from newspapers and magazines, or maybe a photo of yourself on holiday. For each photo, identify what type of shot is being used and the angle from which it was taken. Try to work out why the photographer has chosen to shoot the image this way.

The movie camera is often viewed as an all-seeing eye, which observes without being observed. It is able to follow the action wherever it takes place. It can stalk people, following them without their knowledge, as well as peeping through windows. For moving images, the fact that the camera can move, as well as the subject, allows the creation of images that are more complex and dynamic. Two shots that enable it to do this are:

The pan, in which the camera moves horizontally, either following a piece of action, or shifting across from one image to another, as though making a survey of a scene.

The zoom, where the camera zooms in from a long shot to a big close-up. This shot shows the power of the camera, which controls the action within the frame by moving in to inspect what is going on.

These effects show that the camera can control the action within the frame, either by holding an image as it moves, or by seeking out subjects who are part of the action.

Angle Another decision that you will have to make before you take your photograph is the angle of the camera.

- You may have noticed that images are usually shot at eye-level, so that the camera and the subject are on the same level. This creates a feeling that the viewer is equal with the subject.
- A high-angle shot allows the viewer to look down on the subject, which gives a sense of superiority.
- A low-angle shot has the opposite effect. The viewer is invited to look up at the subject, which may make the viewer feel uncomfortable or dominated.

Other factors Several other factors also influence each shot:

Setting: Where will the photograph be taken – in a back garden, in the street or in a studio? The setting of the photograph will influence how it is interpreted. In film-making, it is very important to sort out the setting, decide what will take place in front of the camera and how it will be shot. These considerations are known as the mise-en-scène.

Framing: Once you have decided on the setting, the next job is to frame the shot. This means you have to decide how your subject will be positioned within the photograph. You do this by looking through the viewfinder until you get the best image for your purpose.

Focus: Is everything sharply in focus, or are some parts of the image blurred? If so, is the blurring deliberate?

Colour: Is the photograph in colour or black and white? Are there reasons for this choice? If the photo is in colour, what sort of colours are most obvious: bright colours or duller ones? Do the colours blend well together?

Lighting: How is the image lit? Is natural light used, or artificial light, such as from a flashgun? Backlighting, where the chief source of light is from behind the central figure, can have a strong impact, as can sidelighting.

Pose and body language: How are the figures displayed within the frame? Are they posed, or do they look natural? Have they been caught in action, or lined up for the camera?

Composition: How have the different elements that make up the photo been put together? When you look at a photograph, think about where you look first. Where is your eye led? Is it drawn to the most important detail in the photograph? If there is a group of people, who seems to be the most important one?

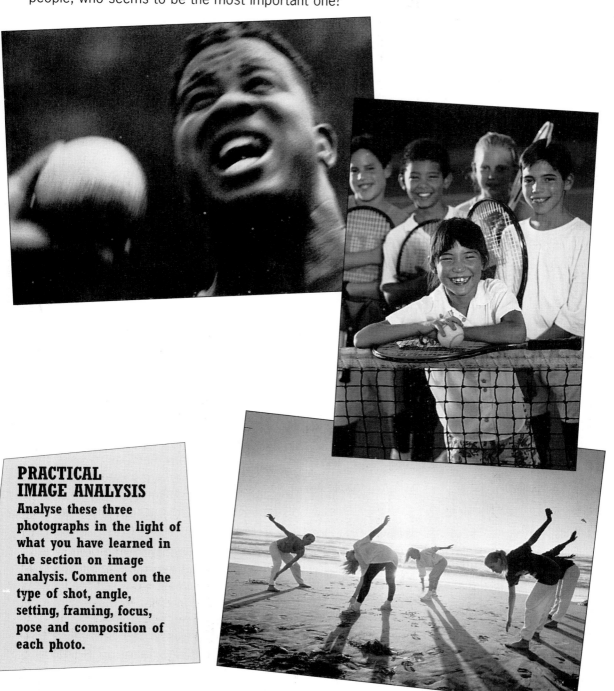

PRACTICAL IMAGE ANALYSIS

Analyse these three photographs in the light of what you have learned in the section on image analysis. Comment on the type of shot, angle, setting, framing, focus, pose and composition of each photo.

Editing

If you are making a film or video, another series of decisions has to be made once the images have been recorded. This is called editing, which is the process of putting the images together into a logical sequence. An editor links the scenes together using a range of devices for shifting the viewer's attention from one scene to another.

The cut is where one scene ends and another scene begins immediately. This is probably the most frequently used of all the edits. An audience is likely to read this device to mean that the action is taking place in a normal time sequence, or that one scene follows on logically from another.

The fade is where the picture slowly disappears until the screen is blank (usually black). After a fade, a new scene may be started by fading up, which is when an image slowly appears from a blank screen. An audience might read this device to mean that a period of time has passed in between the two scenes. Often a shot that finishes in the evening will be followed by one that fades up the next morning, for example.

The dissolve is where one scene gradually fades out as a new scene fades in. It is possible to freeze these images on a video recorder and see both scenes mixed into a single frame in the middle of a dissolve. This device is another method of showing that time has passed, or that people have moved on, say, in a journey. The dissolve is also commonly used when landscape images, such as a misty morning, are set to music to give gentle, romantic views of the countryside, for example.

The wipe is where a new scene wipes over the existing scene from one side of the screen to the other. This kind of edit sharply shifts the viewer's attention from one scene to another. It is especially effective at suggesting that parallel action is taking place elsewhere. Technology has enabled film and TV programme makers to produce a whole series of more elaborate methods of switching scenes, many of which are based on the wipe, for example, a scene folding up and disappearing into the ear of a character in the next scene.

This section has concentrated on how photographs and moving images have codes and conventions, which the viewer learns to read in order to make sense of them. Obviously, this is also true of other media forms. The case study on newspapers (see pages 129–145) looks at how page layout works as a code that suggests to the reader how to read the page.

Activity

Look carefully at the first two or three minutes of any film, video or television programme.

- What type of edits are used to join the different shots and scenes together?
- Are all of the edits the same type, or are different ones used?
- How does the editing influence the audience's expectations about the programme that is to follow?

Narratives

Words and pictures are often combined in media texts in order to create narratives. Narratives are basically stories. From our earliest years, we enjoy narratives, whether in the form of a story told at bedtime to send us off to sleep, or a story told to our class at the end of a hard day at primary school. These stories are sometimes offered as a reward for good behaviour, or are withheld as a punishment for being naughty. As we grow up, the link between stories and behaviour is therefore fixed in our minds. Narratives themselves are often about rewards or punishments for the way that people behave.

Narratives are important to people. One reason for this is that they help to make sense of the world. Religious books, for example, are full of stories that attempt to explain the disasters that afflict the human race. The actual number of possible narratives is, however, limited. New stories are uncommon: most narratives are variations on a limited number of timeless themes. The characters and settings may vary, but the structure remains the same.

CLASS DISCUSSION

■ *What are the first narratives that you remember?*
■ *Where did you hear them?*
■ *How did they affect you?*

IN GROUPS

Think about the following structure for a narrative:
1 Boy meets and falls in love with girl
2 Boy loses girl through a misunderstanding, or some accident of fate
3 Boy gets girl back again.

• Now think of examples of how this narrative appears in different forms across a range of media, such as films, soap operas, magazines, tabloid newspapers and pop songs.
• What other narratives are common to many stories? Make a list of the narratives that occur most frequently.
• Do some narratives work better in one particular medium than in others?

Suspense

If stories occur so frequently, why don't people get bored with them? One reason is that narratives take different forms according to their settings and the characters used to tell the story. They do not simply retell a story that has been told many times before: their effects are more complex. An important element in any narrative is suspense, which is the feeling of excitement or anxiety that you have as you wait for something to happen. Suspense is an example of what is called a narrative code. (A narrative code is a way of describing the conventions or elements that the audience has come to expect to be included in a story.) Suspense works by means of a device called an enigma, which is a puzzle or a riddle. A good narrative teases the audience by giving clues about what will happen next, or making the audience try to work out the answer to the puzzle. Murder mysteries and detective stories are

An old-fashioned cliff-hanger.

popular across a range of media (such as films, TV, comics and magazines) because they work by teasing their audience. Cliff-hangers are a key element of soaps. Originally, the term 'cliff-hanger' described the situation when, at the end of an episode, a character, usually the hero, was left literally clinging to the edge of a cliff. Cliff-hangers keep the audience guessing what will happen in the next episode.

Enigmas also play an important role in non-fiction texts. For example, the news begins with headlines, which tease the viewer with information to get them to stay tuned to find out more. Newspaper headlines whet the reader's appetite for the story: they contain teasing clues about the narrative to follow.

Martians turned my son into an olive

Pop star arrested in drugs probe

Body found in burnt-out car

Terror on the 5.04

GOTCHA!

Is there life out there?

Just one for the road

King Rat

HEADLINES

Each member of the class finds a headline from a newspaper or magazine. The rest of the class then guesses what the story is about, or makes up a story to fit the headline.

Point of view

Another aspect of narrative structure is the point of view from which the audience sees the story. Many films and television programmes are about the eternal battle between good and evil.

The audience is usually placed so that it will identify with the good characters and want them to win. In a police series, for example, the viewer is invited to watch the action from the point of view of the police officer, who is trying to solve a crime and put a criminal behind bars for the protection of society.

Narratives are constructed to ensure that most of the audience will respond in a certain way. One way of placing the viewer alongside the hero or good character is to let the audience see what the hero sees. The viewer shares information with the hero. The hero may even speak directly to you through a voice-over, which allows them to share their thoughts and feelings.

Camerawork is important, too. As you watch a film or TV programme, note how often the camera shows you what the hero sees. The camera becomes the hero's eyes and gives the audience the same privileged view as that of the hero. This shot is called a 'point-of-view shot' and is a very important way of positioning the audience alongside a specific character. A device called a Steadicam has been developed, which allows a camera operator to film while moving or even running, and to keep the shot steady. The Steadicam and lightweight video equipment have increased the opportunities for using a point-of-view shot. A programme such as *The Bill* places the audience right alongside the police as they raid houses or chase suspects.

Needless to say, it is not only fictional programmes that tell their story from the viewpoint of one character. When conflict is taking place between the police and the community, the news often shows pictures shot from behind a line of police officers.

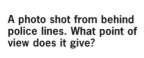

A Steadicam and camera operator.

POINTS OF VIEW
Can you think of any films or TV programmes that show the action from the viewpoint of a character who is operating outside the law?

A photo shot from behind police lines. What point of view does it give?

CLASS DISCUSSION

Notice that the word 'riot' was not used to describe the conflict between the police and the community. If it had been, would it have made a difference to your opinion of the incident? If the police had been described as dealing with 'a mob', would it necessarily be an accurate description of what took place? (Before trying to answer this question, you might like to look at the section on visual language on pages 8-10, which covers the concept of anchorage.)

Conflict

The idea of conflict is important in narratives. Many stories are framed as a fight between two people or two groups. In fiction, this is often depicted as conflict between good and evil. In Westerns, peace-loving communities are frequently threatened by outlaws. The conflict is often resolved by a gunman. Gangster films present a conflict between society and those who flout its laws and values. Narratives based on conflict are found in many unlikely places. Many wildlife programmes are structured as narratives. The plot may rely on conflict between animals that hunt and those that are hunted. The side that the audience supports is often determined by the viewpoint of the group of animals that is 'starring' in the show. In this way, even natural born killers can be presented in a sympathetic light.

In a wildlife programme, an animal can be a hero or a villain, depending on the narrative structure of the film.

The audience is invited to take sides in the conflict, usually supporting the forces of good against those of evil. In the media's coverage of the news, this has important effects, especially in the presentation of stories about politics or international relations. It is often said that the news on television and radio should be unbiased. This means that it should avoid taking sides in a dispute and should simply present the different viewpoints, allowing the audience to form its own opinion. Sporting events on television or in the press require the audience to support one side against the other. In the same way, in responding to the manner in which the news is presented, most people will inevitably take up a position in favour of one viewpoint.

When the UK is at war or in conflict with other countries, the narrative is often told from the viewpoint that the UK is right and its opponents are wrong. Battles are seen from behind British lines, looking towards the enemy. (See the chapter on audience, pages 69–71.) Some people argue that the same is true of industrial disputes. Strikers form part of a narrative in which they are depicted as disruptive forces trying to stop peace-loving people getting on with their lives.

ON YOUR OWN
Make a list of examples from the media in which conflict is a key element in the narrative. For each, explain the position that you think the audience is being invited to take up in relation to each side involved in the conflict.

Motivation

Characters and their motivation are extremely important in narratives. As we have already seen, in narratives the audience is often invited to see the action through the eyes of one particular character. This person is identified as the hero.

CLASS DISCUSSION

How do you know who the main characters in a film or TV programme are? What sort of clues are given at the beginning of a film or television programme about which characters will be important and which will be unimportant?

All the main characters will have a motivation, or a reason for doing something that drives them to achieve their aim. This motivation may take the form of a goal that they set out to achieve. It may be to catch a criminal, to win a person they have fallen for, or maybe just to have a good time. Some characters go in search of themselves, or on a similar quest. These goals may bring them into conflict with other characters, whose goals are in opposition to theirs, for example, a criminal who doesn't want to get caught, a man or woman who doesn't want to be won, or a person who doesn't want the hero to have a good time. Of course, one of the viewer's interests in this narrative is to discover whether or not the hero manages to achieve their goal.

Ideology

We experience narrative from childhood onwards. Narrative also plays a key role in forming our social behaviour and attitudes in later life. There is much debate about the ideas of good and evil, and especially about the question of whose job it is to teach young people about right and wrong. The concepts of good and evil, and right and wrong, are key elements of television programmes, newspapers and even pop music. It is argued that people learn their value system from these media, which decide what is right. They present an ideology, a system of beliefs by which people organize their lives.

An important part of growing up is to learn to see narrative as both a reward and a way of teaching good behaviour. For example, you may learn to believe that if you work hard and don't argue with people in authority, then you will be rewarded. Good behaviour will be rewarded; bad behaviour will be punished. The problem lies in who decides what is good and bad. Many people in authority have a strong interest in encouraging the belief that obedience and respect for people in superior positions is good behaviour. Can you trust the people who control the media to work in your best interests?

In Nazi Germany in the 1930s, the media was used as a powerful instrument of propaganda. Among other devices, it used narratives to persuade ordinary people that those from different ethnic backgrounds were the cause of evil in the world. Sadly, many people were taken in by these lies. In other words, narrative is a powerful means of getting over ideas that can have an impact on people's behaviour. One reason for examining narrative in Media Studies is to make you more aware of its effects and so perhaps less easily influenced by it.

On your own

Choose an issue, for example the use of illegal drugs, that you think is of concern to people of your age group. Collect some examples of how it is presented in the media, including the newspapers, magazines, on television, the radio and perhaps in popular music. Look carefully at the examples. Do they show a clear sense of the rights and wrongs of the issue? Or do you feel that you are given the opportunity to decide for yourself?

Genre In order to hold the narrative of a film or television programme together, a scriptwriter will often seek a device that allows the characters to explore their ambitions. The road movie is an ideal form for a journey of self-exploration, an adventure in which the characters can find their true identity. Disaster films bring people close together, for instance, on a ship or in a burning building, so that conflicts and ambitions can be played out against a dramatic backdrop. Soaps present a series of neighbourhood locations in which the characters meet and the narrative can develop through the reactions of the characters to each other. The pub is obviously a popular meeting place in soaps – far more so than in real life!

In other words, narrative can take different forms according to the type of film, TV series or news report in which it appears. Each form has its own conventions, or common practices, and different types of programme can be identified by looking at the conventions used. The types or categories into which different types of text can be fitted are known as genres. The idea of genres allows you to group texts together so that you can study them and develop ideas about how they work. For example, the Western has already been mentioned as a particular genre of film. A list can be drawn up of distinctive features of the Western. The use of guns and horses, for example, mark out this genre from that of, say, the musical. Also, the setting of most Westerns can be identified as the Wild West. Conflict with the native American is another feature of the genre. Many films show the native Americans as savages who threaten the white man's attempt to bring civilization to the West.

The Western traditionally gave Hollywood's view of how the West was won.

Genre	Setting	Stock characters	Props	Narrative
Western	Wild West, desert, cacti, hot	Cowboys, Indians, beautiful female settler	Guns, lassoes, horses, cattle	Conflict between native Americans and settlers, resolved by a lone gunman
Soap				
Detective story				
etc.				

ACTIVITY

As a class, think of as many different genres as you can. Next, on your own, draw up a chart similar to the one above. Choose six different genres from either television or film and fill in the boxes on the grid with details of the typical settings, stock characters, props and narratives of each genre.

The examples of genre that you have analysed show that it is a useful device for examining media texts and identifying characteristics that are common to groups of them. Of course, it is a useful concept not only to students of media texts, but also to institutions and the consumers of the texts, the audience. It allows the producer to identify a formula that the audience will find attractive and want to consume. If a film or TV programme has been successful, then there is a reasonable chance that one made to a similar formula will also be successful. Of course, this isn't always true. The cinema and TV are littered with unsuccessful sequels and rip-offs of blockbusters.

For the audience, the advantage of identifying a text as a certain kind of genre is that it highlights something that they are likely to enjoy. For example, films are often advertised as being similar to or even better than another film of the same type. This draws the attention of the audience to similarities and gives them certain expectations about the style and content of the text. It also provides a short cut for audiences, because they have already learnt the conventions by which a genre works. The character types may be familiar and predictable, as may many of the storylines. Viewing within a recognized genre, therefore, will not be such hard work as learning the rules of a new one. This is probably one reason why common forms of TV genre, such as soaps and sitcoms, prove so lastingly popular.

Sub-genre

Films and programmes are sometimes classified as a sub-genre, or a genre within a genre. A good example of this is the spaghetti Western, which has many of the qualities that are associated with the typical Hollywood Western. Unlike the typical Western, however, spaghetti Westerns were shot in Europe, mostly in Italy and Spain. Genres can be so wide and all-embracing that they need to be divided into these sub-genres if they are to serve any useful purpose.

As a means of analysing media texts, the idea of genre has its limitations. One problem is that you can easily go round in a circle; soaps belong to the soap genre because they have the qualities that soaps have. This tells you neither why soaps are so popular, nor what you can expect to learn from studying them. Another problem with the concept of genre is that it does not acknowledge the individual's contribution to a text. This is especially a problem with films, where a director may have a distinctive style of making films in the same way that a novelist has a distinctive style of writing books. For example, Alfred Hitchcock made a lot of thrillers, but in some ways they are more distinctive as films made by Alfred Hitchcock than they are as thrillers. Other well-known film directors, such as Jane Campion, Francis Ford Coppola, Kathryn Bigelow, Spike Lee, Penny Marshall and Quentin Tarantino, all bring their own personal signature to the genres with which they have worked.

CLASS DISCUSSION

Are there any people who work in television, film or radio as directors, producers or writers whose work you recognize? What makes it recognizable?

However, media texts are more generally the products of groups of people working together in teams for an organization, for instance, a newspaper or radio station, rather than the creation of an individual. Even a book such as this one relies on a team of editors, designers, artists, photographers and production staff to work on the words that the writers have produced before it is ready to be sold. The organizations that these people work for are called media institutions.

3. REPRESENTATION

Representation is the act of communicating by using symbols, for example using a stick-man to stand for a person. Usually representation takes the form of words, images or symbols. So If I give you an apple, I have given you an apple. If I give you a picture of an apple, I have given you a representation of an apple. The difference between reality and a representation of reality is not difficult to understand. What is not so obvious is that representation is an act or process in which reality is transformed. The picture I give you might be a photograph, a painting or even a drawing of an apple. The drawing might be a detailed still-life, or it could be a simple outline. Or I might convey the idea of the fruit by using the word 'apple'. The message you get in each case will be 'apple'. However, what you think about the apple depends to a large degree on how I represent it. If I want to sell you an apple, I might give you a photograph of the best apple I can find and use computer techniques to make it look even better. If I were an artist and wished to suggest the idea of sickness, I might paint a rotting apple. If I were a journalist, I might use an apple as an image to represent a corrupt organization by describing it as 'rotten to the core'. In each case, the idea of 'apple' will have been worked on to help it convey a meaning. This process of working on an idea or image to convey a specific meaning is called mediation and it is central to our understanding of media messages.

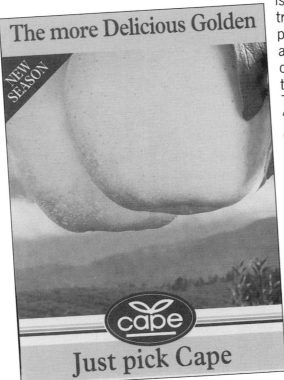

The more Delicious Golden

NEW SEASON

cape

Just pick Cape

Selecting and structuring representations

On your way home, you see a car crash. A car and a van have collided. There is steam coming from the engines. The van-driver is sitting at the side of the road and has blood pouring from his head. Another person is being helped into an ambulance. Traffic in both directions has been stopped by the police. A fire engine arrives and you assume that there must be a person trapped in the wreckage. You hear someone say that the car-driver pulled out in front of the van without looking. But someone else says the car had priority. Everywhere you look there is something going on.

When you get home you tell your family what you saw. But do you? If you told them everything you saw it would take a long time and they would probably get bored. So what you do is select the most interesting facts and tell them. If you tell these facts in the order that you experienced them you would also run the risk of losing your audience. You are more likely to say, 'I saw a bad crash on the way home,' than, 'As I was walking up the road I noticed the police had stopped the traffic. As I got closer I saw an ambulance and what looked like steam rising into the air. Eventually I saw a van and a car had crashed.' In other words, you reorganize and edit the information so that it has more impact. You might also take a stand on the cause of the accident: 'I thought it was the car-driver's fault.' What you have done is to give your own representation of the events you witnessed. The process you have carried out can be illustrated by the diagram below.

Now imagine you were a journalist reporting the same crash. The process you would go through to produce your report would be very similar. You would select what you saw as the most relevant or interesting aspects of the event, and arrange them into a story that would hopefully attract the attention of your audience.

Group Activity

Get some members of the group to perform a short drama: it could be about an accident, a robbery or an argument.

■ *The rest of the group act as reporters and produce individual reports about the event.*

■ *Compare the different reports and the representations of the drama they give. What are the differences? Why do you think they occur.*

Versions of reality

It is important to understand that every report of an event, be it a conversation or a media report, is a representation (or 'RE-presentation') of the event, not a presentation of reality. If we think in terms of the media, reading a newspaper story is equivalent to reading a letter about an event. Listening to a radio report is like receiving a phone call about the event. In both cases, it is easy to see how what you learn about the event is largely controlled by the person writing the letter or making the call – it is their representation of the happening. In the case of television, you may think that it is possible to give a direct presentation of the event being reported; after all, the camera records events as they happen. However, this is not the case. All television reports are edited packages. In TV newsrooms, staff take the raw footage shot at an event and edit it. They select what they consider to be the best images and arrange or reorder them into a sequence that they hope will be of interest to the viewer. They also write a commentary to accompany the visual images, which tells

the story of what has happened. The story makes sense of the images, informing the viewer what is happening. Unlike your report on the accident to your family, there is a time-limit on the amount of information a television report can convey. The average news report lasts no more than a few minutes, so newsroom staff have to cut film and commentary. A lot of film footage recorded at events is never broadcast. Commentaries are never complete; they do not tell you everything that could be said. What the viewer gets is a version of an event, according to the television newsroom.

Even in the broadcast of live events, such as football matches, the coverage is 'edited'. You are shown only what is within the camera shot, which is directed by the camera operator. The camera operator decides to film one part of the action rather than another and controls what the viewer will see. Most sporting events, however, are presented in the form of highlights and, as many football fans who attend games will know, it is very easy to make one side look superior to another by careful selection of film footage. When you consider the selection and reordering that goes into all forms of representation, it becomes obvious that representations are 'versions' of events, not events in themselves.

GROUP ACTIVITY

If you have access to a video camera, film a role-play, of a family argument, or for example, street interviews about a proposed shopping complex development, or a sporting triumph for a local team. Play back the footage.
- Each person in the group makes two lists. On one, put what you would include in a short report and, on the other, what you would leave out.
- Each person then writes a commentary to accompany the video, giving the viewer the story.

- Back in the group, compare your lists and commentaries. How are they different?
- Try to reach an agreement on what should be included or said in the report. You will have to negotiate between different versions of the event.
- If you have editing facilities available, you could actually produce a report.

A representation of an event, an issue, a group or an individual is only one of many possible versions. So it is clear that there must be other versions of the same event and other ways of representing it. So the person viewing the representation has a problem: is the version that they are viewing the true one? In fact, when analysing the media, is it possible to talk about a 'true' representation? To answer this question, the factors that influence the production of representations must be studied.

Whose truth?

Imagine your family photograph album. It is full of pictures of you at different stages of your life. Each picture is a representation of you and gives anyone looking at it information on which to base ideas about the type of person you are.

Suppose you had to choose one photograph from the album to represent the image you would like a stranger to have of you. It is a fair bet that you would choose one that shows you as a really cool character, wearing your most fashionable clothes. One thing is certain: the photograph you would pick of yourself would be different from the one your parents would choose to show to a stranger. They would undoubtedly select one of you looking smart and sensible to create what they would see as a 'good impression'. You would probably reject their choice as embarrassing and not a 'true' representation of yourself. Who would be right?

You must be so proud of her!

In analysing the media the issue is not so much who is right, but rather, what makes people choose to represent events, issues, groups and individuals in certain ways. Think about you and your family: it is clear that you both have an interest in how you are portrayed to a stranger. Your family would doubtless wish strangers to see a pleasant, well brought-up person, who is a credit to them. You, on the other hand, would probably want strangers to see you as a street-wise individual with obvious character.

What if you were a politician and your parents were the owners of a national newspaper that supported the opposition party? The interests that would influence the choice of representation in this case are obvious. It is in your interest to show yourself as a person who is

On your own
Find or take three photographs showing different representations of yourself or another person you know well. For example, the pictures might show you at school, at a party or with your family. How 'true' is each one? Write a paragraph about each one and how it represents the truth.

in tune with the views of most voters. However, as supporters of your opponents, your parents would wish to portray you as someone who is out of step with most people. They might even try to depict you as a danger to the country, to persuade the readers of their newspaper not to vote for you.

A similar argument between the Labour Party and most of the national press, which is traditionally seen as supporting the Conservative Party, has been going on in Britain for many years. The Conservative government of the 1980s and 1990s attacked the BBC, saying that it constantly portrayed their policies and performance in a negative way. Both the Labour and Conservative parties accused the media of selecting and reordering their representations to give a positive or negative impression of their policies. In other words, the politicians accused the media of bias, or favouring one side more than another. Bias usually results from a person having a relationship with the person or thing that they are biased in favour of. For example, if you were selling a car, a potential buyer would probably not believe everything you said about it because you stand to make money by striking a deal. They would say that your representation of the car was biased.

GROUP ACTIVITY

Analyse and discuss the different coverage of one political story in the national press.

■ How does each paper approach the story?

■ What does each approach say about the paper's political loyalties?

Virtually every area of the media has been criticized for the way it represents people and issues. It has been pointed out that heroes in action and adventure films have traditionally been male. Only recently have films with women as the central characters begun to be produced. This has been seen as a representation of the old-fashioned view that women were not as intelligent, brave and resourceful as men and should concern themselves with childcare and housework. What is called sexism (or prejudice against people because of their sex) has also been pin-pointed in the way women are represented in the national press and advertising. A woman's dress sense and appearance tend to be given attention by the press regardless of why the woman is in the news. Some people say that this means that women are not taken as seriously as men are by the press and that their views are given less weight as a result.

Women have traditionally been used in advertising to sell products. This is especially the case when the product is aimed at men. Car adverts in magazines and on television have traditionally shown a man driving and a young woman in the passenger seat. The message is that if you are male, driving the car will make you attractive to females. The same is true in adverts for clothes, shoes, perfume, watches and so on. Women have also traditionally been used in adverts for household goods, such as cleaning materials, food and electrical products. This can be seen as a reflection of the old-fashioned view that a woman's place was in the home. It has generally been the case that in advertising women have been shown as passive, while men have been portrayed as active and adventurous.

However, representations change with the times and the move towards sexual equality has had an effect on how men and women are represented in adverts. More women are now shown driving cars while some men are shown working in the kitchen and taking care of children.

Content analysis

One method of examining how people are represented in the media is called 'content analysis'. This method measures the number of times a particular representation occurs and draws conclusions about it. For example, a content analyst might count the number of women police officers portrayed in crime dramas. If they discovered that very few women were represented as police officers, they would ask why this might be. Is it because the media is sexist and men are seen as more interesting than women? Or does it reflect the reality of the police force, where there are fewer women officers?

To carry out content analysis it is very important to stick to a strict pattern of working known as the experimental method. Most researchers carrying out content analysis use the following steps:

Statement. Select the area you are going to study. Draw up a statement of the idea that you wish to test, for instance, 'More men than women are shown driving in television adverts for cars.'

What will you count? In this case, you would count the numbers of male and female drivers in car adverts on television.

When will you count? Set the times you are going to watch adverts and for how long. You might choose to watch adverts between 6 pm and 10 pm on Tuesdays, Thursdays and Saturdays one week, and Mondays, Wednesdays and Sundays the next week. You might do this for two weeks, four weeks or six weeks, and so on.

Carry out the counting. Make sure that the people who are doing the research know exactly what they are counting and that they are all counting the same thing.

Compile the results. Add up all the figures gathered by the researchers and work out the total for each category counted.

Analyse the results. Judge whether the figures the research has come up with support or disprove the original statement. In this case, are more men than women shown driving in adverts for cars on television?

CONTENT ANALYSIS EXERCISE

Design and carry out a content analysis experiment on the portrayal of families in advertising. Use the experimental method outlined above to design your investigation.
- How are men and women represented?
- How often are fathers shown carrying out DIY and tasks involving machines?
- How often are mothers seen carrying out domestic chores, such as cleaning, cooking and caring for children?
- Do adverts depict an accurate picture of the roles of men and women in families you know, or are the representations stereotyped?
- Does it matter if the representations are stereotyped?

Stereotypes

If a certain sort of person is represented in a similar way over and over again by the media, what is called a 'stereotype' of that kind of person develops. A stereotype is a fixed idea about the characteristics of a certain type of person or thing. Many characters in fairy-tales and pantomimes are stereotypes; the audience recognizes them instantly and believes that they act in certain ways and have certain characteristics. For example, if a woman dressed in black with a pointed hat and a broomstick appears in a pantomime, the audience immediately assumes she is an evil witch and will hiss and boo to show disapproval. A similar process is at work when an old person is portrayed as grumpy or senile in a television soap opera. Other stereotypes include fat people being shown as funny, successful business women as unemotional and people who live in the country as less intelligent than those who live in cities.

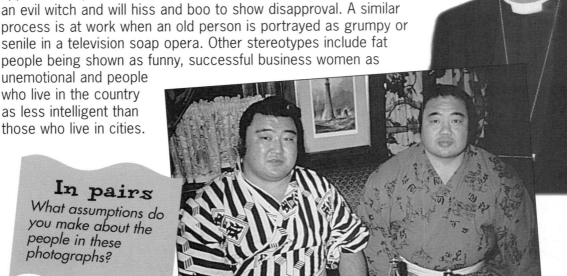

In pairs

What assumptions do you make about the people in these photographs?

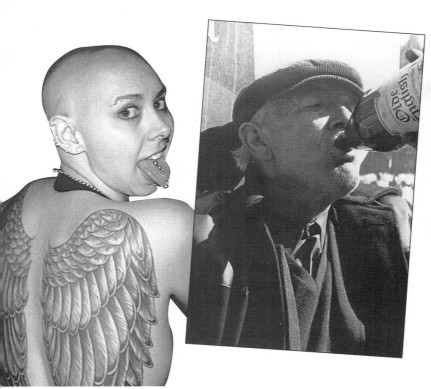

Media stereotypes of some groups have been seen as particularly offensive. It is argued that they increase prejudice in society. This is often true of the representation of people from ethnic minority backgrounds, homosexuals and members of certain religious groups. In extreme cases, the media can be used to encourage violence against certain groups. This happened in Nazi Germany, where Jews were the subject of vicious and twisted propaganda.

CLASS DISCUSSION
List stereotypes you frequently see in the media. Are stereotypes ever true?

Role-play
Rewrite a stereotypical media portrayal of a particular person, group or event, to show it in a different light. For example, you could reverse the roles usually assigned to men and women in films or television shows. Try to imagine a female James Bond and a male Miss Moneypenny. How would the dialogue and action work?

Are you a stereotype?

Perhaps some of the strongest stereotypes portrayed in the media are those of young people. One that is easily recognizable is the youngster from a so-called 'broken home' who gets into trouble with the police. This portrayal has become so common that it is almost taken for granted that in TV programmes any teenager who breaks the law must have family problems. This stereotype ignores those young people from stable family backgrounds who get into trouble and law-abiding teenagers from single-parent homes.

One of the major factors that builds up a stereotype is the way that people in the media dress. Whenever a young person is portrayed as being on the slippery slope to a life of drugs and crime, they are almost certain to be dressed in a way that goes against adult ideas about sensible clothes. If a teenage character in a TV programme is going off the rails, this is not signalled by the character going out and getting a smart haircut and an outfit suitable for an interview; the character is more likely to be dressed in the latest street fashion. Similarly, pop bands use their clothes to present a rebellious image in order to attract fans. Once they are famous, their fans tend to adopt the dress style of the band, which helps to make the stereotype stronger.

Using clothes to represent youthful rebellion has affected the way young people are perceived. Look at the picture on the left. It shows a young man in trendy clothes going through the bag of an old lady. Has he mugged her? Or perhaps the old lady suffers from a heart condition, or asthma, and has asked the man to get her medication from her handbag. Your view of what is going on is determined to a large degree by a stereotype presented to you by the media.

Some young people are stereotyped by the fact that they are hardly ever represented in the media. Young people with disabilities are rarely shown in films or on television. If they do appear, they are shown only to highlight the issue of disability, rather than as characters in their own right.

On your own

Examine popular television shows, such as soap operas and drama serials. How many people with disabilities are portrayed? How old are they? What story-lines are they involved in? What conclusions can you draw about the stereotyping of people with disabilities on these sorts of TV programmes?

Review

Representation is the key function of the media. However, you should always ask yourself the following questions:

- Whose representation is it?
- What reasons could the media have for representing the person, group, issue or event in this way?
- How else could the person, group, issue or event be represented?

4. INSTITUTIONS

Imagine that you wake up one day and decide that you would like to publish your own newspaper. Alternatively, your ambitions may be more limited: you might like to make a new quiz show for Channel 4, or set up a community radio station. The chances are that no matter how enthusiastic you are about your schemes, they are unlikely to get very far, at least not in the short term. This is because however talented or hardworking you may be, in order to do any of these things you will need access to technology and money to pay for the resources necessary to get your idea off the ground. You will need these things because you are going to make a product or commodity that you want people to use, in just the same way that any other manufacturer makes a product to be sold.

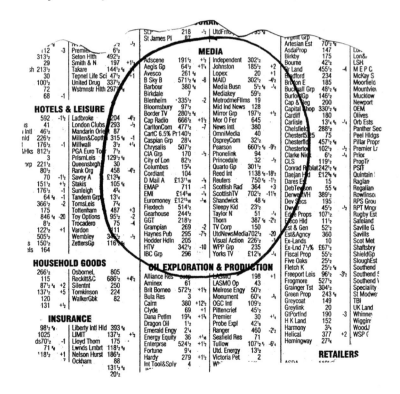

A media institution is a money-making business, just like any other.

Of course, you may be very rich, in which case your dreams could become a reality. Even so, there is no guarantee that your newspaper, quiz show or radio station would be a success and pay back the money invested in it. Media institutions are big business.

They exist to make a profit. Just as car manufacturers or supermarket chains aim to earn money for their shareholders, so media institutions are owned by people who want them to make as much money as possible.

There are, of course, exceptions. For example, the BBC is funded through a licence fee, which everyone in the UK who uses a television has to pay. Even so, the BBC is expected to help to fund itself through the sales of programmes overseas and the publication of spin-off books and magazines, for instance.

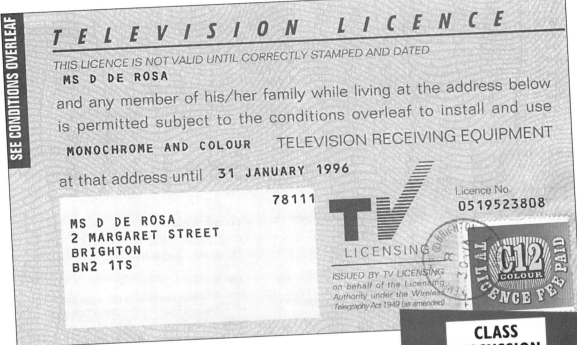

SEE CONDITIONS OVERLEAF

T E L E V I S I O N   L I C E N C E

THIS LICENCE IS NOT VALID UNTIL CORRECTLY STAMPED AND DATED

MS D DE ROSA

and any member of his/her family while living at the address below is permitted subject to the conditions overleaf to install and use

MONOCHROME AND COLOUR   TELEVISION RECEIVING EQUIPMENT

at that address until   31 JANUARY 1996

78111

MS D DE ROSA
2 MARGARET STREET
BRIGHTON
BN2 1TS

TV LICENSING

Licence No.
0519523808

C12 COLOUR

TV LICENCE FEE PAID

ISSUED BY TV LICENSING on behalf of the Licensing Authority under the Wireless Telegraphy Act 1949 (as amended)

Types of institution
Multinationals

A car manufacturer has to invest money in land, buildings and equipment in order to make cars. In the same way, a media producer has to buy or rent such items as TV studios, printing presses or transmitters, in order to deliver their product to the consumer. Car manufacturers maximize their profit by producing cars that are sold all over the world. Such firms with world-wide interests are called multinationals. Many media institutions are also multinationals, with interests in a wide range of media and cultural products. This book, for example, is produced by Collins Educational, which is part of the international company HarperCollins*Publishers*. HarperCollins in turn is owned by News

> **CLASS DISCUSSION**
>
> Much of the money made by commercial TV and radio stations is raised through advertising. Should BBC television and radio carry advertising, instead of depending on the licence fee? Does the BBC carry any advertising at the moment?

International, Rupert Murdoch's vast media empire. Other media interests that are part of News International include *The Sun* and *The Times* newspapers, and Sky Television, as well as other media industries across the globe.

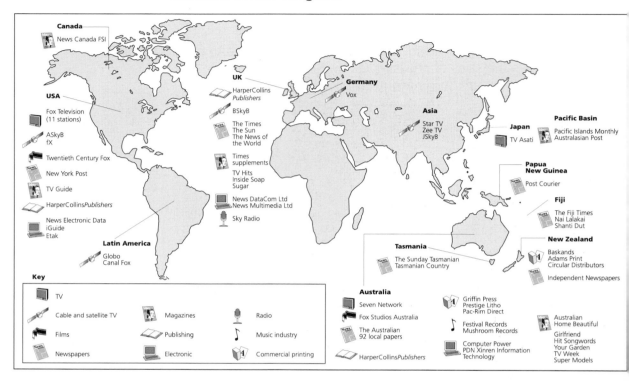

Some companies around the world that are owned (or partly owned) by News International.

Such control of media output in the hands of one organization, and ultimately one man, is a cause of great concern to many people. *The Sun*, for instance, has a circulation of 4 million daily and is read by one in four of the population in the UK. It is so influential in swaying political opinion in the UK that people have argued that it has decided the outcome of general elections. Many people feel that ownership of the media has become too unequal, especially where such corporations as News International control a variety of different media across the world. Too much power, they argue, is in the hands of too few people (see the section on controlling institutions, pages 53–57).

CLASS DISCUSSION

The idea has been put forward that there should be strict controls on how much of the British media any one company or person should be allowed to own, for example, no more than two national newspapers, or one national newspaper and one television company.

- What do you think would happen under a system like this?
- Do you think that there should be such controls?

Small institutions

Small organizations are at the opposite end of the spectrum to the multinational media corporations. They often use limited technology to produce alternative or community media products. Many football supporters will buy a copy of a fanzine written by other fans of the club. Such fanzines exist outside the established media and can offer more radical points of view. Music fans produce fanzines offering a different perspective on the music scene or on a specific type of music. In some cases, they become part of the mainstream of media institutions. *When Saturday Comes* started as a small circulation fanzine and is now on sale throughout the country.

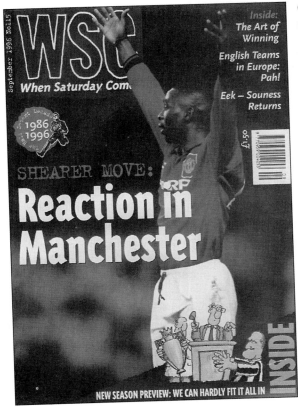

Do fanzines offer the audience something that can't be found in mainstream products?

In the 1960s popular music was not well catered for by mainstream radio. Several pirate stations sprang up to fill the gap. They were sometimes housed on boats anchored off the coast just outside the control of the authorities. This went on until 1967, when the BBC launched Radio 1. Many of the presenters who had worked for these pirate stations were given shows on the new legitimate radio service.

Value systems

Media institutions have so far been discussed as organizations made up of equipment, bricks and mortar, and money to invest in property. The word 'institution' carries with it another important connotation. The place where you are taking your Media Studies course is probably an institution. It is not simply a series of buildings in which people attend lessons, but a system of values and conventions by which people work and study together. Some of these conventions are written down, for instance, rules about smoking. Some conventions exist because people agree that they should, or because they have always existed. Most will make sense to everyone, while others will seem silly to some people.

A media institution will carry with it a similar value system, supported by conventions concerning the way things should be done. You sometimes hear it called 'professionalism', which implies that this is the way that people who are good at the job will do it. Professionalism means sticking to the standards and work practices that are the norm within a particular industry or institution. What makes a good news story is a matter of professional judgement. Which news story is the most important is another matter of professional judgement. In television news, presenters are always smartly dressed and speak directly and clearly to the audience in 'proper' English – they are professional.

These notions of professionalism, or the right way to do things, exist in all media. There is a 'right' way to write newspaper stories, take news photographs or introduce records on the radio. These are part of the conventions that were discussed in the chapter on media language (see page 14). Television comedy sometimes draws attention to these conventions when it pokes fun at them, for instance, when *Spitting Image* or an impersonator parodies news presenters. Anyone who gets a job in a media institution will be expected adopt the same attitudes and approaches to the job as those who already work there. In fact, some people argue that recruitment into the media is limited to people of fairly restricted social backgrounds. To support their argument, they point to the lack of strong regional accents on TV and radio.

IN PAIRS

Different media institutions expect different codes of professionalism from the people who work within them. What do you think professionalism means to each of the following people:
- **A press photographer**
- **The presenter of a show on Radio 1**
- **The editor of a problems page in a women's magazine?**

Commissioning Editor
(Investigative Features & Exposes)

THE BIG ISSUE

We're seeking a successor to our commissioning editor who has just moved to the *Observer*.
- Do you have a talent for exposing injustice?
- Can you back up your worst suspicions with hard facts?
- Are you an experienced journalist (Min 2 years experience) capable of producing dynamic features to impress our 120,000 weekly readers?

If you can research, write, commission and edit features to the above brief, then this is the job for you.

For more information contact Claire Rees on 0171 418 0418 or write with three ideas and a CV to Priya Sher by July 19. The Big Issue 57-61 Clerkenwell Road, Farringdon, London EC1M 5NP.

The Big Issue is striving to be an equal opportunities employer.

Magazine Designer

If you are **young, talented and ambitious** and can **think on your feet**, read on. We are looking for a designer to work on a wide range of contract and consumer titles.

If you are **mad about magazines,** a whizz at Quark, Photoshop and Illustrator and have **1 years experience** send your CV to:

VINCENT STOKES, Art Director, HIGHBURY HOUSE COMMUNICATIONS, 1-3 Highbury Station Road, Islington, London, N1 1SE.

TV QUICK SHOWBIZ WRITER

Apply in writing to:
Lori Miles, Editor,
TV Quick, 25-27 Camden Road,
London NW1 9LL
by 19 July, 1996.

Are you a friend of the stars? Britain's brightest TV magazine is looking for a showbiz writer for a three-days-a-week contract. You must be a smart soap addict who can ask all the right questions. Send us your CV – plus three questions you'd ask Lisa Riley and Paul Nicholls.

FICTION EDITOR
CHILDREN'S

The Children's division of HarperCollins is looking for an enthusiastic editor to work across a diverse fiction list.

You will be confident about working across a wide range of titles, including highly illustrated young fiction. Reporting to the Editorial Director, you will be responsible for a list of authors, editing and copy-editing selected fiction titles. You will oversee their smooth progress through the publishing process which will involve liaising with key departments including Design, Production, Sales and Marketing.

The successful candidate will have excellent editing skills, enjoy building relationships with authors/artists, and be able to work under pressure as part of a committed team. Creative flair with individual texts will be combined with a commercial awareness of the children's book market. This is an exciting opportunity for the right candidate to join the dynamic environment of the HarperCollins Children's division, which produces quality books and audio for children of all ages, from pre-school picture books to award-winning teen fiction.

Experience of children's publishing is essential and a working knowledge of Apple Macs useful.

We offer a competitive salary together with attractive additional benefits.

Please apply in writing with detailed c.v. to:
**Maureen Venton, Personnel Officer,
HarperCollins Publishers Ltd, 77-85 Fulham Palace Road,
Hammersmith, London W6 8JB.**

 HarperCollins*Publishers*

PROGRAMME OUTPUT EDITOR

Channel 4 News needs an experienced output editor to help lead its award-winning team. S/he will have a substantial background in daily television news and current affairs and a proven journalistic record. S/he'll need a keen interest in the conversion of complex issues into appealing television and enthusiasm for an innovative agenda. The ability to lead a team is essential. Please send one A4 side on how you would want to develop Channel 4 News. **Ref: C4N 96/66.**

PRODUCER

We're looking for an experienced television producer who's knowledgeable about both home and foreign issues, can convert their knowledge into attractive television, has first rate journalism skills plus pizzazz, enthusiasm and flexibility. **Ref: C4N 96/67.**

FOREIGN NEWS EDITOR

Channel 4 News needs an experienced TV journalist to work on its foreign desk. The Foreign News Editor helps shape the international output of the programme, organising the on-the-day coverage and some forward planning. You need a strong record in TV production and a good grasp of logistics plus a broad understanding of international affairs. There will be opportunities to work as a general producer. **Ref: C4N 96/68.**

ON YOUR OWN

Look at the job advertisements. What do they tell you about the qualities that the institutions are looking for? What sort of person do you think will get the job? Do you know anyone with the qualities you think they are looking for? Now trying writing some adverts of your own for:
- A quiz presenter on ITV
- The editor of a new unisex teenage magazine
- The host of a radio phone-in programme.

Professional working practices can make anything that is different from them seem amateur. If you look at one of your own attempts at practical production, you will probably compare it to a professional production and feel a little disappointed. It is difficult to produce anything that you can feel proud of if its value is going to be measured against the work of experienced professionals with vast resources at their disposal.

If you look at a home-produced fanzine or listen to pirate radio, however, it becomes clear that some people are not simply trying and failing to imitate what the professionals do. These alternative media may have been created because the major media institutions themselves have failed to address issues that the audience feel are important. The producers of fanzines may, in fact, have rejected the values and conventions of the professionals and opted for a different way of doing things. Of course, the irony is that if they are too successful, they themselves will be swallowed into the mainstream and become part of the system that they were opposing.

As you can see in the chapter on audience (see pages 64–65), media institutions are keen to be seen to involve audiences in their products. They do so using either direct participation, or feedback, which means getting the audience's responses to their products. For the institutions, the nvolvement of the audience has the added benefit of being cheap.

IN PAIRS

■ *Make a list of situations in which media institutions directly or indirectly use the participation of the audience, for example, radio phone-ins and readers' letters to newspapers and magazines.*

■ *How far do you think that the people who choose to participate, or who are chosen, are representative of the whole audience?*

Taking risks

Suppose that you managed to find the money to set yourself up as a media institution. Many people would be quick to tell you that the media is a good place to lose your money. Your investment, as it is called, would be quite risky. This is one of the arguments that multinational media companies put forward in defence of their large and diverse interests. By spreading their risks over a wide range of different products, they stand less chance of losing out completely if they don't get it right.

The problem for media producers is the unpredictability of the audience. For example, most media products are designed to be consumed over a short period of time. The consumer who buys a car or a pair of socks will enjoy them over a relatively long period of time, which makes them seem to be good value for money. A film, on the other hand, lasts for a couple of hours only and consumers judge it on the pleasure they get during that time. This makes the success of a film difficult to predict. Even products that can give a more lengthy enjoyment, such as magazines, rely heavily on an immediate appeal to and impact on the reader.

Unlike the car or sock manufacturer, a media product is rarely a standard item that can be mass-produced. Each television programme has to be different from every other television programme. But as the chapter on language pointed out (see pages 25–27), it will probably contain many similarities with others of its genre. Media producers have to tread a very careful path between identifying and repeating a successful formula, and producing new and innovative products. If they get it wrong, their investment will probably turn into a loss.

Media producers are, however, able to take steps to cut this risk factor to a minimum. On television, one-off pilot programmes are often made to try out a formula before a full series of programmes is made. The pilots will be tested on the market and only if audiences respond positively will a studio commit money to the full project. Similarly, advertisers often try out a campaign in just one region of the country to see if it is worthwhile going national.

As well as working within an established and successful genre, another means of reducing the risk is the use of well-known stars.

This is especially true of Hollywood films, where a star name is a big box-office draw and is likely to provide some guarantee of a film's popularity. Similarly, in the music industry, recording companies prefer to invest money in promoting stars who are already established, rather than risking it on new or up-and-coming talent. In fact, the media industry relies heavily on the concept of celebrity. The famous and not-so-famous appear in TV chat shows, and radio programmes. Some celebrities are said to be famous for being famous!

IN PAIRS

Who are the big box-office draws at the moment? Make a list of stars, male and female, whom you think a Hollywood producer would expect to guarantee the success of a film.

★ What are the most popular films at the moment? Who are the stars of these films?
★ What makes a star or celebrity?
★ How are stars useful?
★ Do you think anyone you know will become a celebrity?
★ Would you like to be one?

CLASS DISCUSSION

Who sets the trend in popular music – the fans or the record companies?

Despite all efforts by the big institutions to make sure that they invest in winning formulas, the media is littered with products that audiences did not want, many of them quite spectacular failures. Each of these products represents an instance of a media producer who failed to guess correctly what the audience wanted.

IN PAIRS

Make a list of media enterprises that have failed. These will include:

- Newspapers, magazines and comics that folded, especially those that produced only a few issues
- Television series that never got beyond the pilot stage
- Blockbuster movies that disappeared after only a short time on general release
- Bands and recording stars who disappeared after releasing a single
- Radio stations that came and went.

Can you think of any examples of spectacular success, for instance, low-budget movies that became box-office blockbusters?

Should we judge the success or failure of a media enterprise on the basis of the money it made or lost? What other standards can you use to judge a media text's success?

Write up your discussion as a report.

Competition between institutions

Market fragmentation

In recent years, institutions have brought about an increasing fragmentation of markets in their desire to sell to audiences (see the section on audience fragmentation, pages 63–64). Market fragmentation is the breaking down of the market for media products into small units. For example, within the market for magazines, specialist magazines with a limited audience and therefore a small circulation can be said to have fragmented the market. Instead of selling large amounts of a product that appeals to a mass audience, products are sold on a smaller scale to much more specialized audiences. Changes in working practices and technology have made printing cheaper, which allows the production of magazines that are profitable with just a small circulation. In fact, many of these small ventures are owned by large media institutions. Quite often titles on magazine racks competing with one another are owned by the same company.

NICHES

Call in at a large newsagent's and look at the titles that cater for specialist audiences, for example:

- **Film and cinema enthusiasts**
- **Computer buffs**
- **DIY freaks**
- **People who like nice food.**

Try to find out by looking on the contents page who owns each title.

The growth of satellite and cable broadcasting has led to an increasing fragmentation in the television market. In urban areas especially, increasing numbers of viewers receive a package of programmes through their local cable operator. The cable operator downloads many of the programmes via satellite and feeds them by means of fibre-optic cable to individual homes. Many homes, however, still rely on a satellite dish to receive programmes. Commonly, these receive a signal bounced off a satellite. The signal is fed from the dish to a combined receiver/decoder, which is able to unscramble the encrypted signal with the help of a smart-card supplied to subscribers. Programmes can then be received on a TV set and recorded on a video recorder, in the same way as is possible with a terrestrial channel.

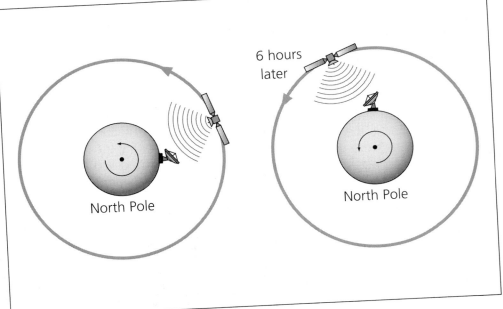

Sky uses a group of four Astra satellites. The satellites are in the same geostationary orbit, which means that they move at the same speed as the earth rotates. Because of this, they stay in the same position relative to the earth, so that a constant signal is maintained across the satellite's footprint (the area of the earth's surface covered by its signal). More satellites are planned in the future.

Sky, the satellite television company, bought the exclusive rights to show live coverage in the UK of premier football. This was a major selling point in its Premium Channels package, which gave subscribers access to film, sports and general entertainment channels. Controversially, the company introduced the pay-per-view scheme for the Mike Tyson–Frank Bruno World Heavyweight Championship title fight in 1996. Many critics of the channel predicted that pay-per-view would be introduced more widely after this event, so that subscribers would pay to see specific films or sporting events on top of the monthly subscription fee.

Access to the Astra satellites gives viewers an opportunity to watch a wide range of minority interest channels, which serve comparatively small audiences. In other words, satellite and cable

TV cater for fragmented audiences (see the chapter on audience, pages 63–64). For instance, Zee TV – which began in India – now broadcasts via the Astra 1D satellite, targeting half a million Asian viewers across the UK and Europe on a subscription basis. It tries to strike a balance in its programming between traditional Asian values and a European lifestyle, through its combination of films, dramas, news and light entertainment programmes. MTV provides 24-hour access to music videos, whilst Sky News offers a rolling news service around the clock. Other satellite and cable channels deal exclusively with such areas of interest as history, travel and science fiction.

Most satellite television viewers use a fixed dish to receive the Astra satellites' signals. It is also possible to motorize a dish, so that it can rotate to receive signals from a range of satellites, providing information and entertainment from around the world and fragmenting the market on a global scale.

Pop music is another area where market fragmentation has taken place. There is now a whole series of charts to demonstrate record sales across a range of types of music, in addition to the UK best-selling singles chart. (For more information, see the case study on the music industry, pages 173–174.)

CLASS DISCUSSION

Nostalgia is an important concept for media producers in a fragmented market. The concept of 'gold' as applied to satellite channels UK Gold and Sky Movies Gold, as well as radio, allows producers to recycle texts from previous years or decades. What do you think is the main attraction of this for:
■ Producers
■ Audiences?

Marketing the product

When a big motor company launches a new car, most people get to know about it. Television, press and radio advertising, features in motoring supplements, bill-board adverts and displays in car-dealers' showrooms announce and promote the new product. Similarly, the media industries have their own marketing ploys for ensuring that a product is likely to reach the audience at which it is aimed.

On TV we are constantly bombarded by trailers for programmes that will be shown later that night, that week or even that month. Continuity announcers tell the audience between programmes about other programmes that they might enjoy. Media institutions promote other media institutions. Television listings appear in all the national dailies. Television news magazines tell us what the papers say. Radio programmes discuss what is on television that night, or what you missed last night. Some game shows are direct tie-ins between TV and the tabloid press. You need to buy a paper to play the game while watching the show on television; you need one to make sense of the other.

YOU SCRATCH MY BACK
Collect examples of how the following pairs of media forms promote each other's texts:
- **Television and cinema**
- **Radio and the record industry**
- **Newspapers and satellite broadcasting.**

Does this mutual promotion ever raise any questions about common ownership?

Scheduling

Of course, despite common ownership, real competition exists between media institutions. Each one wants to obtain the largest share of the market, so that it can charge advertisers large sums of money for the privilege of promoting their products. Even an institution like the BBC needs to attract large audiences for its programmes, even though it is committed to public service broadcasting.

This competition for audiences can be seen across the media. For example, in the press, *The Sun* and *Daily Mirror* are involved in the tabloid wars, a battle for the largest circulation. In the case study on radio, the competition between Radio 1 and similar commercial stations is studied (see pages 183–185). The style magazine market is another circulation battleground, with magazines competing for the prize of advertising revenue for products aimed at the stylish under-thirties.

The most obvious example of competition between media institutions is the battle for prime-time viewing audiences. This fight is mainly between BBC 1 and ITV, with increasing competition from the satellite channels. Each channel wants to maximize the viewing audience for its prime-time slots. Early-evening programming is very important to 'hook' the audience to watch a particular channel, in the hope that they will stay with it throughout the evening. Australian soaps, popular especially with younger viewers, are scheduled into prime early-evening slots to grab the audience in preparation for programmes later that evening.

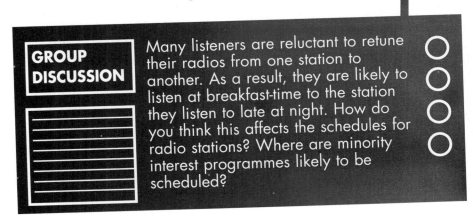

GROUP DISCUSSION

Many listeners are reluctant to retune their radios from one station to another. As a result, they are likely to listen at breakfast-time to the station they listen to late at night. How do you think this affects the schedules for radio stations? Where are minority interest programmes likely to be scheduled?

Drive-time is an important concept in radio listening. Drivers tune in on their way to or from work for news and travel information, as well as for the companionship that the radio provides on a journey. Modern car radios can be programmed to retune automatically to the station that is giving out travel information or a news bulletin, even if the driver is listening to a cassette tape or CD at the time.

ITV

6.00 AM **GMTV**
Starting with The Sunday Review: A signed roundup of the week's TV, including 6.30 News/Sport **7.00** The Sunday Programme **8.00** Dragon Flyz: New series of stories about animals and plants living in a post-apocalyptic city. 50145205

8.25 Disney Club

Anybody this lively first thing on a Sunday deserves to be a success
Craig Doyle and Des meet *Emmerdale*'s Mandy Dingle (Lisa Riley, above). (S) 21204953 Ages 5-10

9.15 Link
Sport for disabled children. (S) (T) 4076798

9.30 Morning Worship
Mass from St Edward's Roman Catholic Church, Chandler's Ford, Hampshire. (S) (T) 16311

10.30 Heavenly Voices
Barry Rose explores the history and tradition of church music. (S) 5561330

10.50 Your Faith And Mine
New series in which children of different religious faiths talk about their beliefs. (S) (T) 4577663

12.30 PM **The Entertainers**
Comic actor Victor Spinetti talks about his career. 13885 Followed by *Regional Weather*

1.00 News/Weather (T) 17323514

1.10 The Agenda
Current-affairs magazine. (S) 6324327

2.00 Theatreland Summer Specials
Featuring Anthony Sher in Stanley. (S) 1309

2.30 The Practice
An inner-city doctor's experiences. (Repeat) 798

3.00 Gold
FILM Action adventure. Drama as a poor man thwarts a conspiracy by gold mine owners. (130 mins. 1974) 58585427
● Films page 33

5.10 Upstairs, Downstairs
For Love Of Love: Elizabeth falls in love with the poet Lawrence Kirbridge. (Repeat) 9188359

MERIDIAN as London except: **12.30pm** 7 Days **12.50-1.00** Regional News/Weather **2.00** The Pier **2.30** Held In Trust **3.00** Highway To Heaven **3.55** FILM: Kim **6.20-6.25** Regional News/Weather **10.45** FILM: Up Pompeii **12.30am** FILM: All's Fair **2.08** Best Of British Motor Sport **2.35** Funny Business **.05** Cyber Café **3.35-4.35** The Crime Hour

ANGLIA as London except: **12.30-1.00pm** Regional News/Weather/Business News **2.00** Highway To Heaven **2.50** FILM: Kim **5.15** Jungle On Your Doorstep **5.45** Homemaker **6.15-.26** Regional News/Weather **10.45** FILM: Protocol **12.30am** FILM: All's Fair **2.05** Best Of British Motor Sport **2.35** Funny Business **3.05** Cyber Café **3.35-4.35** The Crime Hour

CENTRAL as London except: **12.30pm** Newsweek **12.55-.00** Regional News/Weather **2.00** Right Or Wrong **2.30** FILM: The Count Of Monte-Cristo **4.25** Murder, She Wrote **.28** Bullseye **5.50** Our House **6.20-6.25** Regional News/Weather **4.35am** Jobfinder **5.20-5.30** Asian Eye

6.10 PM **Regional News/Weather**
Early-evening bulletin. (T) 520576

6.25 News/Weather (T) 709156

6.35 The Cosby Mysteries
Mirror, Mirror: Angie asks Guy to investigate the suspicious death of her lawyer. (T) 208866

PICK OF THE DAY

7.30 Heartbeat

Old Colonials: PC Nick invites Jo (Juliette Gruber) for a date at the pub, but no sooner have they ordered their chicken in a basket than Nick's called to investigate a burglary. (S) (T) 46576

8.30 You've Been Framed!
Outrageous out-takes from the home-video vault presented by Jeremy Beadle. (S) (T) 2750

9.00 London's Burning
When an armed robbery goes disastrously wrong, the Blue Watch team are called upon to save security guards from a burning van. Hallam meets Jenny by chance. (S) 5717

10.00 Tarrant On TV
Chris Tarrant — the brain behind *Man O Man*, remember — pokes fun at TV around the world, including a game show involving colonic irrigation! Guess which nation has purged this little gem. Answer at foot of page. (S) 86243

10.30 News/Weather
(T) 816427 Followed by *Regional Weather*

10.45 I Love You To Death
FILM Black comedy. When Tracy Ullman discovers hubby Kevin Kline is fooling around, she decides to exact a murderous revenge. (110 mins. 1990) (S) (T) 44072359
● Films page 33

12.35 AM **The Killing Time**
FILM Thriller. Kiefer Sutherland gets into murder, sex and subterfuge in smalltown California. With Beau Bridges. (110 mins. 1987) 559335
● Films page 33
Followed by *News*

2.25 The Flying Deuces
FILM Comedy. Classic Laurel and Hardy slapstick with the daft duo deciding to join the Foreign Legion. (75 mins. 1939, B/W) 9678441
● Films page 33
Followed by *News*

3.40 Not Fade Away
Sporting couple Sharron Davies and Derek Redmond pick soulful musical favourites. (Repeat) (S) 5091118

4.35 Flux
Mayhem from Glasgow. (Repeat) (S) 7991688

5.30-6.00 News 71460

Channel 4

5.50 AM **4-Tel On View**
Pages from Teletext. 7634330

6.35 Early Morning

Shark-steaks the next big thing, are they, pal? 8.00
Starting with The Great Maratha 6693804 **7.00** Madeline (S) 27175 **7.30** The Real Life Adventures Of Professor Thompson 20822 **8.00** Street Sharks *The half-man, half-shark heroes meet Dr Paradigm with his lethal piranha injection.* (S) 8904363 **8.25** Two Stupid Dogs (S) 9318663 **8.50** Cadillacs And Dinosaurs (S) 1189972 **9.20** Saved By The Bell (Repeat) 6409917

PICK OF THE DAY

8.30 Celluloid Icons

9.45 Sister Sister
The sisters decide to throw the party to end all parties, but no-one wants to come. (S) 601156

10.15 Happy Days
Fonzie The Salesman: Just as the feisty new owner arrives, Fonzie quits the garage and starts selling door-to-door. (Repeat) 3749779

10.40 Mission Impossible
Charity: The Impossible Mission Force take an interest in two very professional and fraudulent charity fund-raisers. (S) 3056021

11.40 The Waltons
The Gypsies: John-Boy invites a family of gypsies into the Walton household, despite warnings, so that their baby can recover from illness. (Repeat) (T) 7434595

12.40 PM **Do Not Disturb**
FILM Comedy. Doris Day moves to England with hubby Rod Taylor — cue thick fogs and chirpy cockerneys — and starts a flirtation with an ever-so-continental antique-dealer. (115 mins. 1965) (T) 95114963
● Films page 33

2.35 The Wrong Brothers
Film about the desire to fly. 5743359

2.45 Football Italia
James Richardson brings in the new Serie A season with live action from either the San Siro stadium, where champions AC Milan — boasting Roberto Baggio, George Weah and Paolo Maldini — take on Verona; or from Reggiana's ground, where the visitors are Juventus with their new signings Zinedine Zidane and Alen Boksic. 90064717 Followed by *News/Weather*

5.05 Chasing Shadows
Documentary tribute to Rabbi Hugo Gryn, who died last month. (Repeat) (T) 9170330

6.05 PM **Babylon 5**
And The Rock Cried Out No Hiding Place: Londo's after power in the Centauri Royal Court. (T) 619798

7.00 Equinox
(NEW) *The Curse Of The Cocaine Mummies:* It could well give Tutankhamen a whole new image, as Egyptologists investigate the high levels of cocaine and nicotine present in ancient mummies. As such substances were not 'discovered' until thousands of years later, they raise questions as to the relic's authenticity. (S) (T) 7175

8.00 Celluloid Icons
3/4. This Road Will Never End: When he died of a drug overdose outside a Hollywood nightclub, gay men and lesbians mourned the loss of River Phoenix. Phoenix's assistant Abigail Greenberg and film director Tom Kalin share memories of the star. (S) (T) 1885

PICK OF THE DAY

8.30 Celluloid Icons
4/4. The Street: Coronation Street has yet to introduce a gay character, and yet it's the favourite of many gay men including David (above). Created by a gay man, Tony Warren, and populated by strong female characters like Bet, Elsie Tanner and Raquel, who favour laughter through tears, it has an undeniable appeal for a generation of gay fans. (S) (T) 6232

9.00 Talentspotting
Holed: A friendly round of golf goes horribly wrong for four men when things start to cut up rough on the fairway. (S) 3359

10.00 Blue Steel
FILM Drama. Jamie Lee Curtis dons the navy togs of a rookie cop and immediately falls for a psychopath who frames her for murder. With Ron Silver. (115 mins. 1990) (S) 49732663
● Films page 33

11.50 Sex With Paula
1986: footage of George Michael, Elton John and Dave Stewart chatting frankly to Paula Yates about sex, morals and pop music. (S) (T) 769885

12.55-3.35 AM
The Assault
FILM Drama. A man attempts to deal with the memory of the massacre of his family. (160 mins. 1986) (S) 54994286
● Films page 33

Television news programmes are an important part of an evening's scheduling. Fixed slots for national and regional news, both in the early evening and at 9.00 pm on BBC and 10.00 pm on ITV, form a key element in shaping an evening's viewing for many families. Programmes have to be placed around these slots in such a way that viewers will stay tuned to one particular channel. The ITV network commonly shows the first half of a feature film before its *News at Ten* slot and then shows the second half afterwards.

CLASS DISCUSSION

Many households now have more than one TV set. Does this affect how the television is watched in many houses? How do schedulers think that people watch TV at home? For instance, do they assume that all people watch television as part of a family? Do all people live in families?

Some commentators have made the important point that because news is part of an evening's entertainment, this has an effect on the way in which it is presented. While the news should inform, it must hold the attention of the viewer in competition with programmes that are made to entertain or amuse. In other words, the news is under pressure to compete with other programmes.

Another important aspect of scheduling is what broadcasters call the 9 o'clock watershed. This means the time after which more adult content – swearing, violence and sex – can be included in programmes, because, at least in theory, younger viewers for whom such material is deemed unsuitable will probably be in bed. In other words, scheduling is used to maximize a channel's audience, but there are factors that restrict the schedule. (The ways in which material is regulated are discussed in more detail in the chapter on audience, pages 58–61.)

Not all programmes are aimed at a mass audience. On television, BBC 2 and Channel Four were both deliberately set up to attract minority audiences who were not well catered for by the mainstream channels. Ratings are important for them, too, although audiences are generally much smaller. Snooker, for example, on BBC 2 and, to a lesser extent, racing on Channel Four, are examples of popular programmes attracting audiences who might otherwise be unaware of these channels and what they offer. Even minority interest channels have to take account of the need to attract sizeable audiences.

IN PAIRS

Christmas is a time when the major networks compete with each other for audiences.
- What factors will determine the type of programming shown on each channel from 3 pm until 10 pm on Christmas day?
- Make up a sample schedule for either BBC 1 or ITV. Remember that you are trying to provide entertaining programmes that will appeal to all the family.
- What sort of programmes might audiences for Channel 4 and BBC 2 want to see on Christmas day?

Controlling institutions

The media is controlled in a variety of ways. Such organizations as the Radio Authority (see the case study on radio, pages 189–195) have the power to give and cancel licences for radio stations. They can also criticize, fine or take away the licences of stations that fail to stick to established codes of practice. Similarly, the Press Complaints Commission (PCC) was set up to control and regulate the press. Anyone can make a complaint about a story in a newspaper to the PCC, who will investigate it and make a judgement, which the newspaper in question is expected to print. However, it cannot fine newspapers that break its code of practice (shown on pages 54–56). As a result, many people believe that it is a toothless organization, which acts more in the interests of the newspaper industry than in those of the general public. They feel it should be replaced with laws that would mean the newspapers could be taken to court and punished if they overstepped the mark.

Code of Practice

The Press Complaints Commission is charged with enforcing the following Code of Practice, which was framed by the newspaper and periodical industry and ratified by the Press Complaints Commission.

All members of the press have a duty to maintain the highest professional ethical standards. In doing so, they should have regard to the provisions of this Code of Practice and to safeguarding the public's right to know.

Editors are responsible for the actions of journalists employed by their publications. They should also satisfy themselves as far as possible that material accepted from non-staff members was obtained in accordance with this Code.

While recognizing that this involves a substantial element of self-restraint by editors and journalists, it is designed to be acceptable in the context of a system of self-regulation. The Code applies in the spirit as well as in the letter.

It is the responsibility of editors to co-operate as swiftly as possible in PCC enquiries.

Any publication that is criticized by the PCC under one of the following clauses is duty-bound to print the adjudication that follows in full and with due prominence.

1. Accuracy

i) Newspapers and periodicals should take care not to publish inaccurate, misleading or distorted material.

ii) Whenever it is recognized that a significant inaccuracy, misleading statement or distorted report has been published, it should be corrected promptly and with due prominence.

iii) An apology should be published whenever appropriate.

iv) A newspaper or periodical should always report fairly and accurately the outcome of an action for defamation to which it has been party.

2. Opportunity to reply

A fair opportunity for reply to inaccuracies should be given to individuals or organizations when reasonably called for.

3. Comment, conjecture and fact

Newspapers, whilst free to be partisan, should distinguish clearly between comment, conjecture and fact.

4. Privacy

i) Intrusions and enquiries into an individual's private life without his or her consent, including the use of long-lens photography to take pictures of people on private property without their consent, are only acceptable when these are, or are reasonably believed to be, in the public interest.

ii) Publication of material obtained under (i) above is only justified when the facts show that the public interest is served.

Note – Private property is defined as (i) any private residence, together with its garden and outbuildings, but excluding any adjacent fields or parkland and the surrounding parts of the property within the unaided view of passers-by, (ii) hotel bedrooms (but not other areas in a hotel) and (iii) those parts of a hospital or nursing home where patients are treated or accommodated.

5. Listening devices

Unless justified by public interest, journalists should not obtain or publish material obtained by using clandestine listening devices or by intercepting private telephone conversations.

6. Hospitals

i) Journalists or photographers making enquiries at hospitals or similar institutions should identify themselves to a responsible executive and obtain permission before entering non-public areas.

ii) The restrictions on intruding into privacy are particularly relevant to enquiries about individuals in hospitals or similar institutions.

7. Misrepresentation

i) Journalists should not generally obtain or seek to obtain information or pictures through misrepresentation or subterfuge.

ii) Unless in the public interest, documents or photographs should be removed only with the express consent of the owner.

iii) Subterfuge can be justified only in the public

interest and only when material cannot be obtained by any other means.

8. Harassment

i) Journalists should neither obtain nor seek to obtain information or pictures through intimidation or harassment.

ii) Unless their enquiries are in the public interest, journalists should not photograph individuals on private property (as defined in the note to Clause 4) without their consent; should not persist in telephoning or questioning individuals after having been asked to desist; should not remain on their property after having been asked to leave and should not follow them.

iii) It is the responsibility of editors to ensure that these requirements are carried out.

9. Payment for articles

i) Payment or offers of payment for stories, pictures or information should not be made directly or through agents to witnesses or potential witnesses in current criminal proceedings except where the material concerned ought to be published in the public interest and there is an overriding need to make or promise to make a payment for this to be done. Journalists must take every possible step to ensure that no financial dealings have influence on the evidence that those witnesses may give.

(An editor authorizing such a payment must be prepared to demonstrate that there is a legitimate public interest at stake involving matters that the public has a right to know. The payment or, where accepted, the offer of payment to any witness who is actually cited to give evidence should be disclosed to the prosecution and the defence and the witness should be advised of this.)

ii) Payment or offers of payment for stories, pictures or information, should not be made directly or through agents to convicted or confessed criminals or to their associates – who may include family, friends and colleagues – except where the material concerned ought to be published in the public interest and payment is necessary for this to be done.

10. Intrusion into grief or shock

In cases involving personal grief or shock, enquiries should be carried out and approaches made with sympathy and discretion.

11. Innocent relatives and friends

Unless it is contrary to the public's right to know,

the press should avoid identifying relatives or friends of persons convicted or accused of crime.

12. Interviewing or photographing children

i) Journalists should not normally interview or photograph children under the age of 16 on subjects involving the personal welfare of the child or of any other child, in the absence of or without the consent of a parent or other adult who is responsible for the children.

ii) Children should not be approached or photographed while at school without the permission of the school authorities.

13. Children in sex cases

1. The press should not, even where the law does not prohibit it, identify children under the age of 16 who are involved in cases concerning sexual offences, whether as victims or as witnesses or defendants.

2. In any press report of a case involving a sexual offence against a child:

i) The adult should be identified.

ii) The word 'incest' should be avoided where a child victim might be identified.

iii) The offence should be described as 'serious offences against young children' or similar appropriate wording.

iv) The child should not be identified.

v) Care should be taken that nothing in the report implies the relationship between the accused and the child.

14. Victims of sexual assault

The press should not identify victims of sexual assault or publish material likely to contribute to such identification unless there is adequate justification and, by law, they are free to do so.

15. Discrimination

i) The press should avoid prejudicial or pejorative reference to a person's race, colour, religion, sex, or sexual orientation or to any physical or mental illness or disability.

ii) It should avoid publishing details of a person's race, colour, religion, sex or sexual orientation unless these are directly relevant to the story.

16. Financial journalism

i) Even where the law does not prohibit it, journalists should not use for their own profit financial information they receive in advance of its general publication, nor should they pass such information to others.

ii) They should not write about shares or securities in whose performance they know that they or their close families have a significant financial interest without disclosing the interest to the editor or financial editor.

iii) They should not buy or sell, either directly or through nominees or agents, shares or securities about which they have written recently or about which they intend to write in the near future.

17. Confidential sources

Journalists have a moral obligation to protect confidential sources of information.

18. The public interest

Clauses 4, 5, 7, 8 and 9 create exceptions that may be covered by invoking the public interest. For the purpose of this Code that is most easily defined as:

i) Detecting or exposing crime or a serious misdemeanour.

ii) Protecting public health and safety.

iii) Preventing the public from being misled by some statement or action of an individual or organization.

In any cases raising issues beyond these three definitions, the Press Complaints Commission will require a full explanation by the editor of the publication involved, seeking to demonstrate how the public interest was served.

On your own

Have you read any stories in newspapers that you think should be brought to the attention of the PCC? Write a letter of complaint to the Press Complaints Commission about a story that you have read in a newspaper. Point out the section(s) of the Code of Practice that you feel the story breaks and explain why you are angry, offended or upset.

Class discussion

- Do you think people should have the right to privacy when newspapers are trying to find out about their private lives?
- Should newspapers be allowed to find out about the private lives of famous stars, or members of the royal family?

Controlling access to the media is important for institutions, as it is a way of protecting their profits. Governments, too, have an interest in who is controlling the flow of information. For many governments, controlling the media is an effective way of stifling the voices of people who do not agree with them. In many countries, there is censorship of the media, which means that the government decides what can and cannot be published or broadcast.

One method of international mass communication poses a real threat to efforts to control the information that passes between people across the globe – the Internet. It was originally set up as a means of communication in the event of nuclear war, so that survivors throughout the world could communicate by computer. Because it crosses international boundaries and is made up largely of contributions from individuals, it is hard to police. Already the government of the United States of America has introduced legislation to control what people put on to the Net, especially material that is indecent or pornographic. In Singapore, the

government is trying to control the sites that Singaporeans can access. Many regular users of the Internet predict that it will soon be taken over by big business interests who will use it for commercial gain. As a result, the Net would lose its identity as a forum for people's ideas and opinions. Such is the power of media institutions to swallow up and repackage commercially the individual voice.

REVIEW

To help you find out what you have learned in this chapter, make notes to answer the following questions:
- What different types of institutions are there?
- Does the word 'institution' mean anything more than an organization that makes media products?
- What have you learned about how media institutions market their products?
- In what ways are the activities of media institutions controlled?

CLASS DISCUSSION

- Do you think that there should be controls over what the media is allowed to publish or broadcast?
- Should the media have the right to tell people anything?
- Can censorship be justified in some circumstances, for example, when a country is at war?

5. AUDIENCE

'Audience' is the word used to describe people who consume media products. This includes viewers of television programmes, cinema-goers, radio listeners and readers of newspapers, magazines and comics. The importance of audiences to the media is obvious. All the papers, broadcasts and recordings in the world would mean nothing if no one read, watched or listened to them. Without an audience, the media would be talking to itself. However, the question most often asked in Media Studies is 'Who is in control?' Does the media control the audience, or the audience the media?

The media's effects on its audience

The evil empire

On one side of the debate are those who argue that the media is a very powerful force and that the effects it has on its audiences are largely bad. They believe that people, especially those who are easily influenced, tend to imitate what they see or read. There are many violent and sexual images in the media, which they say lead to more violence and sexual activity in society. This argument has gained support because some people have made links between specific media products and individual crimes. The murder of toddler James Bulger in 1993 by two 10-year-old boys was one of the most shocking to have taken place in Britain. The boys were said to have been influenced by watching a particular horror film, although it is not certain that they actually saw the film. The same film was linked with the mass shooting of holidaymakers in the Australian resort of Port Arthur. One strange illustration of a link between TV, children and violence followed the broadcast of an advert for a soft drink in 1993, which showed a man slapping another person. The advertisement was stopped after there were reports of children imitating it and being hurt as a result.

Some people have also claimed that the portrayal of sex on TV has led to a drop in what are called moral standards. They say that young people have copied characters in television dramas and become involved in sexual activity without considering its consequences.

In Britain in the 1960s, concern over the content of films and programmes on TV and radio led to the creation of the National Viewers' and Listeners' Association in 1965. Its founder, Mary Whitehouse, became a national figure through her campaigns to clean up British television. This concern also led to what is known as the 'nine o'clock watershed' on terrestrial channels. This is an agreement not to show explicit sex or violence before 9.00 pm, so that parents will know that they can let their children watch programmes before this time. However, it is not just television that has been accused of corrupting the young. In America, complaints about violent imagery and swearwords in the lyrics of pop songs led to Parental Advisory stickers being placed on many CDs to warn of potentially offensive language.

Newspapers and magazines have not escaped criticism. Explicit photography and the detailed descriptions of sex and violence in newspapers have been said to have a negative influence on readers. Magazines aimed at teenagers have been attacked for promoting sexual promiscuity by publishing material on contraception and physical relationships. Music and fashion magazines have been slated for their 'glorification' of the bad behaviour of pop stars. The National Lottery has been accused of encouraging people to gamble by leading them to believe that money and happiness are the same thing.

NATIONAL VIEWERS' AND LISTENERS' ASSOCIATION

> ### ON YOUR OWN
> How much violence is there on television? Carry out a content analysis experiment on an evening's viewing (see pages 33–34 for tips on how to do this). Count the number of violent acts shown. Consider:
> - Are there different types of violence?
> - Are some portrayals of violence worse than others? For example, compare the violence in dramas to that in cartoons.

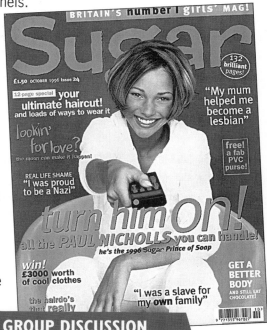

GROUP DISCUSSION
Do teenage magazines encourage their readers to think about sex?

The power of the media to influence, if not to offend, is officially recognized by bodies set up to keep an eye on media output. The British Board of Film Classification (BBFC) gives each film and video a certificate that states whether it is suitable for children or young people to watch. The BBFC can also decide that a film or video is not suitable for public distribution and refuse to give it a certificate. All films and videos have to be certified by the BBFC if they are to be distributed legally to the public in Britain, although local councils have the final decision on whether a film should be shown in cinemas in their area. The BBFC started life as the British Board of Film Censors in 1912. It was set up to advise local councils on which films were suitable for public viewing. It became known as the British Board of Film Classification in 1985 when it was designated under the Video Recordings Act 1984 as the organization that would carry out the classification of videos for sale or rent.

The BBFC certification symbols usually appear on videos and discs, although sometimes you see them on posters advertising films. Each film receives a certificate that states its category, which must be displayed before the film begins. Uc is a category specially invented for videos. Some videos are exempt from classification usually labelled as 'E'. This applies to music and educational videos, for example.

Consumer advice is found on videos. It is in a form laid down by the BBFC.

GROUP DISCUSSION

The BBFC applies different standards of censorship and classification to films and videos. For example, a film may have more scenes of sex and violence cut when it is released on video than when it was shown at the cinema. Why do you think this is?

British Board of Film Classification certification		
Film	Symbol	Video
Universal: suitable for viewers of all ages.	U	Universal: suitable for all.
	Uc	Particularly suitable for young children.
Parental Guidance: whether children should watch the film is left for parents to decide.	PG	Parental Guidance: suitable for general viewing, but some scenes may be unsuitable for young children.
Suitable only for viewers of 12 years and over.	12	Suitable only for persons of 12 years and over. Not to be supplied to any person below that age.
Suitable only for viewers of 15 years and over.	15	Suitable only for persons of 15 years and over. Not to be supplied to any person below that age.
Suitable only for viewers of 18 years and over. Contains scenes or language of an adult nature that are unsuitable for viewers under the age of 18.	18	Suitable only for persons of 18 years and over. Not to be supplied to any person below that age.
For restricted distribution only. To be viewed only at cinemas to which no one under the age of 18 is admitted.	RESTRICTED 18	For restricted distribution only. To be supplied only in licensed sex shops to persons of not less than 18 years.

Video and computer games present new problems of classification. Many games are violent and use realistic graphics. Digital technology has developed, for instance, CD-ROMs (Compact Disc-Read Only Memory), CD-i (Compact Disc-interactive), Laserdiscs and in 1997 DVD (Digital Video Discs). These formats allow video images, including those showing extreme violence and explicit sex, to be stored on disc and generated by computers. Some material of this sort is controlled under the Video Recordings Act (1984). The BBFC is responsible for assessing it, via its video classification system. Many video and computer games, however, are exempt because they do not contain significant violence, sex or criminal techniques. In an attempt to deal with this situation, the computer games industry designed its own voluntary system of categories for games not covered by the Video Recordings Act.

Many CD-ROMs are educational or games-based.

Until 1997 complaints about sex and violence on TV and radio were studied by the Broadcasting Standards Council. In 1997 this body merged with the Broadcasting Complaints Commission, which investigated complaints against broadcasters relating to unfair treatment in programmes. The continued body is still called the Broadcasting Standards Council. The Independent Broadcasting Authority had responsibility for regulating broadcasting on independent commercial television stations until the Independent Television Commission took over in 1991. Their remit includes cable and satellite television.

Independent Television Commission

■ Do media products such as films and CDs need to be classified in terms of how much sex, violence and bad language they contain?

CLASS DISCUSSION

■ How do you judge what is harmful and what is not?

Brainwashing buyers

Perhaps the most sustained attack on the media's effect on audiences has been in response to advertising. Advertising is one of the major ways that media producers make money. Manufacturers pay the media to promote images of their products, which they hope will encourage people to buy them. Many people say that the media's most important function is not to entertain audiences, but to deliver customers to advertisers. An enormous amount of advertising is carried in the media. Up to 60% of a newspaper's content can be made up of adverts. On commercial television, advertisements appear on average four times an hour. On radio stations, adverts are played frequently. Even the non-commercial BBC broadcasts advertisements for its own merchandise, such as videos and books associated with its programmes.

Critics say that the constant bombardment of audiences with advertising is little short of brainwashing. They believe that the sophisticated promotion of products in the media must lead viewers and listeners to buy things that they don't need. The powerful effect of advertising on children causes particular disagreement and discussion. Parents complain about adverts for toys that are shown during and around children's TV programmes. They say that advertisers correctly think that children will beg their parents for toys they have seen advertised on television.

ANTI-ADVERT
On your own, design an advertisement for a product that promises the opposite of what advertisements usually offer, for example, a product that would make you unhappy or unpopular with the opposite sex, such as Bad Breath Mints.

However, it is not only children who are seen as open to the effects of advertising. Success with the opposite sex, luxurious lifestyles, ultimate happiness and freedom from worry are all promised by advertisements for everything from chocolate to floor polish. The Advertising Standards Authority regulates the content of adverts in the media by monitoring such factors as taste, honesty and decency. (See the case study on advertising, pages 206–209.)

Television and computer zombies

The media has also been accused of having an even more sinister effect on its audience: it has been charged with turning people into virtual zombies, addicted to the glow of television and computer screens. A frightening picture is painted of people with glazed eyes whose minds have been hijacked by the media. Children are seen as glued to the TV set instead of playing creatively. Teenagers are portrayed as living in a fantasy world of computer games. Adults are shown as being concerned only with soap operas, newspaper gossip and the latest product advertised on television. The media is charged with the break-up of family life, as adults gather around the television and children are hypnotized by the computer screen.

This picture of the media's effect is known as the hypodermic model. The idea is that the media injects its consumers with the messages and meanings it chooses and that the audience has no real power to resist. In support of this argument, it is pointed out that many people actually believe that what they see in soap operas is real. When a popular character dies, it is common for wreaths to be sent to the studios by grief-stricken viewers. It is also noted that much space, especially in tabloid newspapers, is taken up with news from soap operas, rather than from the real world.

CLASS DISCUSSION
Do computer and video games promote anti-social behaviour?

Audience fragmentation

It is important neither to overestimate the power of the audience, nor to underestimate the ability of the media to take advantage of the audience's demands. Increasingly, media producers are cleverly identifying and splitting off (or fragmenting) particular audiences in order to make money. Satellite and cable TV companies have been particularly good at this. By buying the exclusive rights to show Premier Division football, Sky split viewers of soccer from a general sports audience and charged them to watch the matches.

Pay-per-view television, where viewers pay to receive a particular programme on satellite or cable TV, has become more common in this country. The programmes in question are usually top sporting events. There has been much disagreement and discussion concerning pay-per-view television, because many people think that it exploits viewers.

Audience participation

One method the media has used to increase consumption of its products is audience participation. This means getting the audience involved in the media itself. Some television programmes depend on the audience providing most of the entertainment. These include shows made up of home videos sent in by viewers, or amateur talent contests.

GROUP DISCUSSION

What advantages does audience participation have for media producers?

AUDIENCE PARTICIPATION TECHNIQUES

TALK SHOWS   Quiz programmes

Phone votes   Readers' letters, faxes and e-mails

Open-access television   COMPETITION

Community television programmes   RIGHT TO REPLY

The audience's effects on the media

Are you a radio addict, a TV slave or a computer zombie? Do you live in a fantasy world peopled by characters who don't really exist? When you see something advertised, do you feel that you must go out and buy it? Your answer to these questions will probably be, 'No'. The hypodermic model of the media's effect has been criticized for seeing audiences as too passive and stupid. After all, no one forces you to turn on the television or to buy a magazine. If the media was as much in control as the hypodermic model suggests, then people would watch, listen or read anything that was broadcast or published. This is clearly not the case. Some television shows are unsuccessful, and newspapers and magazines go out of business. Not all products advertised in the media sell and some bands heralded as the 'next big thing' flop. These are examples of the power exercised by audiences.

Audience power has also led to the development of different forms of media. BBC radio used to consist of just one station, the Home Service. It split into Radios 1, 2, 3 and 4, because it was recognized that there were different types of radio listeners; in other words, there were audiences with different tastes. On TV, Channel Four's success is based on catering for so-called 'minority audiences' through programmes on subjects that are largely ignored by the BBC and mainstream television stations. Classic FM, a national commercial radio station that plays nothing but classical music, was launched after it was realized that there was an audience demand for it. All these developments point to the power of the audience to affect what the media produces.

GROUP DISCUSSION

What does the existence of pirate radio stations suggest about the appeal to audiences of legal stations?

To get a clear picture of how the media works in our society, we must consider how audiences can actually influence what it produces. It may be the case that many people enjoy watching soap operas. However, it is not the case that people will mindlessly watch any soap opera that is screened. The TV graveyard is full of soap operas that failed to attract enough viewers. These include *El Dorado*, a soap set in Spain, *Albion Market*, which was about stall-holders in Manchester, and *Castles*, a series about middle-class families. Pressure from viewers can also lead programme makers to change scripts, kill off unpopular characters and even bring others back from the dead.

Finding out about the audience
How does the audience use the media?

In order to study audiences, it is important to consider how people actually use media products. Most newspapers in Britain might support the Conservative Party, but what if the people buying the papers do not read the political comment? They might, for instance, buy the paper for the sport, bingo, stars, television page or even the cartoons. People might watch soap operas for amusement, treating them more like pantomimes than like dramas in which they become emotionally involved. Some people use the radio for companionship. They put it on to hear a friendly voice and are not too concerned which friendly voice it is. Teenagers might like a certain type of music because it is good to dance to, not because of its rebellious lyrics.

This way of looking at the relationship between the media and its audience is called the 'uses and gratifications' approach. It considers how people use media products and what they get out of them. They might use the media as part of their social lives. For example, going to the pictures can play a central role in the development of a relationship between two people. Friends might gather to watch a big game on television, or contact each other through requests or phone-ins on radio shows. For individuals, the media can fulfil personal and psychological needs. Viewers may see a reflection of themselves in characters on TV. They may watch detective shows to test their powers of reasoning in predicting 'who did it'. Or they might enjoy the tension of seeing whether two characters become romantically involved in a drama.

On your own

Make a list of your favourite media products, for example, television programmes, magazines, radio stations and so on. Write a few sentences about each one, saying:
● How you use it
● What you get out of it

What does the audience want from the media?

Media producers need to know what people think about their products in order to increase the size of their audiences. To discover what is popular and what is not, media organizations do a great deal of audience research. There are commercial audience research companies that carry out investigations for media producers. Additionally, organizations set up specifically to investigate audiences include:

The Broadcasters Audience Research Board (BARB), which produces information on television audiences for the BBC and ITV television companies. The information includes the numbers of people watching programmes, their reactions to them and their reasons for watching them.

BARB

BROADCASTERS'
AUDIENCE
RESEARCH
BOARD LTD

BARB produces charts each week showing the top thirty most watched television programmes. Many newspapers publish charts showing the week's top ten programmes, which are are based on BARB'S information.

The Radio Joint Audience Research (RAJAR), which conducts research into radio audiences and the reasons they tune in to particular stations and programmes.
The National Readership Surveys Ltd (NRS), which calculates the number of people reading newspapers and magazines.

Audience research

TECHNIQUES
- **Questionnaires**
- **Interviews**
- Asking people to keep **diaries** of what they listen to or watch
- **Monitoring television sets** to see which programmes are being watched.

These techniques generally produce two kinds of information...

DATA
- **Quantitative data**, or information in the form of numbers, such as how many people watched a particular programme or read a specific magazine.
- **Qualitative data**, or information on people's opinions about media products, for instance, whether they like them and why or how they could be improved.

GROUP ACTIVITY

Carry out a survey among the members of your class to find out which soap operas are the most popular. To do this you will have to produce a questionnaire and carry out interviews. Try to gather both quantitative and qualitative data.

TIP
Keep the questionnaire simple and the interviews short.

To make sense of information gathered through audience research, investigators group similar types of people into categories. This allows them to say what different kinds of people like or dislike particular media products. Measurements used to group people during research include age, sex, income, education and occupation. A very important measurement used in audience research is that of social class. A person's social class is determined by a combination of their income, education, lifestyle and other factors. Social classes in their broadest sense are split into upper, middle and lower or working classes. More complicated measurement scales split these three categories into smaller sections. The one used by many market research organizations is based on the Registrar General's scale of social class set out as long ago as 1911. Newspaper and magazine publishers use this scale to judge what percentage of their readers come from which group. The scale separates people into six groups, depending on the job of the head of the household (or main wage-earner).

A commonly used class measurement scale	
Category	**Description**
A	**Upper middle class** People working in top-level management and professions
B	**Middle class** Middle-level managers and middle-ranking professionals
C1	**Lower middle class** Junior managers, supervisors, clerical workers and lower ranking professionals
C2	**Skilled working class** Skilled manual workers
D	**Working class** Semi-skilled and unskilled manual workers
E	**People at the lowest level of income** For example, state pensioners and casual workers.

GROUP ACTIVITY

■ How would you divide members of an audience if you were doing research into readership of a magazine?

■ Make a list of the factors that would be important to help you to make sense of the information you gathered.

■ How could the information gathered be used to make more money for the publisher of the magazine?

Audience positioning

One of the ways in which the media is believed to inject its powerful effect on audiences is through what is known as audience positioning. Audience positioning refers to the relationship between the audience and the media product. It also refers to how a media product addresses, or talks, to its audience. A media text offers a position to an audience in the way it allows them to see the people, issues and events it covers.

As the chapter on representation discusses (see page 28), media texts are not direct records of reality, but re-presentations of it. Each media re-presentation is the product of a process of selection and editing of information, in the form of film shots, radio interviews or news stories. Because of this process, there will always be other possible re-presentations of the people, events, stories and issues appearing in the media. For example, crime dramas usually position the audience with the main detective character. The viewer follows the detective as if they were looking over his or her shoulder, gets the clues in the order the detective gets them and sympathizes with the detective's point of view. It is very rare for a crime drama to position the audience with the criminal.

However, the position offered to audiences by media texts is not the only possible one. Crime and police dramas could position the viewer with the criminal, showing how they see the world and even encouraging viewers to sympathize with them. However, this does not usually happen. Why? Some say this is because it is in society's interests to promote 'good' behaviour and discourage people from breaking the law. Others argue, however, that what is defined as 'good' behaviour is often biased. For example, people shown taking part in a demonstration in a police drama may be represented as nuisances, because the police may view them from the position of having to control such events. The right to demonstrate peacefully, however, is regarded by many as one of the basic rights of our society. The position offered to the audience in the police drama is therefore seen by many as political, since it may affect viewers' opinions about the right to demonstrate.

★ TODAY Monday January 9 1995 19

DONORS KEBABED

by NICKI POPE, Medical Correspondent

BLOOD given free by British donors is being advertised for sale abroad.

TODAY has obtained documents showing blood by-products from this country being offered to the Turkish medical service.

Sales company Sodhan Vaccine and Blood Products markets itself around voluntary donors.

Doctors set a higher store by voluntarily-given blood because it removes the risk of drug addicts or other unsuitable people giving it purely for cash.

Babies

The by-products are said to come from the National Blood Authority's Bio Products Laboratory (BPL) in Elstree, Herts.

Included on the "for sale" list, are:
● Factor VIII, used by haemophiliacs,
● Human hepatitis B immunoglobulin, giving immunity to the disease,
● Anti-D rhesus immunoglobulin, used on babies, of which there is a UK short-

age. A spokesman for Sodhan said yesterday it bought "unused by-products of blood from BPL".

One brochure for Human hepatitis B immunoglobulin boasts: "It is collected free from voluntary donors."

But BPL's chief executive Richard Walker said the only product sold to Turkey was the protein Albumin, used to treat burns and shock victims, of which there was a huge surplus.

Mr Walker added: "We are not necessarily selling these products but that doesn't mean an agent won't list them.

"Our primary intention is to satisfy UK self-sufficiency and never to bleed a donor to export.

"We plan to export any-

Now they sell your blood to the Turks

TODAY EXCLUSIVE

thing in surplus which we can export. We never sell unless the only option is to burn it." TODAY also has documents showing interest from Bangladesh and Saudi

Arabia in British blood by-products.

The blood-for-sale claims come as the authority appeals for donors. TODAY told last month how the Authority planned to make £14 million exporting blood plasma to Germany.

BLOOD MONEY

You give it free ... they sell it to the Germans

TODAY in December '94

DIABETICS PAY FOR NEEDLES

HOSPITAL chiefs are to make diabetics pay for their needles.

Hammersmith Hospitals NHS Trust, which gave two executives golden handshakes worth more than £120,000, will save just £8,000 a year.

The move hits diabetics who use an insulin pen rather than a syringe.

WHOSE BLOOD IS IT ANYWAY?

Newspapers offer their audience a position on events, which influences who they sympathize with or who they criticize.
- Who does this newspaper story position the reader with?
- How does the story do this?

All media texts also have a way of talking to, or addressing, their users. The way a media text addresses its users also influences the position an audience is offered. Television newsreaders address the viewer face-to-face, as if they were talking directly to them. They use a serious but sincere tone of voice, like that of a concerned friend. This, some argue, positions the viewer with the newsreader and encourages them to believe what he or she is saying. Remember, what the newsreader is saying is only a representation of the news. However, because the newsreader appears to be friendly and worthy of trust, it is argued that viewers will tend to believe almost anything newsreaders say. This may be acceptable if news accounts are accurate, but what if they are biased or filled with lies?

Newspapers also position their readers through the way they address them. Stories in tabloid newspapers tend to be written as if the writer were having a conversation with the reader.

It is assumed that the person reading the story will hold the same beliefs as those expressed in the paper. In fact, most tabloids claim that they do more than just report the news – they say they speak for their readers. For example, in 1984 most tabloid newspapers did not support striking miners during their long industrial dispute. Many printed appeals for an end to the strike. The position they offered their readers was firmly against the strikers and they addressed their readers as if they agreed with that position.

CLASS DISCUSSION

During the Gulf War in 1990, BBC newsreaders referred to service personnel from this country as 'British forces'. ITN newsreaders called them 'Our forces'.
- What difference does each term make to the audience's position?
- How does each description position the viewer in relation to each side in the conflict?

Typical audiences

Most media producers have a typical viewer or reader in mind when they are putting together their products. This is someone whom the media producers believe to be typical of the audience of a particular product. Media producers mould their products to cater for the characteristics of this ideal consumer. For example, a men's lifestyle magazine may have a typical reader who is 35 years old, married with young children, works in an office, drives and takes foreign holidays. Therefore most of the articles in the magazine will be about topics that the publishers think a 35-year-old married man with children, a car and an office job will be interested in. This, then, will be the main audience position offered to the reader of the magazine.

In general, the presumed background and interests of the typical consumer will dictate the position given to the audience of a particular product. The audience position will determine such factors as:

The type of language used. A childrens' TV programme will not use adult words that its audience might not understand. A presenter on a rock music radio programme will use the latest rock world slang, rather than the 'correct' English used on BBC Radio 4.

The tone of voice used. Teenagers would not watch or listen to television and radio programmes aimed at them if the presenters talked in dull, middle-aged voices. So presenters on youth programmes tend to speak in excited, breathless tones, to give the impression that something is always going on. Magazines and newspapers also adopt a particular tone in which they talk to the reader. The tone of such tabloid newspapers as *The Sun* is conversational, while that of such broadsheets as *The Times* is formal.

The subjects covered. A popular quiz show screened during the early evening is unlikely to ask in-depth questions about chemistry. However, *University Challenge* or *Mastermind* may well ask questions on the subject.

Group discussion

• Why do you think that different quiz shows cover different topics?
• What does the choice of subjects say about the audience that is expected to watch each quiz show?

ON YOUR OWN
Draw up a profile of the typical viewers or readers of the following:
• A television soap opera
• A tabloid newspaper
• A pop music show on radio or television
• An action comic.

Media producers would say that they tailor their programmes and publications to the needs of their audience by using these typical reader or viewer positions. Others argue that what the media producers really do is create viewers and readers who live their lives according to what they see on TV and read in magazines.

Media Studies audience research

Media producers are not the only ones interested in audience behaviour. Researchers in Media Studies devote much time and energy to finding out who watches, listens to or reads what. They are particularly keen to discover how people of different age, sex and social class use the media. They use techniques similar to those used by commercial researchers and ask such questions as:
• Are some programmes watched more by men than women and, if so, why?
• Do children take television dramas aimed at them seriously?
• Which social classes read what newspapers and why?
The importance given to certain types of programme by different people is also an area of key interest. For example, men may view documentaries as being of greater value than soap operas.

How and where do we become an audience?

One area of much interest to Media Studies researchers is what is called the viewing, listening or reading context, or where the audience consumes media products. The places in which the audience comes into contact with media products change over time, because of developments in media technology and social trends.

Before the introduction of television, most people relied on the radio as a source of information and entertainment. It became a habit in many homes for families to gather around the wireless set. The tradition was carried on when TV sets became a common feature of most households. If you draw a map of most sitting-rooms, you will find that the television set is the central point around which the rest of the furniture is organized. This has implications for the way family life is structured. The television becomes the focal point of attention, rather than the other people in the room. This, some say, leads to a breakdown in communication within families, as everyone is too busy watching the TV to talk to each other. Others, however, argue that television promotes communication as it provides material for family members to talk about.

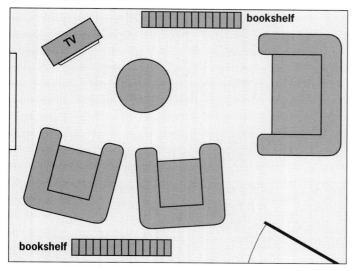

bookshelf

bookshelf

Most sitting-rooms are organized around the television set.

CLASS DISCUSSION

Does the central role of the television in most sitting-rooms encourage families to talk, or does it silence them?

An interesting area of audience research is the issue of who has control over what is watched on the TV – father, mother or the children.

Who's in control?

Monitor who controls what is watched on television in your house.
- *Who keeps hold of the remote control?*
- *Does it depend on what time of day it is?*
- *Who has the final say over what is watched?*

The replacement of radio by television led radio producers to look for other listening contexts. A major new listening context was offered by the development of in-car entertainment. Drive-time, or the hours when most people are driving to and from work, has become a peak period for radio consumption. Many radio stations have tailored their broadcast formats to meet the demands of the drive-time audience by providing a mix of upbeat music, traffic and weather reports. Another listening context targeted by radio producers is the workplace, with such features as office of the day, live coverage of community events and live outside broadcasts.

Drive-time.

The introduction of the VCR (Video Cassette Recorder) into people's homes led to a revolution in viewing habits. The VCR allowed viewers to:

Tape one programme while watching another. This increased the possible audience for a programme, as people did not have to make a choice between watching one programme or another.

Tape programmes while they were out. This again increased the possible audience for a programme, as people who would have missed it could now record it. Also, viewers were no longer tied to the scheduling of TV companies.

Buy pre-recorded tapes and watch them at home. This could reduce the size of the possible audience for a programme, as viewers had a greater range of options from which to choose.

The launch of the VCR also had a major effect on the cinema. It was widely expected that if people were offered the choice between watching a film at the cinema or in the comfort of their own home, they would opt to stay at home. As a result, it was predicted that cinemas would disappear from our towns and cities. To some extent, this did happen and many old independent picture houses closed because of a fall in customer numbers. The rise of the VCR also led to the development of the made-for-video film, which is a production that is not shown at cinemas and can be seen only on video. However, although it went through a radical change, cinema did not disappear. The development of multi-screen cinema complexes attracted a new audience for films. The complexes owed much of their success to the fact that they made going to the cinema into an occasion. Surround sound, luxury seats, fast food, drinks and special showings all contributed to this. In an interesting twist, video rental shops then began to look more like cinema foyers, with popcorn and ice-cream on sale.

Computer games have also affected the way people use the media. Many computer game systems run on television sets. This means that many people use their television sets for playing games rather than for watching programmes, which reduces the audience for TV programmes. Alternatively, some people own more than one television set, so that a spare one could of course be used to watch television programmes when a computer game is being played; this increases both the possible audience for TV programmes and the market for television sets. Other games and education systems run on computers with their own monitors, or hand-held systems, which again reduce the number of people available to watch television. However, it could offer radio producers a new listening context – computer-time.

The Internet, a large system of connected computers all round the world that people use to communicate with each other, has created a new audience that many media producers have tried to exploit. Newspapers and radio stations have set up their own home pages, which Internet users can visit via their computer screens. Advertisers have also put their own 'sites' on the Internet and sponsored others. This is not only exploitation of a new media market, but also a response to a drop in TV viewing figures that has been seen as a result of the Internet.

CLASS ACTIVITY

- Find out how many people in your class have a computer.
- How much leisure time do those who have a computer spend using it?
- How much time does each person in the whole class spend watching television? (Keep two sets of figures, one for those with a computer and one for those without.)
- Compare the two sets of results. Is there a difference between those who have a computer and those who don't?

REVIEW – ON YOUR OWN

When talking about audiences, it is easy to think of them as things and to forget that they are actually made up of people like you. Everyone you know is part of an audience for at least one media project.

- Make a list of all the audiences of which you are a part.
- Do you accept without question everything that you see or hear as a member of each audience?
- Jot down how and why you became part of each audience.
- Do you consume the media? Or does it consume you?

6. SOAP OPERA

Coronation Street is probably the most popular programme on British television. It regularly attracts audiences of over 15 million viewers to four weekly editions. Its following among such a large section of the viewing public is an important source of advertising revenue for the independent TV companies, as well as being fascinating to Media Studies researchers. This case study looks behind the scenes at the production of a programme that has maintained its popularity for over 30 years.

CLASS DISCUSSION

WHAT'S IN A NAME?

Soap operas take their name from the fact that on American radio they were originally sponsored by companies who made soap powders. Today producers prefer to call soaps 'serial dramas'. Why do you think that this is? Why do Media Studies books still call them soap operas?

History

The show was first transmitted on 9th December 1960. Initially, a pilot of 13 episodes was made by Granada Television, which was then a fairly new company in TV production. These programmes were shown only in north-west England on Friday and Monday evenings. It was not until May 1961 that the programme was taken by the ITV network, which meant that it was shown nationally. The programmes were rescheduled to Monday and Wednesday.

LAST NIGHT'S VIEW

A NEW twice-weekly serial came to ITV last night ... screened just before the existing twice-a-week serial "Emergency Ward 10".

Apart from this boob in programme planning I doubt if "Coronation Street" can emulate "Ward 10's" long-running success, writes JACK BELL.

DRUDGERY

The idea of telling the human stories of a single street has already been explored in documentary form this year in Michael Ingram's "Our Street."

And the drama value of such programmes has been culled in Bill Naughton's "June Evening" on BBC.

"Coronation Street" lacks both Naughton's talented observation and "Ward 10's" unusual atmosphere.

I find it hard to believe that viewers will want to put up with continuous slice of life domestic drudgery two evenings a week.

One critic who got it seriously wrong!

In those early days, the Friday evening transmission was live. This meant that if actors fluffed their lines, or if anything else went wrong, there was no second chance to get it right. The

Monday episode was recorded immediately after the live transmission. The programme was an immediate success. The two episodes a week quickly became the most popular programmes on the network, despite the fact that many critics thought that a drama based on northern working-class lives might be too depressing for a mass audience.

Many programmes in the early days of television were broadcast live.
■ Which programmes go out live today?

GROUP DISCUSSION

■ What are the advantages for a television company of recording programmes for later transmission?

■ Try to produce your own short extract (3–5 minutes) from a current TV programme to go out live.
■ What problems did you encounter?

Characteristics of the Street

Coronation Street is an example of a genre known as 'kitchen-sink drama'. This is a play or film with a domestic setting, which is mainly about the lives of ordinary people. During the 1960s, many of the films made by the British cinema industry took working-class life as their theme. For example, *A Kind of Loving*, *Saturday Night and Sunday Morning*, *Billy Liar* and *This Sporting Life* were popular films set in northern towns, which featured the lives of ordinary people.

Many people feel that the real attraction of the Street is that it is character-based. This means that it relies more on strong characters, with whom the audience can identify, than on dealing with issues. This is particularly true of the female characters. Since its creation by Tony Warren, the series has traditionally been centred on strong women with outgoing, forceful personalities. In the early days, this included such characters as Ena Sharples (played by Violet Carson) and Elsie Tanner (played by Pat Phoenix). More recently, such characters as Vera Duckworth (Liz Dawn) have continued this tradition.

Another important quality that has become a hallmark of the programme is its emphasis on comedy. Many of its storylines invite the audience to laugh at, or sometimes with, the characters. In fact, it can be argued

IN PAIRS

⚥ What do you think is meant by a strong female character?

⚥ Give some examples from Coronation Street and other soaps.

⚥ Are there strong female characters in other television programmes or in films?

⚥ Do strong female characters only appeal to female audiences?

that certain characters can only be given comic storylines, as a more serious storyline would seem out of place. When *Coronation Street* does deal with serious issues, it tends to do so when they have ceased to be news headlines, unlike some soaps. *Coronation Street* producers say that they prefer to wait and treat important social issues in a way that develops naturally from one of the established characters.

IN PAIRS

● Make a list of the characters in *Coronation Street* who you think would probably be given only comic storylines.

● Do you think it would be possible to write a more serious storyline around any of them? Explain your answer.

NAMING THE SERIES
The original name planned for the series was Florizel Street. This was later changed to Jubilee Street, until the title Coronation Street was finally chosen.

GROUP DISCUSSION

■ Why do you think the name Coronation Street was chosen? To which coronation might the name of the street refer?

■ Do you know the names of any other fictional streets in the series? What do you think of when you hear their names?

■ If a soap were to be based on the area where you live, what would it be called? Give reasons for your answer.

Visitors all want to pose for their photograph on the set of the famous street.

Writing the scripts

A programme such as *Coronation Street* relies heavily on the work of its writers. At any one time, there are around 14 writers working on the script. They are supported by three storyline writers, part of whose job it is to prepare a scene-by-scene summary of each planned episode. There is also a programme historian, who keeps a detailed archive in which details can be checked. The storyline writers' job is to plan the next three weeks' episodes. They also plan in detail the development of the stories. Each episode must contain at least three storylines, with a balance between a serious storyline, a comic one and an everyday, run-of-the-mill story. Obviously, if there is a serious dramatic event in an episode, a death, for example, comedy will not be allowed to intrude.

The producer calls a script conference every three weeks, at which the writers are given details of the ongoing stories on which they will work. They are asked for ideas about stories that feature characters who may not have been prominent for some time. Each writer attends a commissioning conference, where the storylines and the development of any new characters who are to be introduced are discussed. After this, each writer has about two weeks to script a single episode. Occasionally, a writer may be asked to prepare two episodes, although this is uncommon, because it would take too much time to write so much.

Actors themselves also have a say about what happens to the characters they play. They often make suggestions about how the role might develop, so that a writer can work on appropriate storylines. For instance, much of the writing revolves around groups of characters who relate well to each other, which can determine the storylines that are developed.

On your own

- Watch *Coronation Street* over a period of, say, a week. What are the main storylines? Which of the three categories mentioned do they fit?
- Now do the same with another soap. Is it constructed in the same way?

IN PAIRS

Try to think of groups of characters in Coronation Street who get on well with each other.
- *How are their lives interlinked?*
- *In what situations do they relate to one another? Does this seem natural?*
- *Can you think of similar groups of characters in another soap?*

Charities and other pressure groups often suggest storylines that would highlight issues with which they are concerned. This can provide an effective way of bringing their concerns to the attention

ON YOUR OWN

Imagine you work for a charity, such as Shelter, which represents the interests of homeless people. You want to suggest a storyline that will draw attention to an important issue that you are concerned about. Write notes about a character and plot that would work as a vehicle for introducing this issue.

of a mass audience, without the costs of advertising or publicity. If a drama can be constructed around a specific issue, the producers may respond to these suggestions.

The programme-makers also carry out research to find out how the audience is responding to certain characters and situations. They are particularly keen to learn about viewers' preferences, especially in terms of which characters work together.

ON YOUR OWN

Do your own audience research by asking your family and friends which characters they like and dislike in a variety of soaps. You could show your findings as a table or pie chart.

Not all members of the cast are equally important. There are usually around a dozen or so main characters, with other fringe characters, although the number of characters increased when the transmission of weekly episodes went up to four in 1996. When new characters are introduced, they are usually given a fringe role at first. For example, they may be seen looking for a house in the Street, visiting a friend or relative, or calling at the pub or the shop. Usually, they then disappear for a few weeks, to be reintroduced as part of a storyline. This has the impact of making the phasing in of a new character appear more natural. Perhaps more importantly, it provides the audience with the opportunity to absorb them into the existing set-up.

A visitor to the set sees if anyone is at home.

CLASS DISCUSSION

- Who are the main characters in the show now?
- Who are your favourite fringe characters?

In groups

Imagine you are asked to think up a new fringe character who would appeal to a specific section of the Coronation Street audience, for instance, young viewers.

- *What kind of person would you create?*
- *How would you introduce your character?*
- *What sort of storylines might you develop around the character?*
- *With which major characters would your character be involved?*
- *Which group(s) would your character fit into?*

The age-range of characters is an important aspect of *Coronation Street*: people from the very young to the very old are represented. On one occasion, a character was cast before he was even born: Nicky Tilsley, the screen son of Gail and Brian Tilsley, was cast while he was still in his mother's womb, as both of his real parents had fair hair, like Gail and Brian.

The age-range of the fans reflects that of the characters.

ACTORS' CONTRACTS
Actors are on different types of contracts. Major characters are usually on a 52-week contract, with guaranteed work for a minimum of 40 weeks, during which time they are on full salary. For the other 12 weeks, they are paid at half-salary. Fringe characters are usually on a contract with guaranteed work for just 12 weeks, payable at full salary, with another 40 weeks on half-pay.

Production schedule

Coronation Street, like all programmes using expensive staff and technical resources, must be produced efficiently. In a factory, goods are made on a production line. The production process is broken down into a series of small, manageable steps. The same breakdown of the process into smaller parts is used to make this and other television programmes as cheaply and efficiently as possible.

The production schedule runs on a four-week cycle. Four directors work on the programme. Each director's cycle is as follows:

Week 1: The director prepares for shooting by working on the script. This involves working with a location planner to find and set up any locations needed in addition to the Street and studio sets. Extras are cast and design work is discussed. Design work covers the elements that go to make up the appearance of each scene in an episode. It includes the furnishing of each set with appropriate props, and decisions about the characters' appearance. The director also prepares a camera script based on the script received from the writers. A camera script involves working out all the camera shots that will be necessary to produce material that can be edited into the final version.

Week 2: Production week begins on SUNDAY, with the shooting of any location scenes. These are scenes that are set in any location other than Granada's own set. Examples might include a scene set in a pub other than the Rover's, or the visit of a character to a relative or friend in another part of town. On MONDAY, the scenes shot in the Street itself are filmed on the studio's own set. Scenes set in the studio are rehearsed all day TUESDAY and on WEDNESDAY MORNING. Care is taken to position characters in such a way that the camera operators can get the shots that the director worked out in the camera script. The placing of microphones, especially for close-up dialogue, also has to be sorted out. In addition, make-up and wardrobe requirements are worked out.

Children of Holy Trinity School, Birmingham, looking at the set of Jim's Café on their tour of Granada Studios.

WEDNESDAY AFTERNOON sees the start of the technical run. This is a rehearsal at which the lighting, cameras and sound are checked to make sure that they are all working to achieve the effect that the director wants. A technical run is a kind of dress rehearsal. The lighting director, senior camera operator, sound supervisor and technical director observe in order to plan how they will work, and to try to identify in advance problems that might arise during recording. At the end of the technical run, any difficulties are discussed. All of the observers' different viewpoints are talked through, as well as any aspects of the interpretation of the script that the actors wish to raise. On **WEDNESDAY EVENING**, the props department makes sure that the appropriate sets are in the studio and the moving director and crew light the sets correctly.

The length of each episode is also important. Each episode should run for 24 minutes and 35 seconds. The rehearsals at the technical run are timed and if an episode is too short, the writer may have to lengthen one or two scenes, or even create an extra one. Similarly, any overrun (or extra time) will have to be cut, which is rather easier than adding to an underrun (an episode that is too short).

Recording starts at 9.00 am on **THURSDAY MORNING**. Each scene is rehearsed until everyone feels it is ready to be recorded. Recording goes on until 6.30 pm. **FRIDAY** follows a similar pattern of recording scenes. If recording falls behind schedule, the cast and crew may have to work until late at night.

In groups

Scenes are often not recorded in the order in which they appear on television. What do you think determines the order in which scenes are recorded?

DIRECTOR'S PRODUCTION CYCLE

WEEK 1	WEEK 2						WEEK 3	WEEK 4
	Sunday	Monday	Tuesday	Wednesday Morning	Thursday	Friday		
Work on script Plan locations Cast extras Design work Prepare camera script	Shoot location scenes	Shoot scenes on Street set	Rehearsal of studio scenes	Rehearsal of studio scenes **Afternoon** Technical run **Evening** Prepare sets and lighting	Recording 9.00 am – 6.30 pm	Recording 9.00 am – 6.30 pm	Editing	Episodes are screened

Week 3: The director spends this week in the editing suite, working with an editor to cut the episodes into their final shape. The director will also have collected the scripts to prepare for the next set of episodes for which they are responsible.

Week 4: Transmission of the episodes that have just been edited takes place in this week.

Continuity is very important. Audiences are very quick to spot and point out any examples of inconsistencies on the part of a character, for example, even if they are many years apart. As scenes are not shot in the order in which they are shown, someone has to check consistency. For instance, if a character leaves the house to go shopping wearing a green coat, it would be wrong if they were next seen in the shop wearing a red one. So the production crew have to take great care to make sure that mistakes like this do not happen. In the same way, the writers and the directors need to consult the programme historian to check that any details of past events that are mentioned are correct.

AS A CLASS

Watch a video of an episode of Coronation Street.
- Make a note of each scene's location.
- Decide the rough order in which the scenes were probably shot.
- What continuity problems would the production team need to think about as they shot the scenes?

Soaps and the audience

The massive following enjoyed by *Coronation Street* and other soaps, such as *Neighbours*, *Eastenders* and *Brookside*, has made them the focus of a lot of research by Media Studies experts. In the chapter on audience, the uses and gratifications theory was discussed (see pages 66–67). It examines the way in which people use the media and how they try to get pleasure from it. The soaps attract huge audiences, which suggests that a lot of people enjoy soaps.

One important aspect of soaps that makes them popular is the idea of community that they represent. Community is the ways in which people live in social groups and relate to each other within those groups. People in a community are concerned for each other's well-being. Most people live close to other people, but as the world changes and communications technology advances, traditional communities, where people meet in such communal areas as the pub, the corner shop or the launderette, have declined. For many people, watching television provides a community. Of course, this sort of community has the advantage that others never make demands on you, for example, by borrowing money or asking for favours. Soaps can be seen as a safe form of interaction with the community, in which the audience

There is a community among the fans, as well as in the soap.

can identify with the characters, loving some and despising others. The audience's problems can be identified in the problems faced by the characters on screen. Alternatively, the characters' problems might make those of the audience seem insignificant in comparison.

There is a community among the fans, as well as in the soap.

The next time that the viewers engage with the real community at work, at school or in a shop, they can use their knowledge of character and plot as a source of harmless gossip, to be enjoyed with friends, colleagues and acquaintances. In this way, the viewers are making social use of their knowledge of the soap. Social use is when people use their knowledge to strengthen their social relationships with others. This might mean discussing the programme with other people, arguing about who is right and who is wrong in a dispute between two characters, or predicting what will happen in various storylines. The tabloid press encourages such speculation by revealing future storylines.

Of course, all this means that what is real and what is fictional become blurred. The characters and situations in a soap readily overlap into the viewers' lives. For this reason, people have argued that some of the audience think that soaps are the real world. They cite examples of people writing letters or sending gifts to characters. On balance, it is unlikely that many people really do believe that soaps are real. One theory, however, suggests that audiences get more pleasure from the genre by pretending that the

What is real and what is
fictional become blurred.

characters are real. It is interesting to note that when actors from
soaps make public appearances, such as opening supermarkets,
they generally do so in role, i.e. acting out the part of the
characters they play.

Producers of soaps often pander to this pretence by providing the
audience with a series of tie-ins and spin-offs – products or
services that link directly or indirectly to the series. *Coronation
Street*'s Granada studios tour in Manchester is a typical example of

Visitors to the studio's tour
buying souvenirs to show off
to their friends.

a tie-in. The studios are located on a 3.5 acre site close to the city centre. The main attraction of the tour is a visit to the working set of the show. Here visitors can pose to have their photograph taken outside the Rover's Return, peer through the letterbox of the front door of their favourite character, or peep into the Street's famous back yards.

During the guided backstage tour, visitors get to see such sets as the Websters' living-room and Jim's Café. Strategically placed shops provide an opportunity for souvenir hunters to spend their cash on such spin-offs as key-rings, T-shirts, mugs and an official magazine, as well as a range of Newton and Ridley beverages and bar towels. (Newton and Ridley is the imaginary brewery that supplies, and once owned, the Rover's Return.) Getting the consumer to advertise the product for you is one of the most effective methods of merchandising.

IT'S GOOD TO TALK
The telephone box outside the hairdresser's was once a live British Telecom line. A problem arose, however, when tour visitors made a note of the number and then called during filming, asking to speak to one or other of the characters.

GROUP DISCUSSION

- Why do you think soap operas like *Coronation Street* are so popular with viewers?
- Do you think they are more popular with some sections of the audience than with others?
- What do you think are the pleasures an audience gets from watching *Coronation Street*?

7. TELEVISION NEWS

As human beings, we need to know what is happening in our environment. We need to know, for example, where we can find food and water, where there is shelter, what poses a danger to us, and much more. We need this essential information to survive. However, most of us also have a desire to know things about our surroundings that are not essential. We want to know about other people's triumphs and tragedies, their good and bad deeds, and their loves and hates; about accidents, wars, disasters and famines. In fact, we want to know just about anything and everything. We are very nosy animals.

If you were asked to find out what is going on in the world, who is doing what, and what people should be concerned about, where would you look? It is a safe bet that you would turn to the news. News is central to our way of life today. It exists to satisfy our desire for vital information, as well as for all kinds of facts, figures, views and gossip.

News is a product presented to an audience by the media.

In Media Studies, the term 'news' does not mean simply telling someone about something. News is a product presented to an audience by the media. Most people in our society get their news

from television. The main evening news programmes regularly attract some of the largest TV audiences. This is reflected by the fact that the most expensive advertising slot on ITV is in the commercial break during *News at Ten*. Television news is popular because of its ability to let the viewer be there when the action is happening.

People used to be able to get news only through newspapers, which was like receiving a letter about an event. The invention of radio allowed a more direct experience of happenings, but it was only as good as receiving a telephone call about them. The TV camera allows viewers to look at events as if they were with the camera operator. This sense of immediate reality has been increased by the development of satellite television stations, such as CNN, that offer live news from around the world as it happens.

ROLLING NEWS

The hunger for news, together with the vast increase in the number of TV channels brought about by satellite and cable technology, have led to what are known as 'rolling news stations'. These are television channels that broadcast nothing but news 24 hours a day. The most famous one in the UK is Sky News. Using a communications satellite, Sky News broadcasts to over 70 million viewers in 40 countries. Its offices are in London, but it also has news bureaux in Dublin, Johannesburg, Belgrade, Jerusalem and Washington DC. The rolling bulletins are the backbone of Sky News. They are broadcast on the hour, every hour, throughout the day. As well as its bulletins, Sky News also broadcasts longer news programmes during its schedule.

Sky News schedule

06.00–09.30
Sky News Sunrise
Comprehensive news, sport and weather to start the day.

11.00, 16.00 and **18.00**
World News and Business Report
Concentrates on international and business information.

17.00–18.00
Live at Five
Looks at the day's top stories. Also includes sport, weather and features on fashion, entertainment and music.

19.00 Sky Evening News
Round-up of the day's news, sport and weather.

22.00 Sky News Tonight
Late evening round-up show.

As well as its own programmes, Sky News also broadcasts news shows from America, including *48 Hours*, *60 Minutes* and the *Evening News* from CBS, and ABC *World News Tonight* and *Nightline*. In addition, Sky has links with the major European broadcasters VTM in Belgium, RTL in Germany and the Netherlands, and Vox TV in Germany. It is a member of ENEX, a news-gathering partnership of many of Europe's leading broadcasters.

Sky News has an alliance with Reuters Television, which is run and owned by the world's leading international news agency. Each Thursday, Sky News broadcasts *Sky Worldwide Report*, a magazine programme of news from around the world. It is put together using the joint resources of Sky Television, CBS, ABC and Reuters Television. Sky News produces special news programmes covering fashion, entertainment and science.

CLASS DISCUSSION

- Are fashion and entertainment really news areas?
- Are they covered to fill in the schedule?
- If so, does this mean that there is not enough 'real news' to broadcast non-stop all day?

As the chapter on representation showed (pages 29–30), the impression that television news simply records exactly what is going on in the world is a false one. Most news is carefully packaged for us through the use of editing and the techniques of presentation. Even live 'as-it-happens' news cannot hope to reflect everything that is happening. It is limited by what the camera lens can pick up and by the direction in which the camera operator points the camera.

This chapter will take a close look at how one TV station produces the news for its viewers. You will see that a lot of work goes into making the news, which is a commodity put together by professionals, according to well-established methods.

A typical news day at Calendar

Calendar is the news service of Yorkshire Television. It produces eight bulletins throughout the day, as well as a nine-minute lunchtime news programe and a 30-minute main news programme at 6.00 pm, which is watched by around one million people. Calendar's headquarters is at Yorkshire Television's Newscentre in Leeds, which opened in 1990 and cost £2 million. It uses some of the most sophisticated newsroom computer systems and transmission equipment in the world.

Calendar also has five regional offices in York, Hull, Grimsby, Sheffield and Lincoln, which are all staffed by reporters and camera crews. This network of offices enables Calendar to split its large broadcasting area (which includes all of Yorkshire, Lincolnshire and parts of Nottinghamshire and Norfolk) into three separate sub-regions:

Calendar Central covers north, west and parts of south Yorkshire, as well as north Nottinghamshire and north Derbyshire. It operates from the main Newscentre in Leeds.

Calendar East covers east Yorkshire, Lincolnshire and north Norfolk, via offices in Lincoln, Grimsby and Hull. These offices are served by four news camera crews, a team of reporters and five freelance camera operators.

Calendar South covers Sheffield and Chesterfield, providing one of the smallest localized television news services in the UK. It is staffed by a main presenter and 17 other editorial and technical staff.

Calendar provides each of these sub-regions with its own separate, specialized news service, which concentrates on stories relevant to its areas. Five times a day, Calendar broadcasts three sub-regional bulletins simultaneously. The 30-minute evening show is broadcast from the main Calendar Newscentre at 6.00 pm, with electronic

Calendar's newsroom at Yorkshire Television's Newscentre.

links that allow sub-regional news round-ups to be included in the programme.

<u>06:15</u> **The first bulletin** begins Calendar's day. Bulletins are short programmes that usually last no more than four minutes. They consist of a single presenter reading the news 'to camera'. At Calendar, the presenter sits alone in a small studio facing a camera. Below the camera is an autocue. This is a screen that displays what the presenter has to say during the broadcast. The autocue allows the newsreader to look straight at the camera while reading the script. This means that direct eye-contact is maintained with the viewer. The presenter also has a bulletin script, a typed script of the words that appear on the autocue, along with other information about what will appear in the bulletin.

DAILY NEWS SCHEDULE AT CALENDAR	
Time	**Event**
06:15	First bulletin
06:45	Second bulletin
07:30	Third bulletin
08:30	Fourth bulletin
09:00	News conference
09:55	Fifth bulletin
10:55	Sixth bulletin
12:20	Lunchtime bulletin
13:00	Reporters out with crews
pm	Editing and filing reports
15:25	Afternoon bulletin
16:00	Planning the evening news
17:00	Rehearsal
18:00	Evening news
22:30	Final bulletin

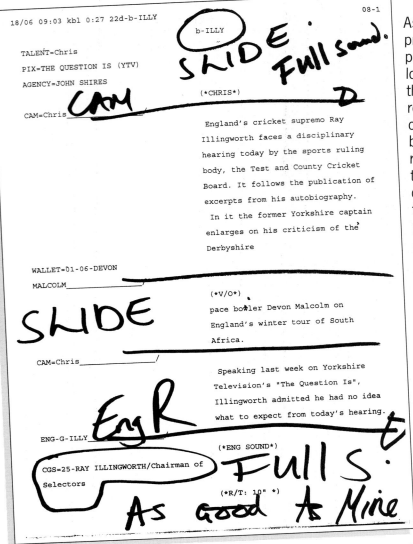

18/06 09:03 kbl 0:27 22d-b-ILLY

b-ILLY

SLIDE Full sound.

TALENT=Chris

PIX=THE QUESTION IS (YTV)

AGENCY=JOHN SHIRES

CAM=Chris CAM

(*CHRIS*)

England's cricket supremo Ray
Illingworth faces a disciplinary
hearing today by the sports ruling
body, the Test and County Cricket
Board. It follows the publication of
excerpts from his autobiography.
    In it the former Yorkshire captain
enlarges on his criticism of the
Derbyshire

WALLET=01-06-DEVON

MALCOLM

SLIDE

(*V/O*)
pace bowler Devon Malcolm on
England's winter tour of South
Africa.

CAM=Chris

Speaking last week on Yorkshire
Television's "The Question Is",
Illingworth admitted he had no idea
what to expect from today's hearing.

ENG-G-ILLY   EngR

(*ENG SOUND*)

CGS=25-RAY ILLINGWORTH/Chairman of
Selectors

FullS.

(*R/T: 10" *)

As Good As Mine

A page from a presenter's bulletin script.

As well as reading the news, the presenter introduces film reports produced by other journalists on location, in other words, where the story is happening. These film reports are played by the bulletin controller, who sits with the bulletin producer in a control room linked to the studio through the camera. Bulletin controllers are responsible for the film reports and still photographs (slides) that are needed for the broadcast. They press the buttons that bring them on screen at the correct time. Bulletin producers make sure that the bulletins run exactly to time and keep up a running commentary on what is going on during each broadcast. This is to let the newsreader know that they are keeping to the schedule and to give them a cue when a film report is coming to an end, so they can prepare themselves to appear on screen again. The bulletin producer has a sheet that lists each news item in the order in which it will appear in the bulletin. This is known as the running order. Each item on it has a name, which is known as a catch-line, to identify it. Also on the running order is the exact amount of time, to the second, that each item will take up in the bulletin. The running order also lists the time at which the item was filed, or was ready for broadcast. The format of the item is among the technical details included on the list, for example:

- E.N.G. = Electronic News Gathering, or a report from the scene on video.
- Cam = Presenter reading to camera.
- Slide = Still photograph of a person, symbol or scene.

06:45 **The second bulletin** of the day is broadcast as part of the GMTV morning show on the ITV network.

07:30 **The third bulletin** goes out to the three Calendar sub-regions, again as part of the GMTV programme.

In the control room, the bulletin controller makes sure that everything runs smoothly.

A running order list for a Calendar bulletin.

```
18/06/96 09:22 kbl ?:?? !12-BELMONT
BELMONT BULLETI    b0 u0 m0 s0    09:22:39
   YORKSHIRE TELEVISION  ** CALENDAR **                        Display
PAGE  CATCHLINE  PRES   TECH-DETAIL  EST    ENG  A B DUR  STAT  FILED  17/06/9
----------------------------------- SEGMENT 1 ---------------------- OUTBACK ---
01     b-sting           ENG                0:05
02    ·b-hello           cam                                          23:57:07
03     b-flames          eng/dupe    0:02          00:02  22b 08:24  23:57:09
04     b-pension         eng/dupe    0:21          00:21  22c 08:57  23:57:30
04a    b-assault         eng/dupe    0:16          00:16  22e 09:00  23:57:46
05     b-dredge          eng/lib     0:18          00:18  22b 09:01  23:58:04
06     b-strike          cam         0:26          00:26  22c 08:36  23:58:30
07     b-speed           eng/dupe    0:19          00:19  22b 08:37  23:58:49
08     b-illy            ENG/dupe    0:25          00:25  22f 08:37  23:59:14
09     b-goodbye         cam/slide   0:27   0:10   00:27  22d 09:03  23:59:51
                                     0:06   0:03   00:06  22a 08:25  00:00:00

XXXXX spares XXX                                                     00:00:00
21     b-care                                                        00:00:00
22     b-verdict         eng/dupe   *0:27          00:27  22b 08:38  00:00:00
23     b-collecte        ENG/dupe   *0:23          00:23  22d 08:38  00:00:00
                                    *0:15  *1:09   00:15  22d 08:38  00:00:00
                                     2:40   0:18
       Total Time:       00:02:58
       Time remaining:    0:02:58 OVER
```

<u>08:30</u> **The fourth bulletin** is broadcast as part of the GMTV programme.

<u>09:00</u> **News conference.** The most important programme of the day is the 30-minute evening show and much of the day's activity at the Newscentre is geared towards getting this programme on the air. At 9.00 am, the production team meets for a news conference, which is called by the producer, who is in overall control of the programme. The purpose of the conference is to decide which stories are likely to feature in the programme. This is done using a news list, which contains information on events and stories happening throughout the Calendar region. It includes details of ongoing court cases, visits by famous or important people, reports referring to the region, stories picked up by reporters or phoned in by the public.

The news list, which
contains information on the
day's stories, is discussed at
the news conference.

RACIAL - Comission for Racial Equality's annual report says one of the causes

of riots in Bradford and Brixton was black and asian youth's feeling of
alienation - there's incisive for you.
****
Sport -

ILLY - Raymond appears before cricket's bosses to explain his controversial
book.

FOOTY - Last of Euro 96 matches in Leeds. Romania v Spain.
****
Belasis
TEACHER - teacher of the year awarded to North Yorkshire teacher.

SUB - Scarborough sub-aqua club discover WW1 submarine with lost crew 80 years
on.

EQUESTRIAN - Feature on North Yorkshire couple chosen to manage British team in
the Olympics in Atlanta next month.

SEALS - Three survivors of recent pollution being released into the sea again.
Presser in Scarbro at 9...released near Grimsby later. Done very similar story
a couple of months ago

BOULES - Teacher from Leeming wins national championship and now needs
sponsorship to go for the world title.
****
Belasis -

LINCOLN - Not before 1200 in London: Judgment on a move to wind up the Ostrich
Farming Corporation.

- kids in Lincoln who are four know more about drugs than their parents. Jim
has feature set up.

HULL - landlord offers free booze at pub because he says trade suffers during
euro 96.

- schools minister visits primary schools that failed OFSTED tests.

- twins' lawyer says legal action is definitely on.

GRIMSBY - editing mud n' stud feature in Hull.

- lecturers on strike at Scunthorpe college. Pics in for 11.05.

WHITES - orchestra being edited am by Alan Hardwick.

- kid picked from thousands to appear at London Palladium in Fagin.

NEWSLINES - suspicious fire on empty estate in gainsborough.
- new type of speed cameras launched in Lincs.

HELD - 5 min Central item on Lincs woman who has set up tourist trap in Franc
****
CAL SOUTH PROSPECTS - JUN 18]

1. Police close road in search for attackers of two men found injured in
Doncaster - both in hospital with head injuries - Bob filming police activity
for first time - Mike/Julie on way out.

2.Hospital nursing staff poised for industrial action over cleaners for nurses

The producer calls on the news editors to run through the news list. They are senior journalists who keep an eye on the stories that come in and the work that is done on them. Calendar has three news editors. The producer allows reporters and other members of the team to voice their opinions on whether a particular item should be covered and in what way. Reporters also come up with ideas for items, which are then discussed by the producer and news editors. Reporters from regional offices take part in the conference using a video link. Once the producer has decided which stories will be covered, then the news editors assign reporters and camera crews to them. The decisions taken at the news conference form the basis of the working day, although time and resources must be allowed to cover any new 'breaking stories' (unexpected stories).

A Calendar news conference. Reporters in regional offices contribute via a video link.

IN GROUPS

Spend five minutes making an imaginary news list; each person in the group should contribute three or four items to it. Decide who will play the roles in the production team (producer, news editors and reporters) and role play a news conference. Each person should try to explain why they think that certain stories should be included in the bulletin.

SOURCES OF STORIES

Without stories, news programmes would have nothing to broadcast. How do they get the stories? Sources for news stories include:

• **Emergency services.** Reporters keep in close touch with police, fire and ambulance services, so that they will hear of any major incident as soon as possible.

• **Press releases.** Thousands of organizations send out press releases to draw the media's attention to their news and events.

• **Contacts.** These are people who are a good source of stories. They usually have jobs dealing with the public and so are able to pass on snippets of information.

• **Local councils.** News organizations receive agendas and minutes from local council meetings, which provide a great deal of information that might be of interest to their viewers.

• **Tip-offs.** Members of the public phone in with stories or subjects that they think should be investigated.

• **Other news organizations.** These may be in the form of 'wire services', which are computer systems that transmit updates of news to news organizations for a fee. They are provided by such companies as the Press Association (see the section on news agencies, page 137). The news media use wire services to get stories and information that they do not have the staff or money to cover themselves. Alternatively, news programmes may buy stories from freelance journalists, who work for themselves. Or they may simply follow up stories reported in newspapers or other news programmes.

The Fugees (Refugee Camp) - "The Bootleg Versions"
Available from 25th November - Limited Edition Only

With "The Score" approaching one million UK sales and breaking new ground here each week comes the "Bootleg Versions".................All the mixes from all the singles on one limited edition album dropping November 25th 1996.

The album includes sought after mixes from the first album "Blunted On Reality" as well as mixes of the current single "No Woman No Cry", a live version of "Killing Me Softly" from their stunning Brixton Academy show, and the Clark Kent Mix of "Ready Or Not" available nowhere else on CD.

This album will be limited to the first 70,000 copies.................when they are gone, THEY ARE GONE.

Tracklisting is as follows:

1. Ready Or Not (Clark Kent Remix)
2. Nappy Heads (Mad Spyda Remix)
3. Don't Cry, Dry Your Eyes
4. Vocab (Salaam Remix)
5. Ready Or Not (Salaam's Ready For The Show Remix)
6. Killing Me Softly With His Song (Live From Brixton Academy)
7. No Woman No Cry (Steve Marley Remix)
8. Vocab (Refugees Hip Hop Mix)

Fugees "Bootleg Versions" is available from 25th November on vinyl, cassette and CD.
Cat No: 486824 1/4/2.

For further information please contact Carl Fysh, Head Of Press, Columbia Records on 0171 911 8409.

Columbia Press – Release
10 Great Marlborough Street London W1V 2LP.
Tel – 0171 911 8200. Fax – 0171 911 8606

GREENPEACE News Release

For immediate release:
12th September 1996

**PLUTONIUM FLIGHT EN ROUTE TO UK DESPITE ACTIVISTS'
BLOCKADE**

**NUCLEAR INDUSTRY BEGINS PUSH TO INCREASE NUCLEAR FLIGHTS
AROUND THE WORLD**

An air cargo of plutonium is now en route to the UK despite a blockade by
Greenpeace activists at Ostend airport in Belgium. Between 10 and 12 activists have
been removed following attempts to prevent a dangerous air transport of radioactive
plutonium mixed oxide (MOX) fuel destined for the Dounreay nuclear reprocessing
plant in Scotland.

The plutonium, which travelled by road through southern Germany into Belgium, is
being carried in a 'type B' container which can only withstand a fall of 9 meters and
which was originally designed for road transportation. It will arrive at Wick airport in
North Scotland at approximately 13.15 to 13.45 hours local time.

Greenpeace activists had surrounded the BA 147 aircraft operated by TNT Transport
to prevent it leaving. This flight, which is opposed by shipping and transportation
unions, comes as the Nuclear Industry gears up for increased nuclear flights around the
world.

It is believed that the transport contains 13.2 kg of plutonium and 31 kg of highly
enriched uranium in 40 MOX fuel assemblies. The plutonium MOX is unirradiated and
is due to be stored and possibly reprocessed at Dounreay. It came from the abandoned
KNK-11 experimental breeder reactor located at Karlsruhe in Germany.

Greenpeace Nuclear Campaigner Shaun Burnie said, "The German authorities are
getting rid of their plutonium by dumping it on the UK, in the process they are
threatening nuclear devastation over the continent and the United Kingdom. This
madness has to be stopped."

On your own

Write and design a press release to publicize an event and make a list of all the people you would send it to. The press release might be about a real or imaginary event, for example, a protest about a new road, or a school play that is based on local history.

__09:55__ and __10:55__ **Two more bulletins** are broadcast.

__12:20__ **Lunchtime bulletin.** A longer bulletin is broadcast just before the main national news from ITN. By this time, the content of the bulletin will have changed, as new stories from reporters and camera crews will have come in during the morning to replace older ones that came in overnight. Throughout the morning, the producer of the evening programme and the news editors have been monitoring what was going on and deciding whether to include stories from the bulletins in the later programme.

__13:00__ **Out with a crew.** Reporters and camera crews are out and about gathering information and footage for the evening programme. Television news programmes are mainly made up of reports filmed on location. The reports are put together by a reporter working with a camera crew. Calendar reporters work with one- or two-person camera crews. A typical film report starts life when the reporter researches the story. Research can involve speaking to people connected with the story, collecting facts and figures, or getting 'background'. (Background is information that will help a viewer to understand a story fully. For example, the background to a story about a factory that burnt down would include such information as who owned the factory, what it manufactured, how long it had been used and how many people worked there.) The reporter also arranges times and places for interviews and liaises with the news editor and producer to find out what they want from the story and how long the report should be.

Reporters research stories before going out on location with a camera crew.

IN PAIRS

During their research, the reporter must decide who should be interviewed to get a full picture of an event or issue. Make a list of the people that you would choose to interview about the following stories:

- A major road accident in which people were injured
- A row over planning permission for a new supermarket
- A factory closure involving the loss of over 1 000 jobs
- A local football team signing a famous Italian striker.

Once all the research that can be done from the office has been completed, the reporter sets off with a camera crew. A reporter and camera operator know what makes good TV and they go out with a fairly clear idea of the kind of footage they want. As a visual medium, television is at its best showing action and colour. It is rare for a film crew to be present when such events as accidents, disasters or crimes occur. Despite this, camera crews try to make their footage dramatic by getting shots of damage, police vehicles with lights flashing, or interviews with eyewitnesses. Some events, such as shows, parades and festivals, offer the chance to film 'action' as it happens, while others, such as official openings and publicity stunts, can be set up specifically for camera crews to film.

To make a full film report, a reporter needs a variety of types of film footage. They may require:
• Interviews with people involved in the story
• Action shots of an event
• Shots of the reporter speaking directly to the camera
• General or cut-away shots. A general shot is film that is used to add atmosphere to a film report, for example, in a report about Christmas shopping, it might be pictures of a busy high street, or in a report about a football match, it might be shots of a crowd. A cut-away shot is a shot of a person involved in a news story not speaking to camera, for example, in an interview with an artist, a cut-away shot might show the artist painting. These are used between interviews to give a sense of atmosphere, or to allow the reporter to do a voice-over, which is when film footage is shown without sound and the presenter reads a commentary to accompany it.

Camera crews always shoot more footage than will be used in the finished report when it is broadcast. This is to allow reporters a greater variety of shots to choose from when they put the report together back at the studio.

Interviews are a vital part of any film report.

IN GROUPS

Imagine that you are camera operators sent out on the following assignments. Make a list of the types of shots that you might need to compile each news report:
• A demonstration against fox hunting
• A festival parade
• A feature on Christmas shopping
• A football match.

PUTTING TOGETHER A NEWS STORY

Every news story is unique, because each one has a different subject. However, most of the questions to which a viewer would like answers are the same. While the details of each story will differ, the following points must be covered in every report:
- What has happened or will be happening?
- Where is it happening?
- When did it or will it happen?
- How did it or will it happen?
- Who was or will be involved?
- Why did it or will it happen?

On your own
Watch the news on TV. Study one i̇
(you might like to video it if you ca
and explain how all the questions
listed above are answered in it.

pm **Editing.** Once the reporter has all the material that is needed, the crew returns to the Newscentre where they begin the process of turning the raw film footage into a finished report that can be broadcast on television. To do this, the reporter works in an edit suite with a picture editor. The reporter selects shots, the editor joins them together and sound is recorded over the pictures, if it is required.

To put the report together, the reporter:

Edits the raw film footage into a running order. This means deciding the order of the shots. The reporter selects the shots that they think tell the story best and places them in an order that leads the viewer through the report in a logical way.

The reporter is responsible for editing the report. This happens in the edit suite.

Scripts the commentary to go with the film footage. This involves writing the words that explain to the viewer what the story is about. The voice of the reporter usually delivers the commentary over general shots, where no one is being interviewed. It is the commentary that holds the report together, as it gives it a storyline with a beginning, a middle and an end.

Once the report is complete, the reporter 'files' it by adding it to the news list. The producer then knows that there is a completed film report that can be placed in the running order for the evening's programme.

IN PAIRS

Write the script for a news report on your breakfast or lunch. Think of how you would describe what you ate, how it was prepared, how you ate it, what it tasted like and so on. Draw up a list of the camera shots that you would need for your report and put them into the order in which you think they should appear. If you have access to video and editing equipment, you could have a go at producing the report.

15:25 **The afternoon news bulletin** is broadcast.

16:00 **Planning the evening news.** Throughout the afternoon, the producer working with the news editors has been deciding what will actually be broadcast as part of the evening show. Together, they have reviewed stories, looked at film reports and kept an eye on what is going on in the region, to make sure that no breaking story slips through the net. Working with production assistants and a director, the producer comes up with a plan for the programme, which involves:

A running order, which is a schedule showing the order in which reports, interviews and features will appear on the show. Each item is timed to the second so that every minute of the show is accounted for. The producer must make sure that there is a variety of different types of story in the programme, to cater for the different interests of viewers. There must be serious news items to inform the audience. However, light-hearted or amusing stories to entertain are also usually included. As well as film reports and news stories read by the presenters, the producer may arrange for guests to come into the studio to be interviewed. There is usually also sports news and perhaps weather in the programme. In Calendar's case, the producer must decide how much time will be taken up by contributions from the three sub-regional news services.

A script. The producer writes the script for the newsreaders who present the show. This includes:
• Headlines
• Stories read to the camera by the presenter

- Introductions and conclusions to film reports
- Voice-overs that are read by presenters
- Links between different items.

Legal issues. The producer must also consider any legal issues, such as libel, a law aimed at preventing false and damaging statements about people being broadcast, and decide on matters of taste, and whether the reports are fair to those mentioned.

Pick members of your group to play the roles of producer, news editors and production assistants. From the list below, choose the items that you think should be included in your 30-minute evening broadcast. The broadcast is split into two parts, so you will have to decide which news goes into which half, in which order and how long each item should last.

FOOTBALL RESULTS

Fashion feature

Road safety campaign

Interview with local author

WEATHER

IN GROUPS

Motorway pile-up

Dance group's new show

PENSIONER MUGGED

Dog learns how to skateboard

Brother and sister reunited after 40 years

Local marathon runner wins

<u>17:00</u> **Rehearsal.** It may seem strange that a news programme has a rehearsal. A live programme gives the impression that things are happening for the first time. However, before the programme goes out, the presenters go onto the set and run through the programme. They practise reading the script and alter it if they can make presentation easier. Around them, technical staff make the preparations necessary for the broadcast.

The director, who sits in a control room separate from the studio set, is in charge of the rehearsal. The director sits in front of a bank of TV monitors. At Calendar, three of these screens are linked to the three sub-regional studios, so that the director can watch what is being broadcast from them. Other screens are linked to different cameras on the studio set, which allows the director to use shots of the presenters taken from different angles. In the centre of the bank of television screens is a large clock, which is a constant reminder that everything must run to the second.

The director sits behind a control desk. Beside him or her sits the production assistant, who has a stopwatch to time each section of the show to check that it matches the running order schedule. Also at the desk are the vision mixer, who is responsible for making sure that the camera shots appear in the correct order, and a camera operator, who controls the shots coming from the studio set. Next door, in another room, a sound technician monitors levels from microphones and film reports.

During the rehearsal, any slides that will be needed to illustrate a story are prepared, and headlines are read and rewritten to gain maximum effect. Throughout the rehearsal, a TV monitor shows what the ITV network is broadcasting, so that the director knows how close Calendar is to its programme's slot.

The director, who works in the control room, is in charge of the programme.

IN GROUPS

On your own, write a short news story and read it out to a group as if you were a newsreader. (If you have access to a video camera, you might like to film it.) Discuss the story with the group:
- Does the way you have written the story make it come alive for the viewer?
- Is it difficult to read?
- How could it be improved?

<u>18:00</u> **Show time.** The producer sits at the control desk with the director. All the film reports are cued up and the autocue is ready to roll. On the studio set, technical crew are in place to supervise lighting, cameras and make-up. They are linked by microphones to the control room and receive instructions from it throughout the show. The presenters are sitting behind the newsdesk facing the cameras, ready to take their cue from the director. At the end of the national weather forecast that follows the ITN News, the Calendar titles are run and the show goes live to over a million viewers.

The show is hosted by two presenters, one male and one female. This male–female combination is common to many television news programmes. The presenters act out roles very much like those of married couples and viewers almost expect a 'chemistry' to exist between them. This image is promoted through unscripted conversations between the presenters. For example, they may have a conversation about a particular news story. The approach of the presenters is usually friendly. They appear to be talking directly to each viewer, as if they were long-standing friends. Even when they read amusing headlines, their tone is one of sincerity and concern.

The presenters are known as 'anchors', because they hold the show together. They introduce the programme and the camera returns to them between film reports. They are the programme's figureheads and they provide continuity, not only during individual shows, but also night after night. Many presenters become celebrities in their own right. They become identified with the region in which they broadcast and appear on other shows as local personalities. The same is true of many sports and weather presenters who are regular faces on news programmes. Calendar's two main anchor presenters are Christa Ackroyd and Mike Morris. They are the faces that people in the Yorkshire Television broadcast area associate immediately with Calendar.

Calendar's 30-minute evening show has a basic format that it almost always sticks to. It is divided into two sections, which are

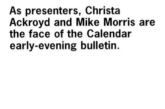

As presenters, Christa Ackroyd and Mike Morris are the face of the Calendar early-evening bulletin.

separated by a commercial break. The programme begins with the headlines, which involves the two main anchor presenters reading over clips taken from the film reports that will appear later in the show. After the headlines, the two presenters welcome the audience to Calendar and mention any other headlines and features that will be coming up in the programme. The headlines act as an index to the show, letting viewers know what they can expect to see.

The presenters then begin working down the running order, introducing film reports or reading stories straight to camera. Mike and Christa usually present alternate stories. The change of presenter indicates a different story and helps to keep the viewers interested. The major and serious stories tend to come towards the beginning of the programme. The tone usually gets lighter as the show approaches the commercial break. As well as introducing film reports, the presenters may also conduct interviews with people who feature in the news.

A distinctive characteristic of the Calendar programme is its use of different presenters for its sub-regional services. In both sections of the programme, time is given to news from different parts of the region. This lets the programme offer viewers a specific news service for their area, as well as provide a region-wide summary of the day's events.

The second section of the Calendar bulletin has a different feel. Although serious stories are included, there is a more relaxed atmosphere. Film reports offer more depth and tend to be largely 'human interest' stories. Celebrity interviews and funny stories also tend to feature in the second half of the show. Sport is a regular feature in the second section. At the end of the show, the presenters usually engage in a short conversation about some aspect of the news to wind the show down, before they say goodbye to the audience.

<u>22.30</u> **The final bulletin to Calendar's region.**

IN GROUPS

Try to produce your own short news programme. Choose a producer, director, newsreader and reporters. Using material from newspapers, or stories made up by members of the group, draw up:

❾ A running order
❾ A script
❾ A schedule.
You could produce the show as a short play, or, if you have a video camera, you might film it.

NAME: KATIE LAMPERT
AGE: 27

Katie Lampert prepares to read a bulletin. She is Calendar's youngest presenter.

Q How did you get into television?

A After completing a Media Studies degree at Liverpool, I did a radio journalism training course at Falmouth. Through this, I learnt how to find stories, interview people and edit reports. After leaving Falmouth, I worked for a number of radio stations, including Metro Radio and BBC Cumbria. My last job in radio was as Deputy News Editor for Century Radio on Tyneside. I got the job at Calendar after the producers saw a video of me reading the news.

Q What hours do you work?

A I have a five-day working pattern, usually starting at 9.00 am and finishing at 6.45 pm The hours are long, but they are necessary to get the programmes out.

Q What does your work involve?

A I present a lot of bulletins, both from the main Calendar Newscentre and from our South Yorkshire studio in Sheffield. This involves reading the news to camera in a small, one-person studio. My script appears before me on an autocue. I have to speak as clearly as possible and give each story the emphasis it requires. It would be no good laughing during a serious story, or keeping a straight face during a funny one. I do film reports with film crews. This involves researching stories and going out on location to interview people and get camera shots.

Q What makes a good TV news story?

A Pictures are what television is about and you must remember that at all times. A story has to be visually interesting if it is to keep the viewer's attention. That means action and colour. After all, if the story is not interesting to look at, the audience might as well listen to the radio instead. You also have to keep the pictures in mind when you are writing the commentary for the report. The reporter's words must be linked to what is happening on the screen.

Q What do you enjoy most about your job?

A The buzz. Every day we are reporting on something different. We work to tight deadlines and it is always a challenge to get the story before the programme goes out.

Q Have you encountered prejudice in the industry because you are a woman?

A I do not feel my career has been limited by prejudice. Certainly not at Calendar. It may be different elsewhere.

Q What advice would you give to someone who wants to get into the media?

A Start working towards your career now. While I was at college I worked as a volunteer on hospital radio and it helped me win a place on the radio journalism course after I graduated. You have got to prove to people that you really do want to work in the media by putting the effort in.

On your own

Draw up a list of qualities that a good TV news reporter should have if they are to be successful.

What is the news?

As the study of Calendar shows, the news on TV is the result of a long production process. It is constructed by a group of professional journalists and technical staff, who make the decisions about what the audience will see and how they will see it. Certain factors influence the form that television news takes:

Visual impact. News stories that are visually exciting will always be chosen instead of those that are not. Big stories that do not lend themselves to TV may not be covered, while more frivolous stories that have a strong visual element may be included.

Journalistic decisions. Producers and news editors decide which stories will be covered. Some serious stories may be dropped and replaced by light-hearted ones to add variety to a news programme. Producers and news editors also decide how a story will be told and from whose point of view.

Production decisions. Camera footage that may shed a different light on a story may not be included in a report because it does not 'fit', or is of poor quality. Commentaries may be cut or rewritten to fit in with time constraints.

GROUP DISCUSSION

Study your local news programmes.
* *What sort of stories appear on them?*
* *What sort of people do they concentrate on?*
* *What subjects do they deal with?*

* *What are the similarities and differences between news programmes on different channels?*
* *Are you getting the news you want or need?*

Review

Television is the most popular of the news media, with millions of people tuning in to find out the latest. On the surface, TV news seems to be a 'window' through which the viewer sees events happening in the world. However, television news is actually the product of a long manufacturing process, which involves journalists selecting, ordering and editing information and film reports. What the audience sees on the screen is not 'reality', but a representation of events that has been put together by professional news-makers.

8. CINEMA

To watch a film at the cinema is to be part of a piece of trickery. Film is an optical illusion, a play of light on to a screen that the audience reads as a three-dimensional space in which the joys and fears of people's lives are acted out. In 1994, the people of the UK made 124 million visits to the cinema, paying nearly £530 million for the privilege of being tricked, such is the popularity of the cinema today.

In this case study, we will be examining in detail the cinema as an industry, the making of films and their exhibition both at cinemas and at home, on video and television.

CLASS DISCUSSION

☆ When did you last go to the cinema?
☆ What did you see?
☆ Was it good?
☆ How often do you go to the cinema?
☆ Are young people more likely to go to the cinema than older people?

Sound and vision

Film is able to weave its magic spell over us through a phenomenon called persistence of vision. Most of you will have seen a simple flick book, or even a device like a zoetrope, in which a series of still images is animated to create the illusion of movement. This happens because images remain within your vision after they have actually disappeared, which means that your brain will link a series of still images together to create continuous movement.

When we watch a film at the cinema, a strip of celluloid film is pulled through a projector, a machine that consists of a powerful light behind a lens. As each frame passes between the light and the lens, it is projected on to the screen for 1/24th of a second, before the next frame is pulled into the gate and appears on the screen. At the same time, a shutter opens and closes in synchronization with the frame movement, so we don't see one frame replacing another.

What we are seeing is very like a slide show in which the images are shown so quickly that we are deceived into believing we are watching a continuous sequence of events. If you watch early silent movies, you will notice that they flicker (the cinema used to be called the flicks) and that the movement of the characters is jerky. This is because they were shot and projected at 16 frames per second (fps), rather than the present-day 24 fps.

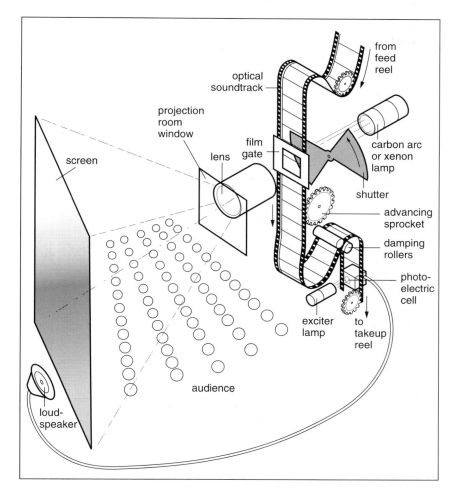

A projector is basically a movie camera in which the light is on the inside. A powerful bulb is needed to enlarge the 35 mm image of the frame to 300,000 times its size on the screen.

Sound first came to the cinema in the 1920s, when films were known as the 'talkies'. Today, sound plays a key role in the enjoyment audiences get from watching film. Film sound usually comes in the form of an optical soundtrack, as part of the 35 mm print (a positive copy of a film) on which most films are distributed. This track has a light shone through it by a small bulb called an exciter lamp. The beam of light is then picked up and read by a photoelectric cell, which converts light into electrical impulses. These impulses are then fed through an amplifier into the speakers, where they appear as sound.

When the talkies first began, a single loudspeaker behind the screen produced the sound for the audience. The auditorium of a modern cinema contains a number of strategically placed speakers to produce dramatic sound effects, including surround sound, whereby the audience can be made to feel a part of the action of the film. One of the earliest films to exploit the technological possibilities of surround sound was Francis Ford Coppola's *Apocalypse Now*, which was set during the Vietnam War. The director made the film to be projected with quintrophonic sound – three speakers at the front and two behind the audience. This gave the audience the impression that they were not just watching a war movie, they were in the midst of the fighting.

One of the most recent innovations is digital sound, which comes either as part of the film print or as a separate CD, which is electronically synchronized with the film image. Digital technology can produce sound of a very high quality.

When a film arrives from the distributor for exhibition at the cinema, it comes in reels. On each side of the 35 mm print with its optical soundtrack are sprocket holes, which sprockets on the projector use to pull the film through the gate. The film slowly unwinds from a spool above the projector and winds back to one below it.

Going to the cinema

Going to the cinema has always been an exciting experience. In 1946, before the arrival of television, the British made a total of 1,640 million visits to the cinema. The popularity in the early 1980s of the mass-produced video recorder, together with the chance to rent the latest releases on video, reduced this grand number to under 54 million in 1984, less than one visit to the cinema that year for each member of the population.

Today cinema has recovered much of its popularity, with audiences more than doubling to 124 million in 1994, which means that on average we all go to the cinema twice a year. The apparent threat posed by the VCR, video rental outlets and, more recently, satellite movie channels has, in fact, stimulated interest in film-going and led to an increased demand.

One of the chief reasons for this increase in cinema audiences in the past decade is the arrival of the multiplex (a cinema complex with numerous screens). The first multiplex cinema, based on an American concept, was opened in 1985 in Milton Keynes, a town that previously did not have a cinema. Now there are nearly 700 screens across 80 multiplex sites throughout the UK. It is estimated that this number will grow at the rate of 60 screens a year up to the year 2000. (The largest multiplex cinema in the world

ON YOUR OWN

When TV first arrived, the cinema industry was worried that this new competitor would ruin its business. To try to maintain its lead, the cinema introduced several technical innovations. Some, such as CinemaScope or widescreen, were a success; others, such as 3D and Cinerama, were less successful.

- Find out what you can about the innovations listed above
- Why do you think they succeeded (or failed)?

is the 30-screen complex operated by AMC Cinemas in Kansas City. Complexes in Brussels and Antwerp each have 24 screens.)

MULTIPLEX CINEMAS

★ **IS THERE A MULTIPLEX CINEMA NEAR YOU?**

★ **WHY HAS IT CHOSEN THE LOCATION THAT IT HAS?**

★ **HOW DOES IT ATTRACT ITS AUDIENCES?**

A typical multiplex cinema is situated out of town, with good access by road. It is close to other amenities, such as shopping facilities and restaurants. It gives the cinema-goer access to around ten screens, each offering a different programme. Shared projection rooms, box office and kiosks mean that the costs of running so many screens are comparatively small in terms of labour and capital. It also means it is more likely that audiences will find at least one film that they will want to see.

Persuading people to attend regularly is an important ploy in the marketing of cinemas. Of course, their out-of-town location, often at a major motorway junction, makes it almost essential to have or use a car to get to a multiplex. This has an important bearing on the type of audience that they attract, as does the fairly expensive admission prices they charge.

IN GROUPS

There must be several films that you would like to see that you can't.

❥ *Make a list of these films.*

❥ *List the reasons why you can't see them, and compare your list with those of the other groups.*

There could be many reasons why you can't see a film, such as expense, difficulties of getting to the cinema or the age restriction of the certificate.

The multiplex is geared to showing mainstream commercial films, usually Hollywood products, which have been well hyped in the media. Occasionally, films that do not have a mass appeal are screened, but these are very much a minority.

The timing of the release of films is quite important to distribution companies in their efforts to ensure a good financial return on a film. Most films have their première in London before going on general release (shown across the country), usually a week or so later.

Increased interest in the cinema has also led to a more secure position for what are sometimes called art house, or independent, cinemas. These are cinemas committed to showing films that would not normally be on general release. They may be foreign films, or those made by independent production companies that may not have the mass appeal of Hollywood films. The finances of some independent cinemas are supported by organizations like the British Film Institute, which helps fund a network of regional film theatres committed to showing films that otherwise might not be commercially viable. There may be one in a town or city near you.

Independents Cinema

You saw them here first:
The First Wives Club's Goldie Hawn in Rowan And Martin's Laugh-In (1969)

Christopher Doyle 11.30am (Odeon Haymarket) Gravesend 11.30am (ICA) Snakes & Ladders 1.15pm (Odeon WE) Polygraph 1.30pm (Odeon WE) Films From The Heart 1.45pm (NFT) Flight 2pm (NFT) Nostalgia For Countryland 2.15pm (ICA) Dead Heart 3.45pm (Odeon WE) Microcosmos 4pm (Odeon WE) Wives III 4pm (NFT) Indian Summer 4.15pm (NFT) Slanted Vision 4.30pm (ICA) Temptress Moon 6pm (Odeon WE) The Quiet Room 6.15pm (Odeon WE) Days Of Democracy 6.30pm (MOMI) Dog In The Manger 6.30pm (NFT) Palookaville 6.45pm (ICA) Focus 8.30pm (NFT) When Mother Comes Home For Christmas 8.30pm (MOMI) Good News From The Lord 8.45pm (NFT) Intimate Relations 8.45pm (Odeon WE) American Buffalo 9pm (Odeon WE) Esperanza & Sardines 9pm (ICA)

MON 18: Taxi 1.15pm (Odeon WE) Love And Other Catastrophes 1.30pm, 6.30pm (Odeon WE) The Village Has No Walls 1.30pm, 6.15pm (NFT) Alchemy 2pm, 6.45pm (ICA) The Cry Of The Silk 2pm, 6.30pm (NFT) Kids Return 3.45p

Men [...]
The H[...]
Disap[...]
4.15pm [...]
(ICA) Ro[...]
6.15pm [...]
9pm (NF[...]
Robert [...]
TUE 19: [...]
6.30pm [...]
1.15pm, 6[...]
Honeym[...]
(NFT) Gall[...]
House 2.1[...]
Shine 3.1[...]
Robert Ryland's Last Journey 3.45pm, 8.45pm (Odeon WE) The Scent Of Desires 4.30pm (NFT) BFI New Directors 4.15pm (NFT) The Keeper 4.30pm, 9pm

Mayfair) Me & My Matchmaker 6.30pm (MOMI) Pretty Village Pretty Flame 8.30pm (MOMI) Conspirators Of Pleasure 9pm (ICA) Kansas City 9pm (Odeon WE) THU 21: The Emperor's Shadow 1.15pm, 6.15pm (Odeon WE) Le Bonheur 1.30pm, 6.30pm (Odeon WE) The Promise 1.45pm, 6.15pm (NFT) Big Night 2pm (NFT) Close-up 2.15pm (ICA) Welcome To The Dollhouse 3.45pm, 8.45pm (Odeon WE) If These Walls Could Talk 4pm, 9pm (Odeon WE) The Sandman 4pm, 8.30pm (NFT) The Sensual Art Of Animation 4.15pm (NFT) Things I Never Told You 4.30pm, 9pm (ICA) Beyond Childhood 6pm (NFT) Weird & Wonderful Worldwide Animation 6.30pm (MOMI) Close-up 6.45pm (ICA) Musicals Great Musicals 8.30pm (MOMI) Guardian Interview: Harry Belafonte 9.15pm (NFT)
FRI 22: Nenette & Boni 1.15pm, 6.15pm (Odeon WE) Trees Lounge 1.30pm, 6.30pm (Odeon WE) A Hot Roof 1.45pm, 6.30pm (NFT) A Summer In La Goulette 6.15pm (NFT) Carla's Son 3.30pm, 9pm (Odeon WE)

6.30pm The Incredibly True Adventure ... 6.30pm Phenomenon 9pm; also Thu 4pm
THU 21: Multiplicity 1.30pm

● RIO (0171-254 6677) [WA]
SAT 16: Pebble And The Penguin 11am; also Tue 4.15pm Adventures Of Pinocchio 1.30pm, 3.45pm Michael Collins 5.45pm, 8.30pm, 11.15pm; also Sun, Tue

Sat, Sun 1pm, 7.30pm The Pillow Book Sat, Tue-Thu 3.15pm, 9.30pm; also Sun 3.15pm, 9.30pm, Mon 2.45pm, 9.15pm The Secret Of Roan Inish Sat, Sun 5.15pm Exotica 11.45pm
SUN 17: Rancho Notorious 11am
MON 18: The Last Supper Mon-Thu 1pm, 7.30pm L'Avventura 5pm; also Tue 11am
TUE 19: Le Colonel Chabert

[...] Secrets And Lies 8.20pm
THU 21: Splendor 6.30pm + Il Postino 8.45pm
FRI 22: City Of Hope 6pm + Lone Star 8.30pm

SAT 16: Twister 11am The First Wives Club Sat, Mon-Fri 2.30pm, 4.45pm, 7pm, 9.05pm; also Sun 7pm, 9.05pm
SUN 17: Dekalog 1-5 1.20pm

● IPSWICH FILM THEATRE (01473-215544). [WA]
SAT 16: The Swan Princess 1pm, 3.30pm Lone Star 6pm A Matter Of Life And Death 6pm

ON YOUR OWN

From a copy of your local paper or listings magazine, make a list of films that are on at your local cinemas.

■ Which films on the list are showing for the first time in your area?

■ Which films have been shown previously, or have been retained by the cinema for another week?

■ Have any films been shown for more than a week?

■ Are any of the films on your list independent films?

Films on TV and video

Of course, you don't have to go to the cinema to see a film. Films on television have always been popular and people in Britain are especially fond of the video recorder for playing back tapes, either rented or bought; in fact, three out of four homes now possess a video recorder. The British public spent a total of £438 million on video rental in 1994 and nearly £700 million on video retail sales, although this figure includes sales of tapes other than feature films. The rental market is slowly declining in face of competition from cable and satellite, while the retail market is growing, having nearly doubled between 1990 and 1994. Much of this growth comes from videos targeted at young children, such as Disney films.

Films become available as video rentals only after being shown on the general release circuit, and perhaps after they have replayed in one or two smaller independent cinemas. Films available from video rental shops usually have a 'satellite hold-back'

IN PAIRS

- What types of video other than Disney films are people likely to buy?
- What is the advantage of owning these titles, rather than renting them?

period of around six months, during which time the distribution company will not make them available for showing on the satellite channels. This means that the video rental shop has an opportunity to recover its outlay on the film before satellite audiences can watch it. Finally, the rights to a film are bought by one of the terrestrial channels to be shown across the network.

Films form part of the basic programming of the terrestrial TV channels. When a major film is shown for the first time on one of these channels, it is often accompanied by a similar hype to when it was first released at the cinema. In addition, satellite subscribers have access to two 'premium' movie channels, with other channels showing older films as part of the package.

Some people like to create in their own home the viewing conditions that cinema audiences enjoy. Terrestrial television broadcasts many films in NICAM stereo, which gives stereophonic sound through a compatible TV or through a hi-fi system. Satellite offers some films in surround sound. Viewers must set up five speakers in the viewing area in order to enjoy the full benefits of this system.

Another innovation is the development of widescreen TV. The standard aspect ratio (see below) of a television is 4:3, roughly equivalent to academy ratio, the Hollywood standard before CinemaScope. Films shot for the cinema in widescreen have to be cropped or have part of their image selected for viewing on a standard TV, a technique called 'pan and scan'. Alternatively they can be shown in 'letterbox', with black spaces at the top and bottom of the screen. Widescreen TV, with a ratio of 16:9, allows almost all of the image of a CinemaScope film to fill the screen. This system is far less popular in the UK than on the continent, where many subscription channels broadcast the bulk of their films in this format. The cost of widescreen televisions is thought to be preventing them from becoming popular in the UK.

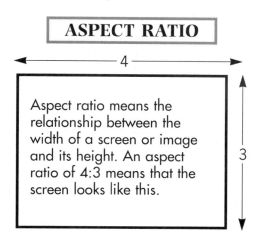

ASPECT RATIO

← 4 →

Aspect ratio means the relationship between the width of a screen or image and its height. An aspect ratio of 4:3 means that the screen looks like this.

3

WIDESCREEN - THE FUTURE OF TV

Widescreen TVs are the buzz product in the consumer electronics industry. They look sleek and present movies the way the director intended in their original cinematic 16:9 ratio. Widescreen TVs really come into their own during tailor-made widescreen broadcasts and movies, which result in rich, panoramic images.

SONY
28" WIDE SCREEN TV
"This good-looking set has all the features you'll need for those goose-bump-inducing home cinema moments."
● 67cm visible screen
● FST
● Wide screen format
● Dolby Pro-Logic Surround Sound
● Nicam digital stereo
Model KV28WS2
(Detail of cabinet may vary)
9 MONTHS INTEREST FREE OPTION▼

GUIDE PRICE
£1099.99

BEST BUY
WHAT VIDEO & TV

TOSHIBA
28" HOME CINEMA TV/VIDEO PACKAGE
28" HOME CINEMA TV
"This Pro-Logic TV delivers a sharp picture with well saturated colours – with five speakers included, the total sound effect is gorgeous."
● 66cm visible screen ● FST ● Fastext
● Dolby Pro-Logic Surround Sound
Model 2857DB
NICAM STEREO VIDEO RECORDER
"Competent sound performance with good picture quality to boot – an ideal match for a Dolby Pro-Logic TV"
● Nicam digital stereo ● 4 head
● Long play ● Built-in Videoplus+™
Model V705B
12 MONTHS INTEREST FREE OPTION▼

GUIDE PRICE
£1199

STOP PRESS
JUST VOTED
VIDEO PROJECTOR
OF THE YEAR
HOMECINEMA 96

CINEMANIA
SIMON
SOUND & VISION

Specialising in Multi Room Audio, design, supply and installation, of complete cinema rooms from start to finish, whether its a hidden screen in your lounge, a dedicated cinema room, or a loft conversion. With the introduction of the New LS5001-ws from RCF we believe this to now be the No1 choice for The Ultimate Home Cinema Experience

Visit our Demonstration rooms.

UNIT 10 PATCH PARK, ONGAR ROAD
ABRIDGE
ESSEX RM4 1AA

THE BIG PICTURE
AT
MUSICAL IMAGES

Dual Format (1.85 : 1) WIDE SCREEN
and TV (4 : 3) on the same WIDE SCREEN screen!

The Best of Both Worlds

RCF
VIDEO

CLASS DISCUSSION

As you can see, technology makes it possible to create a cinema in your living-room. Do you as an audience watch a film in different ways according to the viewing conditions? Consider the following viewing conditions:

■ At the cinema
■ At home watching a rented video
■ At home watching satellite TV
■ At home watching terrestrial TV
■ At home watching a recorded TV programme.

Among other things, you need to consider the extent to which you personally have control over the medium you are watching, as well as the amount of effort and cash you have invested in getting to see it.

You also need to think about the interaction between the film and the audience, such as the amount of discussion (or silence) that occurs in each viewing condition.

Hollywood and the film industry

Whether you watch a film at the cinema or at home, there is a good chance it was produced in the USA. Hollywood is almost the same thing as the film industry, and the majority of films on show at your local cinema are likely to have been made there.

There are, of course, other film industries. In India, films are in great demand, not only for the home market, but for export to Asian communities across the world. The Indian film industry is sometimes known as Bollywood (a mixture of the words 'Bombay' and 'Hollywood') and produces more than of 900 films a year. In Europe, the French have always been active film producers ever since the first public showing of a film by the inventors of the 'cinematograph', the Lumière brothers, in Paris in 1895. Film is seen by many European countries as an important part of their cultural identity.

In the UK, many of the films made are financed by the US film industry with an eye for US box-office success. In 1994, 84 films were made in the UK at a total cost of £455.2 million, which means that the average budget for each film was £5.46 million. Of this figure, investment from the US represented £279 million, well over half. By contrast, the average Hollywood film costs £22 million. To this should be added £9 million of marketing costs by way of prints for distribution and advertising in the US alone.

A poster advertising a product of 'Bollywood'.

The British film industry itself, however, is still capable of producing movies that make a lot of money on both sides of the Atlantic. Made for a mere £2 million, *Four Weddings and a Funeral* took nearly £28 million at the box office in the UK and £34 million in the US.

Every Hollywood producer dreams of producing a blockbuster – a film that, it is hoped, will produce huge box-office receipts, for example, Steven Spielberg's *Jurassic Park*. Increasingly, the box-office takings of such a film are only one part of its success story. Spin-offs from a film, including sweets, games, toys and, of course, such clothing as T-shirts, are a key ingredient in maximizing profits. They also fulfil an important role in the marketing of the film, not only by drawing attention to it, but by holding the audience's interest for longer than success at the box office alone would normally manage to.

Films such as *Star Wars* and *Batman* have grossed more from their spin-off earnings than they actually took at the box office. (The 'gross' is the total revenue that a film brings in.) These are sometimes called event movies and are often accompanied by a huge amount of hype across the media before their nationwide release, which is often timed to coincide with school holidays, when families are most likely to go to the cinema.

ALL-TIME FILM RENTAL CHAMPIONS, 1960s–1990s			
Film	Director	Studio	Total film rentals (US & Canada)
1990s			
1 *Jurassic Park* 1993	Steven Spielberg	Universal	£130,000,000
2 *Home Alone* 1990	Chris Columbus	Fox	88,839,000
3 *Terminator 2* 1991	James Cameron	TriStar	71,338,000
1980s			
1 *E.T. The Extra-terrestrial* 1982	Steven Spielberg	Universal	144,685,000
2 *Return of the Jedi* 1983	Richard Marquand	Fox	107,288,000
3 *Batman* 1989	Tim Burton	Warners	95,434,000
1970s			
1 *Star Wars* 1977	George Lucas	Fox	122,877,000
2 *Jaws* 1975	Steven Spielberg	Universal	82,149,000
3 *Grease* 1978	Randal Kleiser	Paramount	61,065,000
1960s			
1 *The Sound of Music* 1965	Robert Wise	Fox	50,713,000
2 *Doctor Zhivago* 1965	David Lean	MGM/United Artists	38,658,000
3 *Butch Cassidy and the Sundance Kid* 1969	George Roy Hill	Fox	29,139,000

GROUP DISCUSSION

What does this information tell you about trends in cinema over the last four decades?

How a film is made
The team

Wherever a film is made, the process is likely to be very similar. A key player at all stages of the production is the producer. Before any film is shot, a good deal of planning has to take place: with such vast sums of money at risk, pre-production – as the planning stages are called – is vitally important. The producer's job at this stage is to come up with an idea for a film, get it scripted and raise the money to make the picture. The idea may be the producer's own, or one bought from someone else. Wherever it comes from, a writer will be needed to turn the idea into a screenplay (script).

Once a producer has come up with or acquired an idea, commissioned a writer to produce a screenplay and found people to put up money for the film, then he or she must hire actors and technicians to work on the film.

On your own

Obviously, some screenplays are produced specially for the cinema. Many, however, begin life in other forms. Make a list of what you think are some of the main sources of ideas for films.

The most important member of this team is the director. The director's job is to turn the screenplay into a motion picture. He or she is concerned mostly with the artistic qualities of the film, in other words, the interpretation of the screenplay into a full-length movie. This artistic interpretation on the part of the director is likely to be one of the hallmarks of the film. Many directors give their films a personal stamp or signature, which makes it identifiable as their work.

CLASS DISCUSSION

- Who are the great film directors of the past and present?
- Are some directors as well known as stars?
- Are there directors whose films you would make a point of trying to see?

Although a film may be seen as the personal vision of a director, he or she is only the head of a large team of people who are responsible for making the film. As the music plays over the end credits of a film at the cinema or on television, notice the long list of names and jobs that appears. Each person has contributed in some way to making the picture, including the vitally important function of providing food on set for the actors and technicians.

WHAT'S IN A NAME?

There are quite a lot of unusual names given to the jobs in the film industry. Here are some that you are likely to come across most frequently:

- **Gaffer:** chief electrician on the set, takes charge of the lighting
- **Best boy:** the gaffer's assistant (who can, of course, be a girl)
- **Focus puller:** assistant camera operator, whose chief job is to keep the shot in focus when the camera is moving
- **Key grip:** in charge of the grips, or stagehands, who look after the set and the props
- **Animal wrangler:** trains and looks after the animals.

Shooting

Once the producer has got a team together, work can start on the shooting of the film. A schedule has to be drawn up that makes the best use of available resources, locations, the stars and other actors and technicians. Things like stunts, which take a lot of organizing, are built into the schedule. Obviously, it makes sense to shoot all the scenes that take place in one location together, regardless of the order in which they appear in the finished film.

The film footage shot each day is called the rushes. These are processed quickly so that the director and other key members of the crew can view them before the next day's shooting.

Film is generally shot on 35 mm film (this figure measures the width of the frame), which is the same size that is used in many still cameras. Formats such as 16 mm and 8 mm are also available. Eight mm film in the form of Super 8 was very popular with amateur film-makers, but has been largely superseded by video. Occasionally film-makers use Super 8 to give a home-made quality to a sequence of film. Sound is recorded separately. The clapperboard, on which are chalked details of each take (that is, each uninterrupted sequence between edits), is used to ensure that at the editing stage sound and vision will be in perfect 'sync'. This is especially important for dialogue: audiences quickly spot the slightest error in lip sync, when an actor's lips move in different time to the words spoken.

Many films are dubbed into a different language. This means that the original pictures are used, but other actors speak the words translated into a different language. Of course, it is immediately obvious that the lip sync is completely out in this situation, as the movement of the actors' lips does not match the words that are being spoken.

IN PAIRS
Look at this photo of a film crew on location. Can you identify some of the personnel and see what they are doing?

The process in which everything is arranged in front of the camera is called the mise-en-scène, as we explained in the chapter on language (see page 16). Each shot at this stage has to be carefully planned to ensure, for example, that continuity will be achieved at the editing stage (see below). Continuity means that all details in a shot will match the details in the next one, even though they may be filmed several weeks apart. An actor who is seen to board a plane in Los Angeles will need to look the same when he or she leaves the plane in New York. If their clothes and hair length are different, for example, an audience will notice the lack of continuity between the two shots.

Editing

Once a film has been shot, then the business of editing it can begin. Modern techniques of editing film involve the use of computers and video equipment. Film is transferred to video tape and edited electronically, with a computer coding each frame of the original film. Many of the traditional skills are still used by the film editor. Much of the time, film is literally cut and stuck together with tape to join scenes. This is called splicing. (Originally, before tape was used, two frames were glued together, which meant that two frames were lost each time an edit was made.)

An editor's first job is to choose which of a series of takes to use. One scene may have been shot a number of times in different ways. Some of these takes may be unusable for technical reasons, for instance a problem with lighting or sound. In others, actors may have forgotten or fluffed their lines. (Takes that go wrong and are not used are called out-takes and are very much in demand as the source of such programmes as *It'll Be All Right on the Night*.) The editor's other main job is to join the chosen shots together into a logical and coherent narrative. In addition, sound has to be added from a separate magnetic sound source; this has to synchronize perfectly with the movement of an actor's lips on screen.

The Steenbeck allows a film editor to view the footage shot on a small screen. He or she can then stop the film, roll it back and chop out any sections that are not needed. These lengths of rejected film often end up discarded on the floor of the cutting room.

THE KINDEST CUT

• It is said that if an editor has done a good job, the audience won't even know it has been done at all. When you watch a film, can you tell where the edits come?

• Some films use long takes, whereas others use edits in quick succession. What does the style of editing tell you about these films?

Again, continuity is also an important element in the editing process. If a character is seen to walk in opposite directions when two scenes are edited together, it can be hard for the viewer to make sense of the action.

The edited version of a film is called a cut because the film literally has been cut into its final shape. This may not, however, be the cut that you see in the cinema. Different countries have different attitudes to censorship, and this is one reason why the version you see in the cinema in this country may be different from that shown elsewhere in the world. Equally, there is a growing fashion for different cuts, in the same way that there are different mixes of sound recordings. A video release version may even contain scenes not shown in the cinema.

CLASS DISCUSSION

Are there any films that you would like to recut yourself? A sad film that you would like to give a happy ending, for example?

Marketing the film

The star system

In the chapter on institutions, we looked at the importance of stars as a means of helping a producer ensure the success of a media product (page 46). Nowhere is this system more powerful than in the film industry based in Hollywood. The stars are the public face of the film industry; they are the people with whom audiences are most familiar. As such, their key function is to get people to the cinema. Audiences will go to see a film because of the star.

NEWS OF THE WORLD, November 10,

LIZ QUITS HOLLYWOOD FOR NEW LIFE IN PARIS

...and gets a Hugh sigh of relief!

GOOD FRIENDS: Liz and Lord Henry Brocklehurst

LOVER: Hugh dislikes Henry

NEWS OF THE WORLD EXCLUSIVE

By GEORGE CLARE and JAN JACQUES

LIZ HURLEY is quitting Hollywood to live in Paris—far from the company of a filthy rich aristocrat who lavishes her with expensive gifts.

And according to pals, Liz's lover Hugh Grant couldn't be more pleased.

He has rarely got on with Lord Henry Brocklehurst who swans around Beverly Hills in a £60,000 Mercedes convertible.

The peer—who inherited £50million this year—has admitted: "We represent another world to Hugh. I'll always see more of Liz on her own."

While Hugh was 3,000 miles away in New York two weeks ago Lord Brocklehurst, 30, was spotted taking Liz out for a £160 Sunday lunch.

It began at midday at the opulent Ivy Restaurant in Los Angeles. At 2pm Estee Lauder-girl Liz left with Henry to go shopping.

At the Agnes B boutique Henry bought her a £450 sweater. At another store he got her a mini-skirt . . . for £2,200.

A Hollywood insider explained: "Liz really adores Henry's company. He's mega-rich and very handsome. She loves the attention he gets."

Actor Jim McMullen, another pal, said: "Liz and Henry have stayed close throughout the ups and downs of her relationship with Hugh.

"In fact, whenever Hugh's away, Henry seems to take his place. It's all a bit weird."

Addict

Brocklehurst, a former heroin addict whose father when he was four, met Liz party in 1993. By then she been dating Hugh for than two years.

Soon after, Liz began s at His Lordship's home

Hollywood hills. She also goes pheasant shooting at his stately home, Sudeley Castle, in Gloucestershire. But Hugh refuses to accompany her.

It was Lord Brocklehurst who gave her a shoulder to cry on when Hugh, 35, was caught with hooker Divine Brown.

But he has said: "Sh

APPE

Yo
sta
Si

POP ve
is app
News
memor
1958 ⌐
He r
progran
cert tic
years.
Fans
thems
next ⌐
with ⌐
Th ⌐
write
PO ⌐
Pev ⌐
BN2⌐

YOUR STARS

Collect newspaper cuttings, or make a diary of TV and radio stories over a period of a month about a star who is in the news.
* What sort of stories appear?
* How is the star represented in the media?
* Does this publicity, including such events as chat show appearances, coincide with the release of a film in this country?

What stars do off-screen is often as important or even more important than their performance on screen. Gossip is an age-old method of keeping stars in the public gaze. Stories of stars' private lives, whether true or not, are a way of ensuring constant media coverage and speculation amongst their fans.

Stars attract fans, who will not only want to watch their films, but are interested in their lives and lifestyles. Some may even try to be like them. Stars, therefore, are a powerful force in the marketing of a picture; they are often at the forefront of fashion and lifestyle, introducing the public to new ways of doing things. As trend-setters, stars often become associated with products that they are seen to endorse. Equally, the manufacturers of luxury goods such as cars and clothing are keen to have their products associated

The film industry has always been clever at promoting itself and its products. Such events as the Oscar ceremonies, and film festivals such as Cannes, held each May in the south of France, attract a vast amount of media attention from across the globe.

Media Studies for GCSE

with the glamorous lifestyles of the stars. You will often see these items used as props in films. This is known as 'product placement'. It is an effective method of advertising, especially if the film is a huge box-office success.

The more important a star, the more power he or she has. Stars like Clint Eastwood, for example, are able to set up their own companies and direct their own films. This is a far cry from the days of the studio system, where all the major stars were under contract to make a certain number of films to studios such as Warner Bros, MGM and Paramount. Stars who were not co-operative in fitting in with the demands of the studio bosses would find their careers in ruins.

Reviews

The film industry relies heavily for publicity on the other media, such as radio, television, magazines and newspapers. Reviews are an important source of information about films. They appear in a number of forms, for example on TV programmes where experts or members of the public offer their opinion of a film. Many magazines carry reviews of films released each month at the cinema, as well as video rental and retail releases. Specialist film magazines, such as *Empire* and *Premiere*, try to cover all the feature films that are released.

Newspapers provide similar information, some of it more detailed and considered than others, and radio stations often have slots in programmes in which newly released films are discussed.

A good film review should be more than just the reviewer's opinion of the film. It should provide potential viewers with information about the film that will allow them to decide whether it is worth seeing or not. For some people, the decision whether or not to see a film at the cinema may rest on the opinion of a reviewer whom they trust.

ON YOUR OWN

Earlier in this chapter you were asked to find out which films were showing at your local cinema. Now try to find out about each of these films.
* Where did you get your information about these films from?
* How reliable is the information?
* Do you trust the judgement of some reviewers more than others? Why?
* Did you find any sources of information about the films other than reviews?

Sight and Sound

'Friends': the great comedy of the 90s by Andy Medhurst

Re-release: the inside story of Orson Welles and 'Touch of Evil'

Exclusive interview: Lars von Trier on 'Breaking the Waves'

Revealing special effects: 'Frankenstein' to '2001'

Twisted desire and film noir: Edgar Ulmer's 'Detour'

Britgrit

Christopher Eccleston: from 'Shallow Grave' to Michael Winterbottom's...

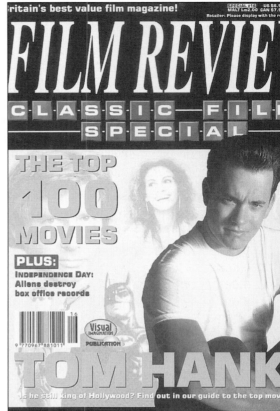

Britain's best value film magazine!

SPECIAL #16   US $6.9
MALT Lm2.00 CAN $7.9
Retailer: Please display with the re

FILM REVIEW

CLASSIC FILM SPECIAL

THE TOP 100 MOVIES

PLUS:
INDEPENDENCE DAY: Aliens destroy box office records

Visual IMAGINATION PUBLICATION

TOM HANK

Is he still king of Hollywood? Find out in our guide to the top movi

---

marie claire review

Film   BY CHRISTOPHER HEMBLADE

KANSAS CITY

Marking a return to form for Robert Altman, after his fashion industry spoof *Pret A Porter* flopped last year, the film is set on the eve of vote-rigged elections in 1934 Kansas City. Drunken socialite Carolyn Stilton (played by Miranda Richardson) is married to President Roosevelt's special advisor Henry Stilton (Michael Murphy). Henry, a sharp politician with a vested interest in a Democrat victory, is keen to avoid any scandal involving his wife. But his desire for a quiet election is foiled by brassy Blondie O'Hara (Jennifer Jason Leigh), who hatches a wild plan to kidnap Carolyn. Blondie plans to hand her over to local mobster Seldom Seen (played splendidly by Henry Belafonte) to secure the release of her own husband, who was caught after a botched robbery. The plot is deftly woven together and the ensuing two hours are an intriguing journey into the changing relationship of two women inadvertently thrown together through circumstance.

ALSO OUT THIS MONTH
● **BREAKING THE WAVES**
Director Lars Von Trier has bestowed an eerie beauty to this film about love in a remote Scottish village. Newcomer Emily Watson, above (see profile on page 147), puts in a remarkable performance as the village girl who marries an 'outsider', much to the chagrin of the local villagers. When an accident paralyses him, she must make agonising decisions. A little traumatising, but worthy of attention.

● **THE CRAFT**
This is a nonsense comedy drama about four high-school girls, who, having decided to explore the power of magic, end up pursuing a tantalising path of darkness. There isn't a bewitching moment in it, but Fairuza Balk (the prostitute from *Things To Do In Denver When You're Dead*) is great.

NEW RELEASES

BRASSED OFF
Following the changing fortunes of Yorkshire's Grimley Colliery Band in 1992, as management fight to close down the coal mine, *Brassed Off* is also a love story of childhood sweethearts - miner Andy (Ewan McGregor) and British Coal Board employee Gloria (played by Tara Fitzgerald), above. The band returns triumphant from the semi-final of a national music competition to find the colliery closed and the community on the verge of disintegration. What follows is a gritty fight to win back pride for all concerned. Sue Johnston (Brookside's Sheila Grant) puts in a good performance as a wise and witty housewife married to a man with a

roving eye, while McGregor is convincing as a frustrated young mine worker. A range of dynamic characters compensate for a particularly dull story line.

THE PILLOW BOOK
This new film from Peter Greenaway is set in Kyoto in the 1970s, where a young Japanese girl, Nagiko (Vivian Wu), below, is transfixed by a calligrapher who daubs a birthday greeting on her face. In adult life, Nagiko searches to find an ideal calligrapher/lover to use her body as his paper. Most of the film is set in her adult life, but we are constantly referred back to the childhood experience to remind us of its emotional resonance. In Hong Kong, she meets

British translator Jerome (Ewan McGregor again). He flips the scenario around by convincing her that she should write on his whole body and that he will carry her writing on his skin to a publisher. From here on in, things become bizarre and dark - and a little far-fetched besides. The quintessential Greenaway trademarks - beautiful scenery, exquisite costumes (designed by Koji Tatsuno and Margiela) - are all here. But it takes great effort to enjoy the film's sumptuous splendour.

THE EIGHTH DAY
Jaco van Dormael's pan-European riposte to *Rain Man* has lead actors from France and Belgium, with Daniel Auteuil as the new Tom Cruise character and Pascal Duquenne in the role of Dustin Hoffman, above right. *Eighth Day* tells the story of a chance encounter one night

between Harry, a stressed-out businessman, and Georges, who has Down's syndrome, and the strange and often difficult partnership that develops between them. The film follows their exploits on trips out together, and details the sometimes improbable discoveries they make about each other - and themselves. *Eighth Day* is touching without being cloying: a scene in which an actress is horrified to discover that Harry's friend has Down's syndrome is a measure of how far the film goes to avoid sentimentality. A winner at Cannes (in the Best Actor category jointly awarded to Daniel Auteuil and Pascal Duquenne), this is a subtitled feel-good movie

● **TWELFTH NIGHT**
A comic tale of love and intrigue, *Twelfth Night* is also an examination of gender. Trevor Nunn, recently appointed Director of the Royal National Theatre, has assembled a strong cast, including Imogen Stubbs and Nigel Hawthorne, in a pleasing rendition of this Shakespeare play.

FILM REVIEW

Choose a film that has just been released at the cinema. Collect as much information as you can about the film in the form of reviews from newspapers and magazines and information from TV and radio.

■ Do all the reviewers agree about the film, or is there a difference of opinion about it? If so, why do you think this is?

■ Now go to see the film. Which review, in your opinion, gave the most accurate evaluation of the film?

Raging Bull ★★★★
US   1980   119m   bw/colour
UA/Chartoff-Winkler

The rise to fame of an unlikeable middle-weight boxer, based on the autobiography of Jake La Motta.

Tough, compelling, powerfully made ringside melodrama. A poll of American critics voted it the best movie of the 1980s.

w Paul Schrader, Mardik Martin d Martin Scorsese ph Michael Chapman m from library sources pd Gene Rudolf

☆ Robert de Niro, Cathy Moriarty, Joe Pesci, Frank Vincent, Nicholas Colasanto

'Scorsese makes pictures about the kind of people you wouldn't want to know.' – *Variety*

'A bravura display of cinematic skill.' – *Daily Mail*

🏆 editing (Thelma Schoonmaker); Robert de Niro
   best film; best direction; Cathy Moriarty; Joe Pesci; Michael Chapman
▽ editing

The Raging Moon ★
GB   1970   111m   Technicolor
EMI (Bruce Cohn Curtis)

aka: *Long Ago Tomorrow*
A love affair develops between two inmates of a home for the physically handicapped.

Appealing romantic drama which nearly became a big commercial success.

wd Bryan Forbes, *novel* Peter Marshall ph Tony Imi m Stanley Myers

☆ Malcolm McDowell, Nanette Newman, Georgia Brown, Bernard Lee, Gerald Sim, Michael Flanders

Raging Waters: see *Green Promise*

Una Ragione per Vivere e Una per Morire: see *A Reason to Live, a Reason to Die*

'What a time it was, an incredible time, a good time, a bad time . . .'

Ragtime ★
US   1981   155m   Technicolor   Todd-AO
Ragtime/Sunley (Dino de Laurentiis)

Just before World War I, various Americans are affected by world events, and a chapter of accidents turns a placid Negro into a revolutionary.

The fascinating patchwork of the novel has been virtually abandoned in favour of its least interesting episode, which is even further drawn out by the decision to bring on the aged James Cagney as a comic turn not in the novel. The early sequences show what might have been.

w Michael Weller *novel* E. L. Doctorow d Milos Forman ph Miroslav Ondricek m Randy Newman ad John Graysmark, Patrizia von Brandenstein, Anthony Reading

☆ James Olson, Mary Steenburgen, James Cagney, Pat O'Brien, Elizabeth McGovern, Howard E. Rollins Jnr, Brad Dourif, Moses Gunn, Kenneth McMillan, Donald O'Connor

'It's limp . . . it always seems to be aiming about halfway toward the effects that Doctorow achieved in his literary extravaganza.' – *New Yorker*

'The book, despite its defects, was funny, radical and angry. The film, despite its virtues, is solemn, liberal and passive.' – *Sunday Times*
† The film cost 32 million dollars and took eleven.
   screenplay; Miroslav Ondricek; Randy Newman; Elizabeth McGovern (supporting actress); Howard E. Rollins Jnr; art direction; song 'One More Hour'

Raiders of the Lost Ark ★★
US   1981   115m   Metrocolor   Panavision
Paramount/Lucasfilm (Frank Marshall)

In the thirties, an American archaeologist and explorer beats the Nazis to a priceless artefact, the magical box containing fragments of the stones on which God wrote his laws.

Commercially very successful, this attempted wrap-up of the Saturday morning serials of two generations ago spends a great deal of money and expertise on frightening us rather than exciting us; in Dolby sound the experience is horrendous. Second time round, one can better enjoy the ingenious detail of the hero's exploits and ignore the insistence on unpleasantness; still, there are boring bits in between, and the story doesn't make a lot of sense.

w Lawrence Kasdan d Steven Spielberg ph Douglas Slocombe m John Williams pd Norman Reynolds
☆ Harrison Ford, Karen Allen, Ronald Lacey, Paul Freeman, John Rhys-Davies, Denholm Elliott

'Both de trop and not enough.' – *Sight and Sound*

'Children may well enjoy its simple-mindedness, untroubled by the fact that it looks so shoddy and so uninventive.' – *Observer*

'Kinesthetically, the film gets to you, but there's no exhilaration, and no surge of feeling at the end.' – *Pauline Kael, New Yorker*

'An out of body experience, a movie of glorious imagination and breakneck speed that grabs you in the first shot, hurtles you through a series of incredible adventures, and deposits you back in reality two hours later – breathless, dizzy, wrung-out, and with a silly grin on your face.' – *Roger Ebert*

† Tom Selleck was the first choice for the lead, but was tied up with his TV series *Magnum*.
‡ It was followed by two sequels: *Indiana Jones and the Temple of Doom* and *Indiana Jones and the Last Crusade* (qqv).

🏆 editing (Michael Kahn); visual effects
   best picture; Steven Spielberg; Douglas Slocombe; John Williams
▽ Norman Reynolds

Rain Man ★★
US   1988   133m   DeLuxe
UIP/United Artists/Guber-Peters (Mark Johnson)

A fast-talking salesman discovers, on his father's death, that he has an autistic elder brother.

An intelligent road movie, but one that does not move far enough from more conventional buddy-buddy movies.

w Ronald Bass, Barry Morrow d Barry Levinson ph John Seale m Hans Zimmer pd Ida Random ed Stu Linder, Thomas R. Moore

☆ Dustin Hoffman, Tom Cruise, Valeria Golino, Jerry Molen, Jack Murdock, Michael D. Roberts, Ralph Seymour, Lucinda Jenney, Bonnie Hunt

🏆 best picture; best director; best original screenplay; Dustin Hoffman
   best original score; best cinematography

Review   As you have seen in this chapter, cinema is an important and complex medium. Like other media products, it is a commodity, produced, in the main, by large and influential institutions. As a commodity, it has to be carefully marketed to ensure that it appeals to as wide an audience as possible. Indeed, as an industry, its survival depends on this ability to manufacture products that audiences want to consume.

9. NEWSPAPERS, MAGAZINES AND COMICS

History

On street corners throughout the world, newspaper-sellers invite people to read the 'latest'. In airports and stations, kiosks and shops offer eye-catching displays of magazines to entice travellers. In doctors' waiting-rooms, dog-eared piles of old magazines help patients to take their minds off their troubles. Newspapers, magazines and comics are some of the most familiar objects on earth.

Humans have communicated using writing for thousands of years. However, it was the development of printing in the 15th century that made the written word so powerful. It meant that large numbers of copies of a document could be made, using printing blocks that were covered with ink and repeatedly pressed onto paper. This was revolutionary, as it meant that, for the first time, written information could be circulated to a large number of people. Previously, documents had to be copied by hand, which limited both their number and people's access to them.

However, at first, the development of printing meant little to most people, because they could not read. That is why the first newspapers and magazines in the UK were produced for and read by the rich and powerful. The first recognized newspaper or pamphlet to contain information about world events was the *Oxford Gazette*, which was first published in 1665. It was produced to keep the royal court (which had fled to Oxford to escape the plague) informed of events in London. It later became known as the *London Gazette* and is still published today. The first daily paper was the *Daily Courant*, published for the first time in 1702. The news it contained was hardly hot off the press, as it carried only stories from papers published on the continent. The history of newspapers really began in the UK in 1885, with the first appearance of *The Times*.

The development of newspapers and magazines into items familiar to virtually everyone in the UK was brought about by two main factors: education and distribution. The development of road, and especially rail, transport meant that newspapers and magazines published in London and other big cities could be distributed throughout the country. However, it was only in the 20th century, when most people could read as a result of education reforms, that large audiences for printed material were created.

NEWSPAPERS

Thousands of different newspapers are published in the UK each week. They can be separated into groups according to where they are published, and when and how often they are published. Virtually all newspapers fall into the following categories.

Types of newspaper

National daily papers

The national daily papers are the big papers that everyone is familiar with – *The Sun*, *Daily Mirror*, *The Times*, *The Guardian* and so on. They are published in London each night and are on the news-stands every morning, except Sunday. In the UK, there are ten national daily newspapers. They can be divided into two groups, depending on their size.

Broadsheet newspapers are printed on sheets of paper 116.83 by 81.28 cm (46 by 32 inches). There are five such broadsheets: *The Daily Telegraph*, *The Times*, *The Financial Times*, *The Guardian* and *The Independent*. *The Daily Telegraph* is the best-selling broadsheet paper, with sales of around 2.5 million copies a day.

Tabloid newspapers are half the size of broadsheets, with pages measuring 58.42 by 40.64 cm (23 by 16 inches). There are six national daily tabloids: *The Sun*, *The Star*, *Daily Mail*, *Daily Mirror*, *Daily Express* and *Daily Sport*. *The Sun* is the tabloid that sells most copies, around four million a day. This makes it the UK's best-selling daily paper.

National Sunday newspapers

The *Sunday Times* is the UK's biggest selling Sunday broadsheet and, thanks to all its sections, its heaviest.

As well as national daily newspapers, the UK has nine national papers that are published only on a Sunday. There are five national Sunday broadsheets: *The Sunday Times*, *The Sunday Telegraph*, *The Observer*, *Independent on Sunday* and *The European*. *The Sunday Times*' sales are the largest – over 3.5 million every week.

There are five tabloid papers published nationally every Sunday. They are: *News of the World*, *The Mail On Sunday*, *The People*, *Sunday Express* and *Sunday Mirror*. The *News of the World* sells around 12 million copies each week, making it not only the biggest selling Sunday paper, but also the UK's best-selling paper overall.

Regional papers

Dailies In addition to the national papers produced in London, the UK has a strong regional press. Nearly 90 daily papers are published in cities and towns throughout the country. Regional papers tend to be grouped according to what time of day they are published (either in the morning or the evening), rather than according to whether they are broadsheet or tabloid in size. There only a few morning regional papers. They include the *Daily Record*, which is published in Glasgow and is the UK's biggest selling regional daily paper, with sales of nearly three-quarters of a million copies a day. Most regional daily papers are evening papers. The London *Evening Standard*, for example, is the second largest regional daily with around half a million copies bought every day. Regional morning papers were once popular, but went into decline, largely as a result of competition from national morning papers.

Weeklies Most regional papers are published only once a week. These publications can also be separated into two groups, according to whether they are paid for by the reader or given away free. The idea of giving papers away free to readers and making money only from the adverts that they contain, became popular in the 1970s. However, economic recessions that led businesses to reduce their advertising budgets forced many free newspapers to close.

The UK has a very strong regional press.

Sundays There are also a number of regional papers that are published only on a Sunday. These include such papers as the *Sunday Life*, which is published in Belfast, *Wales on Sunday*, produced in Cardiff and the *Sunday Sun*, published in Newcastle.

Specialist newspapers

As well as national and regional papers, there are newspapers that cover specific areas of interest. The *International Herald Tribune* is a daily paper that covers world news. The *Racing Post* and *Sporting Life* are national daily papers that cover events in the worlds of racing and sport. The *Morning Star* and *Newsline* are daily left-wing political papers that are published nationally. The *New Musical Express* and *Melody Maker* publish the latest news from the music world, along with reviews and features each week. The *Angling Times* is among many weekly newspapers that cater for leisure interests.

ON YOUR OWN

Go into a large local newsagent's and jot down the names of as many papers as you can. Decide which type of paper they are and draw up a chart to show the results of your research.

What's in a newspaper?

The process of putting any paper together is basically the same, although there are thousands of newspapers, each one of them different. Most newspapers have several distinct departments:

• Editorial, which consists of the words written by reporters and the pictures taken by photographers.
• Advertising
• Production
• Sales.

Who does what?

The advertising department

Like all media organizations, newspapers have to make money if they are to survive. They get their money from two sources:

Cover price. The price of the paper, which is paid by the reader when they buy it.

Advertising fees. These are paid to the publishers of the paper by the businesses that buy space to promote their products.

The amount of money that a paper makes from its cover price and advertising fees depends on its circulation, or the number of papers that it sells each day or week. If a lot of papers are sold, as is the case for national dailies, then a large part of the publisher's income comes from the cover price. If fewer papers are sold, for instance, in the case of local weeklies, most of the money comes from advertising. The general rule is that the smaller a paper's sales, the larger the percentage of adverts in it. Free papers that are delivered through every door in a set circulation area make all their money from advertising.

The advertising sales department, under the control of the advertising manager, has the task of selling advertising space to businesses. The advertising manager has a team of sales representatives, who contact businesses either by visiting them, or by phoning them, which is known as telesales. Advertisers can pay for their adverts to be put in specific places in the paper, such as on the front or back, or can simply leave the position of the advert up to the newspaper, which is known as 'run-of-paper advertising'.

The types of adverts found in papers include:
Display adverts, or adverts for products, with photographs and graphics, placed by businesses.
Classified adverts. These are small adverts in columns, usually placed by individuals. They cover such topics as second-hand goods, cars and births, marriages and deaths.
Advertorials. These are advertising features about products, which are written like news stories and are usually accompanied by pictures.

Press advertising is covered in more detail in the chapter on advertising (see pages 198–200). However, at this point it is important to realize the crucial role that advertising plays in newspapers. Without money from adverts, most papers would go out of business. (In fact, for hundreds of years, the front page of *The Times* consisted of nothing but advertisements.) Because of this, great importance is given to advertising by publishers. Adverts are usually placed on a page first and the stories produced by reporters are arranged around them. This means that the way a newspaper page looks depends to a large degree on the adverts that are on it. They make up what is called the 'page scheme', which the editorial department has to work around. Page schemes are plans of news pages that have been drawn up by the advertising department. They show where the adverts that have been sold on the page are placed.

Advertising is crucial to newspapers. *The Times* used to carry nothing but adverts on its front page.

IN PAIRS

Contact your local newspaper and get an advertising rate card. Look at a copy of the paper and work out:
• How much of it is advertising.
• How much money the newspaper made from the advertisements in that particular copy of the paper.

The editorial department

The editorial department produces the 'news' in newspapers, in other words, the stories and photographs that appear around adverts. The editorial department is usually made up of:

The editor, who is in charge of the whole department. Editors make sure everything runs to plan and have the final say on what appears in the paper. They work closely with the advertising manager to make sure that the paper makes as much money as possible.

The chief sub-editor is a senior journalist with design and layout skills. Chief sub-editors receive page schemes from the advertising department and decide which stories will go on each one. They distribute the page schemes and stories to sub-editors.

Sub-editors are journalists who place stories and photographs on page schemes. They do this on computer screens. Before placing a story and writing a headline for it, they must first check that it is accurate, does not break the laws of libel and is spelt correctly. They do all this under the guidance of the chief sub-editor.

The news editor is a senior journalist who is in charge of a team of reporters. News editors look at all the stories coming in and decide which ones to follow up. They give the stories that they are interested in to reporters and tell the photographic department what pictures will be needed. They also check stories written by reporters before they are sent to the chief sub-editor.

Reporters are senior and junior journalists who research and write stories. Reporters may cover all kinds of stories, or they may be specialists, concerned with a specific area of the news, such as sport or crime.

Photographers take and develop the pictures needed for each edition of the newspaper. They are usually controlled by a chief photographer and report to the picture editor, who oversees the photographic needs of the newspaper.

Designers are artists who produce graphics for editorial features and advertisements.

ON YOUR OWN

Look at a copy of any newspaper.
■ Look for the 'by-lines' (the names that show who a story or photograph is by).
■ Note down the names and titles (for example, Julian Honer, Chief Reporter, or Jane Turner, Crime Reporter, if any are given.
■ Next to the names, write the titles of the stories, or a description of the photographs for which each person is responsible.
This will give you an idea of the editorial structure of the newspaper.

The production department

The production department is responsible for putting the paper together in its final form, as well as for having it printed. The production editor oversees the printing of the paper, working with a team of plate-makers and printers. Printing is the most expensive area of newspaper production; the cost of printing presses runs into millions of pounds.

Printing presses are the most expensive equipment used in the newspaper production process.

Over the last 30 years, developments in printing technology have revolutionized the production of newspapers:

Hot-metal printing. Until the 1960s, papers were printed using movable metal type, which was built up into pages. The ink was placed onto the type and newsprint was then run over the top of the plates. This form of printing was known as 'hot metal', as the metal type could be melted down and remoulded to make different letters, words and symbols.

Photo-typesetting. With the invention of photo-typesetting, stories (or 'copy') were typed on computers and then printed onto a special type of photographic paper called bromide paper. This paper was then cut to size and pasted onto page plans, which were photographed. Printing plates were made from the photographs.

Offset litho printing, however, was the invention that changed the face of UK newspapers. It involves using photographic negatives of bromide pages to make printing plates with raised images. The plates are placed on printing drums and rotated so that they come into contact with ink rollers. The drums then impress an image onto rubber sheets. Newsprint is pressed onto the rubber sheets and the pages are printed.

The sales department

Once the newspaper has been printed, it has to get to the readers. This is the responsibility of the sales department. Under the sales manager, the department tries to maximize sales of the paper through as many outlets as possible. Outlets include:

• Newsagents and other shops
• Paper sellers on the street
• Home deliveries.

Sales representatives try to persuade shops to take more copies of the paper. They also contact individuals at home to encourage them to have the paper delivered. Special offers are often used to tempt readers to order regular copies of a newspaper.

IN GROUPS

You are a publisher who is launching a newspaper for schools or colleges in your area.

You have to decide how many copies of the paper you will need to distribute to your readers and how much it will cost. To do this, you will have to:

• Work out your potential readership. How many schools or colleges will you target? How many students does each have?
• Find out how much it would cost to print the number of papers that you would need. You will have to contact printers to do this.

In groups

❥ Investigate the ways in which newspapers have tried to increase their sales. To do this, you will have to look at advertisements for newspapers on television and in other media, special offers, competitions, free gifts, cheaper prices or coupons for holidays. Most promotional activities have very little to do with 'news'.
❥ Use your findings as the basis for a class discussion on the subject of what these developments tell us about the role of newspapers in our society.

Distribution

Newspapers are distributed using all forms of transport. National newspapers use road, rail and air links to send out their publications. Local paper delivery vans are a familiar sight in most towns, as they take the latest edition to the shops. Paper-sellers go to a distribution point to pick up bundles of papers, before setting off for their carefully chosen spots throughout towns and cities. Many students are part of a newspaper distribution network, working to deliver papers for a newsagent.

From story to page

Newspaper stories, like all media products, are the result of a production process that involves a team of workers. To reach the printed page, a story goes through the following stages.

Choosing the story

'News' does not just happen, it is created. Someone has to decide it is news before it is printed or broadcast. The people who decide this are journalists. In the case of newspapers, it is the news editor who usually judges what the news is. They sift through the stories that come in and decide whether to follow them up or not (for a list of sources of stories, see the chapter on television news, page 96). There is a difference between:
• The stories that are reported to a newspaper, and
• The stories that a newspaper reports.

NEWS AGENCIES

News agencies are private companies who sell stories to the news media. They exist because news organizations' coverage of events is limited by the number of staff and the amount of money that they have. Agencies have their own reporters, photographers, film and radio crews, who produce ready-made news that newspapers, radio and TV can reproduce. Agencies range in size from small, regional press agencies to multinational, multi-media companies.

The Press Association is one of the UK's biggest news agencies. It supplies news, sports coverage and photographs to newspapers, radio and television. It even publishes reports on the Internet. Each day the Press Association produces over 40,000 words, 1,000 ready-made pages and 100 photographs for its customers. Reuters is one of the most famous agencies and supplies news to media organizations throughout the world.

Not all the information that arrives on a news editor's desk ends up as news in a paper. The news editor decides whether the material that comes to their attention will become news by being turned into a story, or remain unreported information. In this way, news editors influence what the audience thinks of as news. By sorting information and deciding what to follow up, they set a news agenda, which is drawn up on the basis of the news editor's personal decisions, not on the basis of the information that they receive. This is why the news is something that is created, rather than simply reported.

News values

Several factors influence whether a story will be selected for coverage. These are often called news values and include:

Where the event occurred. If an event happened within the area covered by the newspaper, it will be more interesting to readers than an event that took place outside it.

When an event occurred. An event that has just happened is more news-worthy than one that happened a week ago. This is simply because people are more likely to know about something, the longer ago it happened.

Who is involved in the story. A story is more likely to be reported if the person involved is famous or well known in the newspaper's area. Also, a story about someone who lives in the newspaper's circulation area is more likely to appear in a paper, even if they are not well known, than one about someone who lives outside it.

News sense. This is a word used by journalists to describe a gut-feeling about what makes a good story that will interest readers. It is often talked about as if it were a kind of magic power. However, it is really a professional way of looking at information, which is built up through working in a news environment.

IN GROUPS

Each group represents a national daily newspaper.
● Look closely at copies of the newspaper that your group represents and decide what its news values are.
● Which three stories from the following list does each group think that their paper would be most likely to cover? Use the news values you have identified to help you to make your choice.

- A top pop band splits up
- A plane carrying diplomats crashes in China
- The goverment announces a drop in taxes for the rich
- The star of a TV soap has a baby
- Russian minister is sacked
- A big fraud case involving city bankers comes to trial
- A princess wears a daring dress to a film première
- The space shuttle is launched on another mission.

Getting the information

If a news editor thinks that a story is interesting enough, they give it to a reporter. It is the reporter's job to gather all the information that they think is necessary to write the story. The news editor briefs the reporter on what the story is about and supplies any information that the newspaper has about it. This may be addresses and telephone numbers, a press release, a report from the emergency services, or copy from a news agency. The reporter then begins to add to this information by interviewing people face-to-face or on the telephone, visiting the site of the event and gathering information from organizations, libraries or other newspapers.

Writing the story

Once the reporter has enough information to write the story, they sit down at a computer and key in the words that make up the copy. This is done using a set of professional codes, or ways of writing that have been learnt from other journalists (see the chapter on language for an explanation of codes, pages 13–14). In writing the story, they select what information will be included and what will be left out, and decide the order in which the information will appear.

It is the reporter's job to research and write news stories.

Most news stories are written in the following format:

Intro. This is the first paragraph of the story and it is the most important one. Research into how people read newspapers shows that most people read the headlines first and, if they find them interesting, will then read the first paragraph of the story. If the first paragraph is not interesting, most readers will not continue with the story. As a rule, the most exciting or interesting aspect of the story is written about in the first paragraph. After reading the intro, readers should be able to tell what the story is about. The intro paragraph acts as a 'hook' to drag readers into the story.

Elaboration. The next few paragraphs tell readers more about the story outlined in the intro. They tell readers what happened, when and where, and to whom it happened. The elaboration should also say how it happened and, if possible, why. In all news stories, the more important the information is, the closer it is placed to the beginning of the story.

Quotes. Virtually all news stories contain comments from those involved. These are called quotes and are meant to be word-for-word records of what the person said. They usually come after the story has been elaborated and are an important element in keeping a balanced view of a story (see page 140).

Projection. Many, though not all, news stories tell the reader what might happen next in relation to the event or people in the report. This may take the form of a police officer saying what they will be doing in an enquiry, or an MP outlining what action they will be taking over a particular issue. This sort of information is generally used to end stories.

An important element that a journalist must keep in mind when writing a story is that of balance. Journalists must try to give equal weight to the point of view of all those involved in the story in order to avoid bias. In theory, if a story is critical of a particular person or organization, the person or organization should be offered the chance to respond to the criticism. In practice, however, balance is a controversial issue, as many people believe that they have been unfairly treated in the way they have been portrayed. Journalists may find it difficult always to represent equally the views of those involved in stories. Some people, however, accuse journalists of misrepresenting people in order to spice stories up. The issue of balance is important in debates about how different groups in society are represented. As was discussed in the chapter on representation, many groups feel that the media is biased against them (see page 32). Many left-wing councils have complained that stories written about them by journalists who work for right-wing newspapers are biased and without balance. The Press Complaints Commission, discussed in the chapter on institutions (see pages 53–55), was set up to deal with complaints about unfair treatment in news stories, amongst other things.

The typical structure of a newspaper story.

Intro ──────▶
Elaboration ──────▶
Quotes ──────▶
Projection ──────▶

Air stowaway seeks asylum

A MAN is claiming asylum in Britain after stowing away in the baggage hold of a flight from New Delhi to Heathrow. The man, an Indian national, was treated for hypothermia after his 10-hour ordeal in the freezing hold and is now at Harmondsworth immigration detention centre.

He must have slipped through the tight armed security at New Delhi airport, aviation experts say. The man was found much the worse for his journey wandering around without the necessary identification documents at Heathrow's Terminal 4 by a British Airways dispatcher.

One official said: "He stowed away in the baggage hold of an aircraft where temperatures drop extremely low – he is very lucky to be alive."

Airlines face fines of up to £2,000 for bringing into Britain anyone without the necessary travel documents.

CLASS ACTIVITY

Examine stories from a range of newspapers, both broadsheet and tabloid, and local and national. Are the stories 'balanced'? Does everyone mentioned in the story get fair hearing? Can you spot any bias?

TYPES OF STORY

Journalists separate stories into types, depending on their length or the position they are intended to take on a page. Some of these story types are:

SPLASH – the main story on the front page of a newspaper.

PAGE LEAD – the main story on a newspaper page. It is usually the longest story on the page and has the biggest headline.

SUPPORT – usually the second longest story on a newspaper page, 'supporting' the main story.

SHORTS – stories usually between three and eight paragraphs in length.

FILLS – stories of no more than one or two paragraphs, which are used to fill gaps on a page.

NIB – or news in brief. Nibs are one- or two-paragraph stories that give only basic facts. Nibs are often arranged in lists with small headlines on the front page of a paper. They usually refer to stories carried inside the paper and give the page number on which the full story appears, so that readers can find it.

NAG – or news at a glance. These are short news summaries that give the main points of a story.

In pairs

Take a page of any newspaper. Look at each story and decide which type of story it is.

The deadline is the time by which the reporter has to have a story ready. The reporter must make sure that the copy appears on the news editor's screen in time for it to be checked, before being sent to a sub-editor. The news editor reads through the story to make sure that it makes sense and that the reporter has followed up all the possible avenues of information. If they are not satisfied, they will send it back to the reporter with suggestions as to how it could be improved, for example, by interviewing another person.

Getting the picture

Every news story is considered not only in terms of words, but also in terms of the photographs or graphics that could accompany it. The news editor looks at each story and decides if there is a photograph that could go with it. If they think that there is, they discuss with the picture editor or chief photographer what sort of picture would be suitable. It may show an event happening, for instance, a demonstration or a meeting, or it may show a person involved in the news. Once it has been decided what sort of picture is wanted, the task is given to a photographer, who goes out and takes it. The photographer has a deadline for the photograph and has to make sure that it is developed in time to be used in the newspaper.

As well as photographs, the news editor may decide that a story could be illustrated with graphics in the form of illustrations, tables or decoration. In this case, they talk to the design department and a graphic designer is briefed to come up with the necessary graphics.

Sub-editing the story

When the copy and the photographs are ready, they are sent to a sub-editor. Sub-editors are given page schemes by the chief sub-editor. They are also given a list of stories and photographs to fit onto the page scheme. Their job is to display the stories and photographs to the best effect in the space surrounding the adverts. Their job involves:

In newspapers, photographs are as important as words.

Making sure stories do not break the law by libelling people.

Libel is a law that defends people's right not to have things said about them in print that are not true and damage their reputation. If a newspaper prints a story that libels someone, the victim can take the newspaper to court and demand cash in compensation.

Correcting spelling and grammar. Even trained reporters make mistakes.

Writing headlines. Headlines are 'doors' through which readers get into stories. They have to be interesting and inviting, or the reader may pass the story by. This is especially true on the front page, as it is the main headline that often persuades a reader to buy the paper.

Sub-editors place stories and write headlines.

Placing photographs to best effect. Photographs are 'windows' through which readers see what is going on in a story. If the photograph is used badly, it will be ignored and fail to attract the reader to the story. As with headlines, this is especially true on the front page. The picture that is used on the front page of a newspaper has to be good to encourage readers to buy the paper.

Writing captions for photographs that tell the reader what they show.

Making sure the story fits into the space set aside for it on the page, usually by cutting words from it. Once a sub-editor has laid out the page, it goes to the chief sub-editor on the computer network to be checked. If it is approved, the page is then sent to be printed.

Newspaper identities

All newspapers have their own identities, which are expressed through a combination of the following:
- Design and layout
- Content
- Language.

Design and layout

Most papers are either broadsheet or tabloid in format. The size of a newspaper has an effect on how it looks, for example, broadsheet papers have more stories on a page because the pages are bigger. However, the design and layout of broadsheet and tabloid newspapers are very different in other ways too.

Tabloid newspapers tend to be brasher in their presentation. They use large photographs and big headlines. In fact, the front pages of most tabloid newspapers are dominated by the splash headline and a striking photograph. Stories in tabloids tend to be short. Many of the photographs are used simply because they are visually interesting, rather than because they are newsworthy. Pages are designed to be eye-catching, with lots going on.

Broadsheets are more restrained in their presentation. Headlines are usually informative, rather than startling. Photographs are used to illustrate stories, rather than used as stories in their own right. Stories are laid out in blocks on the page and tend to be longer than those in tabloid papers.

IN PAIRS
Try to come up with headlines for the following stories:
- Angry mothers march on a school to protest about the lunches
- Local dog wins Crufts' dog show
- Martians land in your town.

Terms used to describe elements of newspaper layout.

DATE · PRICE · MASTHEAD · TAG · SPLASH · PICTURE CAPTION · LURE · HEADLINE · SUB-HEADLINE · SUPPORT STORY · LEAD STORY · BY-LINE

Content

Newspapers also develop their own identities through the type of story they print. Tabloid papers, especially the popular ones such as *The Sun*, *The Star*, *Daily Mirror*, *News of the World* and *The People*, generally carry stories concerned with crime, sex, gossip and scandal. This has led to them being called the 'gutter press'. They have been condemned by some for lowering moral standards through stories regarded as being in bad taste. Tabloid editors, however, argue that they aim to entertain their readers as much as to inform them. They also say that the fact that their papers have the highest circulations shows that their readers are interested in the subjects they cover. Of course, not all tabloid papers are like this. What are known as the 'quality' tabloids, such as the *Daily Express* and *Daily Mail*, take a less sensational approach and carry a lot more 'serious' news.

Broadsheet newspapers see their job as that of informing their readers as to what is going on in the world. Their stories tend to deal with political, economic and international news. It is unusual for a broadsheet to lead on a sex scandal, unless it affects politicians or people in positions of authority.

IN PAIRS

Carry out a content analysis exercise on two broadsheet and two tabloid newspapers (see the chapter on representation, pages 33–34, for tips on how to do this). Which subjects feature more heavily in one type of paper than the other?

Language

A major part of a newspaper's identity is the language that it uses in its stories. The type of words used play an important role in the way the paper addresses its readers. In the chapters on language and audience, it was shown that different media products use different tones of voice to communicate with their users. Tabloid newspapers use short, simple words. They tend to use slang, as people do in conversation, for example, 'cops' instead of police, and 'squaddies' instead of soldiers. They often refer to famous people by nicknames, like 'Jacko' and 'Gazza'. They also use puns and word-play to make headlines entertaining. Popular tabloids have been attacked for using sexist and racist language to describe minority groups and foreigners.

ON YOUR OWN

Can you find examples of language used in tabloid newspapers that may be offensive to particular groups of people?

Broadsheet papers tend to use more formal language. Stories often contain longer words and sentences than are used in tabloids. Headlines are written 'straight', in that they rarely use humour or word play. People in stories are usually given their proper titles, such as Mr Blair, Mrs Gupta or Ms Anderson.

PAGE FEATURE PROFILE

The Star is Yorkshire's biggest selling newspaper.
TYPE: Evening paper.
FORMAT: Tabloid.
PUBLISHED: Six days a week.
CIRCULATION: Around 100,000 copies a day.
EDITIONS: *Sheffield Star, Rotherham Star, Doncaster Star* and *Barnsley Star*.
HEAD OFFICES: Sheffield.
PRINTING PRESSES: Produce 50,000 copies of the paper an hour.
EMPLOYS: Around 600 people.
OWNER: United Newspapers.

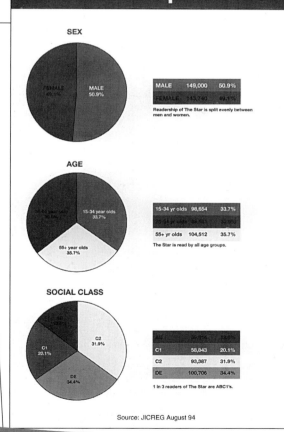

IN GROUPS
Using this profile as a guide, produce a profile of your local newspaper.

9.NEWSPAPERS CASE STUDY   **145**

MAGAZINES

The word 'magazine' comes from the French 'magasin', which means 'storehouse'. This is an appropriate name, as magazines tend to be storehouses of knowledge and information about a particular subject or area of interest. The first magazine to be published using the word in its title was the *Gentleman's Magazine of London*, which was first published in 1731.

Magazines are very different from newspapers. They are generally thicker, printed in colour on glossy paper, and are published less frequently. One major difference between newspapers and magazines is their content. As magazines are published less often, they cannot keep readers informed of day-to-day happenings, as newspapers do. Therefore, magazines tend to focus on feature material, in the form of interviews with 'newsworthy' people, or investigations of particular subjects (although some magazines, such as the American *Newsweek*, do concern themselves with current events).

Magazine publishing is one of the most lively areas of media production. There was a big rise in the number of titles during the 1980s and 1990s. According to the Periodical Publishers Association, which promotes the interests of magazine producers, from 1986 to 1996 there was a 68% increase in the number of business magazines and a 38% rise in the number of consumer magazines. In 1996, people spent 140% more on magazines than they did in 1986 (PPA review).

So many magazines

Over 7,500 different magazines are presently published in the UK. They range from the *Radio Times* to *What's New in Farming*. Magazines are generally divided into two groups:

CLASS ACTIVITY

Do a survey of the different magazines read by members of your class. Which magazines are the most popular and why?

Business and professional titles. These are specialized publications aimed at people in specific areas of business and industry. Such magazines make up the majority of magazines published in the UK: around 5,250 titles fall into this category.

Consumer. These are magazines aimed at the general public, or at specific segments of it. There are around 2,500 titles in this group in the UK. These include the publications that most people think of when the word 'magazine' is mentioned, for instance, *Just Seventeen*, *Cosmopolitan*, *The Face*, *More*, *GQ*, *TV Times*.

There are so many magazines because they are relatively cheap to

There is a magazine for virtually every subject you can think of.

produce, in comparison with newspapers. This means that there is less risk involved in setting one up. As most magazines do not have their own printing presses, all they need is staff, computer equipment and enough start-up cash to pay a printer. Desk-top publishing (DTP) packages that allow professional-looking pages to be produced on personal computers have revolutionized magazine publishing. Working from a rented office, a small team can have a magazine in the newsagent's within months of the initial idea to set it up.

In the chapter on audience, audience fragmentation, or the splitting of audiences with particular interests from wider audiences, was

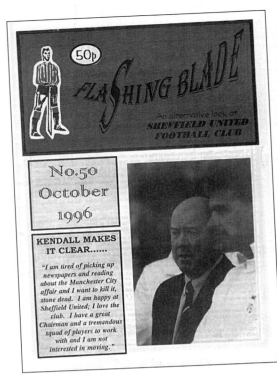

FLASHING BLADE

An alternative look at
SHEFFIELD UNITED
FOOTBALL CLUB

50p

No.50
October
1996

KENDALL MAKES
IT CLEAR......

"I am tired of picking up newspapers and reading about the Manchester City affair and I want to kill it, stone dead. I am happy at Sheffield United; I love the club. I have a great Chairman and a tremendous squad of players to work with and I am not interested in moving."

discussed (see pages 63–64). The magazine market has seen a large degree of audience fragmentation. The low cost of publishing means that very small readerships with special interests can be catered for at a profit. So a publisher might look at existing fishing magazines, decide that they are too general and that money could be made by launching a magazine solely for those interested in fly fishing.

However, not all magazines are published to make a profit. Fanzines are magazines with a small circulation that are produced by fans about their particular area of interest, for example, a band or a football team. Fanzines are published on very low budgets, often using nothing more than a typewriter and a photocopier. They tend not to make a profit and are produced out of love for the subject they cover.

Making money

Like newspapers, magazines can make money from their cover price (which the reader pays to buy a copy), from advertising or from a combination of both. Most business magazines are sent free to readers and make all their money from advertising. Consumer magazines generally charge for copies. However, advertising is still their major source of revenue.

Magazine advertising departments work in a similar way to those on newspapers. They sell adverts on the basis of how much space they take up on a page, and which page the advert is on. Most quote a price for a full-page advert in their magazine and, for a smaller advert, work out a percentage based on that price. The more copies a magazine sells, the more it can charge an advertiser, as it can say that more people will see the advert. In 1996, taking out a full-page advert in the *Radio Times*, which had a circulation of 1,433,223, cost £18,500. In comparison, a full-page advert in *Pony* magazine, with a circulation of 37,300, cost £1,245.

One way in which magazines create income that they can rely on is through the subscription system. This is where a reader pays for a set number of copies of the magazine in advance, usually at a price lower than they would pay in a shop. The magazine is then sent to the reader by post. The advantage for the magazine is that it receives a lump sum of money that it can invest in its operation.

A major factor affecting how much money magazines make is the cost of paper. From 1986 to 1996, the price of paper rose steeply, causing some magazines to close and forcing most to increase their cover price.

IN PAIRS

Imagine that you were launching a new skin cream for men and women. Draw up a list of five magazines in which you would like to place a full-page advert. Contact them to see how much it would cost.

Setting up a magazine

More and more magazines are being launched. Unfortunately for their publishers, many sink. To make sure that a magazine has a chance of success, potential publishers have to take many factors into consideration.

Identifying a market

A publisher must be sure that there are people who will buy their magazine. It is no use producing a magazine for worm racers if there are only three in the country. Publishers must also be sure that there is enough to write about and photograph on a specific subject to fill a regular magazine. The number of worm racing facts and action shots may be somewhat limited.

Low production costs mean that magazines can be published for very small readerships.

Assessing the competition

Before launching a new magazine, a survey of the market must be done to see what magazines are already published in the same subject area. If there are already a lot of them, it may be difficult to justify launching a new one, as readers only have so much money to spend. The publisher may decide to go ahead with the magazine, however, if they are convinced that it will be better than others already being published and will lure readers away from them. When a particular subject area is seen to be completely covered by magazines, it is known as 'market saturation'. It could be argued that men's lifestyle and computer magazines have reached market saturation point.

Most new magazines are produced because their publishers believe that they have spotted a gap in the market, or an area that is not catered for by existing magazines and that could generate a profitable readership. A good example of this was the launch of *The Oldie* in 1992, a magazine specifically for older people, which had very little competition. Another area that has produced a lot of new magazines is that of UFOs. There used to be only a few publications covering this area, for example, the *Fortean Times*. However, the success of such TV programmes as *The X-Files* generated a lot of interest in the subject, and publishers were quick to spot the gap in the market. *Encounters*, *Nexus*, *Sightings* and *UFO Reality* soon appeared on newsagents' shelves. It will be interesting to see how many magazines this area can support before market saturation is reached.

Attracting advertisers

As most magazines depend on advertising to survive, a publisher has to be certain that some businesses will want to buy space in the new publication. The publisher will have to convince businesses that enough people will read the magazine to make it worth paying for an advert. To do this, they will outline to potential advertisers the readership that they have identified.

Securing finance

The publisher will need cash to set the magazine up. They will have to buy or rent offices and equipment, employ staff and pay for printing. The money may come from a bank loan or from investment by other businesses in the project.

Organizing distribution

For a magazine to make money, people have to be able to buy it. Most magazines are sold in newsagents'. The two biggest sellers of magazines in the UK are W. H. Smith and John Menzies. To be successful, a publisher must persuade newsagents' and other shops to stock their magazine.

CLASS DISCUSSION

In 1996, W. H. Smith announced that it would no longer stock 350 low-circulation magazines that did not make a lot of money. Some were political or religious publications. This led to an outcry from many concerned with the freedom of the press. Why do you think this was?

ON YOUR OWN

Come up with an idea for a new magazine by answering the following questions:
• What would your magazine be about?
• Who would read it?
• Who would advertise in it? (Make a list of firms and products that would be of interest to the readership.)
• What would it be called?
• How often would it come out?
• What would the competition be?
• Could the market support your magazine, or has saturation point been reached?

Producing a magazine

Magazines, like newspapers, are all different. However, like newspapers, their individual production processes are essentially the same. A typical production process includes the following stages:

Planning. The editor and advertising manager discuss how many pages the magazine will have. This is called pagination and is decided on the basis of how many adverts have been sold for a particular edition.

Writing. The content of the magazine is produced. Like newspapers, this comes from two sources, the advertising department and the editorial department. Most magazines carry classified advertisements and the glossy, full-colour format of the majority of magazines offers a good platform for eye-catching display adverts. Editorial in most magazines is made up of a combination of features, photographic spreads, columns, news items and readers' letters. A lot of feature articles are written by freelance journalists, who are writers who work for themselves and sell articles to many magazines. Journalists who are employed just to work on a particular magazine are called staff writers. Photographs are also often taken by freelance photographers.

Designing. Designers and sub-editors lay out the adverts and editorial copy on pages. They work according to what is called a flat plan, which is a map of the magazine that shows every page and what will appear on it.

A flat plan is a map of the magazine, which is used to decide where everything will go.

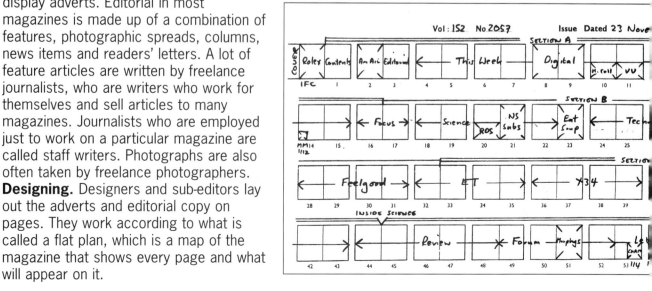

Printing. Most magazines are published in full-colour. To produce them, special printing plates have to be made of each page using a technique called 'colour separation'. Pages are printed using only four colours: black, yellow, red (or magenta) and blue (or cyan). Every photograph has to be 'separated' into these four basic colours by being photographed four times, using filters that allow only one of them through. This produces four pieces of film, which are laid over one another and exposed onto a printing plate. All the colours needed to produce a full-colour photograph are made by mixing different sized dots of these four basic colours. Colour separating and printing are usually done by printing companies, not by the magazines themselves.

CLASS ACTIVITY

Have a go at producing your own magazine.
- *To do this you will have to appoint an editorial team, with an editor, an advertising manager, writers and designers.*
- *Set a production schedule with a deadline for each stage.*

- *You will have to:*
  Find and write stories
  Get and design adverts (these could be made up or produced for local businesses
  Design the magazine and put it together.
You could produce one copy of the magazine for the class or, if you have a budget, print copies to distribute around the school or college.

COMICS

Development

You may think comics are something produced simply to keep young children amused. However, comics are an important part of the modern magazine market and they have a long and eventful history. They are also big business, and not just for children. In fact, in Japan, comic books out-sell most leading newspapers.

Comics are books of stories that are told in the form of cartoons. They started life as comic strips, which were introduced into newspapers at the end of the 19th century to attract more readers. In the early 20th century, comic strips began to be collected from newspapers and published as magazines in their own right. Comics really became popular in the UK in 1937, when D. C. Thompson published *The Dandy*. A year later, *The Beano* was launched and became the UK's best selling comic.

The Beano and *The Dandy*, the UK's first really popular comics.

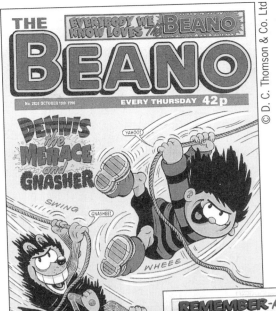

Captain America was one of the first superheroes to appear in the United States.

In America, the 1930s saw the birth of many of the cartoon characters that have become household names throughout the world – Superman, Batman, Wonder Woman, Buck Rogers and Flash Gordon. Most of these characters appeared in comics published by Marvel.

Comics have never been aimed only at children. In the 1960s, the adult comic was born. Some of these comics dealt with serious subjects, using cartoons to make political statements. Others were sexually explicit or depicted extreme violence. It was during the 1960s and 1970s that a recognizable comic culture developed, complete with serious collectors and specialized shops. The introduction of 'manga' comics from Japan into the UK and America in the early 1990s led to an explosion of interest in comics. Manga is a style of Japanese animation.

The introduction of manga comics into the UK led to an explosion of interest in comics.

Cartoon animation was an early development in the history of cinema and there has always been a close relationship between comics and films. Many cartoon characters that first appeared on the cinema screen, such as those of Disney, have their own comic books, as do such television characters as Sooty and Scooby Doo. Other comic characters that were created for the page have gone onto the screen, many of them being played by real actors, for example, Judge Dredd and Tank Girl. Japanese comics inspired 'anime' (the Japanese word for 'animation'), which is the video animation of popular manga publications. Even toys, such as the Care Bears and Barbie, have their own comics.

Genres

In the chapter on language, the concept of genre was examined (see pages 25–27). Genre is the word used to describe types of media text that can be grouped together because of their shared themes and structures. Genres are very important in the field of comics. Comic genres include science fiction and fantasy, war, superhero and educational. Each genre has its own 'rules' that readers expect to be followed, for example, that the superheroes will always win. Genre influences how the cartoons are drawn, the storylines that characters are involved in and the language that they use.

ON YOUR OWN

If you have a specialized comic shop in your town, make a visit and see how many different genres of comic you can spot. What is typical of each genre? Are there genres within genres, for instance, science fiction westerns?

Elements of comics

Comics communicate a narrative to the reader through a combination of images and words. The story is told through a series of scenes in the form of boxes. Each box is like a snapshot, in that it depicts one piece of action. In themselves, the scenes mean little, but arranged in a sequence they build up to form a narrative.

The narratives are usually:
• Simple, dealing with straightforward situations
• Action-based, dealing with adventures
• About a set character or group of characters. New superheroes do not usually appear each week
• Self-contained, with a beginning, middle and end. They tend not to continue over several issues.

The images may be:
• Simple line drawings, as in children's' comics
• Artwork that is very complex and even beautiful, as in many comics aimed at adults
• Photographs, as in photo love stories.

The characters depicted can be:
• Fantastic, for example, monsters
• Superhuman, or human with special powers, for example, Spiderman or Judge Dredd
• Anthropomorphic, in other words, animals with human characteristics, such as the ability to speak
• Realistic, either because the characters are drawn realistically, or because the stories are made up of photographs.

The words in comics are usually kept to a bare minimum. They are secondary to the images. However, they still have important functions to perform:
• Words anchor the image – they tell the reader how to interpret the pictures
• Words express information that is difficult to communicate visually, for instance, thoughts and feelings
• Words give extra information, such as introductions that set the scene for the comic narrative.

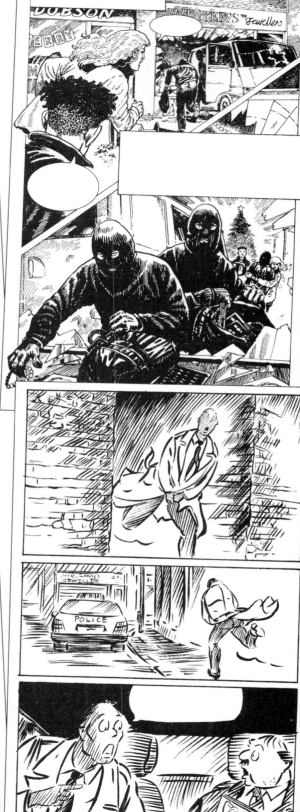

ON YOUR OWN

Look carefully at the four examples of comics on the left. Decide which genre each example belongs to. Choose one of the examples and imagine the narrative that it is part of. Write down the words that might fill the blank areas with captions and speech.

Producing a comic

Comic stories are the result of a production process that involves creative input from two types of people:

Writers, who come up with ideas for stories or scripts. They may invent a character and then write storylines involving that character, or they may be asked to write stories involving existing characters.

Illustrators, who draw the cartoon images. They may come up with the idea for a character, or be asked to draw a character that has been suggested by a writer.

The production process of putting a comic book together is similar to that of a magazine. The comic book is a combination of editorial (in this case the comic strips) and advertising. The editorial and advertising departments work together to produce a flat plan of the comic. The comic strips are designed and placed onto pages along with adverts. The finished pages are then sent to be printed.

Produce your own comic strip, using computers or art materials. Remember, you must first come up with characters and a script. Your comic could be in the form of a cartoon, or you may want to produce a photo story, using members of the group as models.

Comics, sex and violence

Controversy has dogged comics since they were introduced. They have been attacked for corrupting not only children, but also adults. In America in 1954, the Comic Code was passed to limit what was seen as most comics' love of crime and violence. Comic producers were encouraged to create more wholesome comic characters and storylines. Despite this, comics have been criticized for being:

Violent. Adult comics have been condemned for being too graphic in their depiction of violence. Children's comics have been attacked for treating violence as funny and not showing its tragic effects.

Racist. There have been complaints that some comics, especially those dealing with war, portray people of different races in an offensive way, for example, in some British comics with stories about the Second World War, Japanese and German soldiers are shown in this way.

The character of Tank Girl goes against the sexual stereotyping that is sometimes seen in comics.

Sexist. Children's comics have been criticized for reinforcing sexual stereotypes (see pages 32–33). They do this, it is said, by showing girls to be passive and well behaved and boys to be adventurous and violent. Adult comics have been attacked for sexist depictions of women. Critics say that women in science fiction and horror comics are shown semi-naked and are used only as props for the male characters. Some cartoon characters, such as Tank Girl, have gone against this stereotype somewhat by showing a strong female character who is at the centre of the action.

Immoral. Comics have also been condemned for promoting bad behaviour. In children's comics, characters who are well behaved and study hard are shown as swots. In adult comics, violence and crime are often shown as the only way to gain power or enjoy life.

IN GROUPS

- Collect examples of comics and identify characters, storylines and language that could be defined as racist, sexist or immoral.
- Do you think that the examples you have found could influence the views of those reading the comics?

INTERNET PUBLISHING

The growth of the Internet offers a new way to publish newspapers, magazines and comics. Users can input material on their computer and people all over the world can access it by typing in an electronic address. Publications on the Internet are called web sites (after the World Wide Web, which organizes the information) and can range from one 'page' to whole magazines.

Putting information on the Internet is relatively cheap and this has led to millions of different 'publications'. Most national newspapers have web sites. The Internet offers them a chance to expand their readership without printing papers, as one web site can be accessed from all over the world. Publishers can also sell advertising on their electronic pages. Most Internet publications, however, only appear in electronic form on computer screens.

A page from HarperCollins' web site.

IN PAIRS

Look at some media web sites that cover:
Newspapers, for example:
http://www.the-times.co.uk
http://www.scotsman.com/index.html
http://www.barnsley-chronicle.co.uk
Magazines, for example,
http://www.connect.org.uk.merseyworld.stf
http://www.erack.com/empire
http://www.envirolink.org/oneworld/toc/html
Comics, for example,
http://www.cet.com/~rascal/
http://www.usyd.edu.au/~swishart/looney.html
Books, for example,
http://www.harpercollins.co.uk
http://www.penguin.co.uk
Compare the sites that you look at with the traditional, printed media and write a review of two or three of the sites.

NB
The addresses given may change, so be ready to search for new ones.

REVIEW

Looking along a newsagent's shelf takes only a few seconds. However, a survey of the print media shows how much work goes into producing just one of the publications that can be seen in the newsagent's. Next time you are in a newsagent's, take down a magazine and look at how much information it contains. Imagine how long it would take you to read every newspaper, magazine and comic in the display. Our society is awash with printed words and the companies that produce them play a major role in our lives.

10. MUSIC INDUSTRY

Whatever we're doing and wherever we're going, we can now have music there with us. Car stereos, radios as small as coins, portable CD players, Walkmans and other technology allow us to listen to our favourite tunes anywhere. Billions of CDs, tapes and records are sold worldwide and the lives of pop stars make headline news. The music industry has ensured that the human race is truly wired for sound.

However, all this is a relatively recent development. Until the early years of the 20th century, there was no such thing as a music 'industry'. This is because before the invention of sound recording there was no way of selling music to a mass market. The only way to hear music was to attend a performance or play it yourself. In order for music to become an industry, a way had to be found of turning it into a product that could be sold. The birth of recording technology was the spur for the development of a business now worth around £27 billion.

From phonograph to DAT

The music industry owes its beginnings to Thomas Edison, who made the first recording of a human voice in 1877. A year later, he patented the first phonograph for playing back recordings, using cylinders made of tin foil. Tin foil cylinders were soon replaced by wax ones, but there was still no way to mass-produce them. It was Emile Berliner who really set the turntables spinning by patenting the gramophone in 1888. The gramophone used flat discs to produce sounds and it was easy to make copies of them. This opened the way for the mass marketing of sound recordings, and the 1890s saw the first sales of commercial recordings.

Sound reproduction technology took a big step forward in 1896 when Johnson Eldridge fitted a motor to the gramophone, doing away with the need to wind it up with a handle. Johnson set up the Victor Talking Machine Company and in

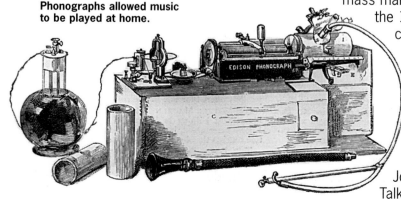

Phonographs allowed music to be played at home.

1906 it produced the first gramophone with an internal horn, or amplifier, known as the Victrola. Victor went on to become RCA Victor, one of the world's largest record companies.

The birth of KDKA, the first American commercial radio station, in 1919 was a mixed blessing for the early recording industry. Record sales fell initially as people could listen to music on the radio for free. However, record companies soon realized that radio was the perfect advertising vehicle for their products. The invention of the jukebox in the 1930s led to a new demand for records. The 1930s also saw the publication of the first 'hit parade', or chart listing the most popular recordings.

Getting it taped

The next leap forward for the music industry was the development of sound recording using magnetic tape. The German firms BASF and AEG first demonstrated the use of tape recording with their Magnetophone in 1936. The technique was developed in America by 3M, and Ampex produced recorders that could match the quality of recording onto wax.

The 1950s saw the introduction of stereo recording. This involved recording two separate channels of sound onto one tape. It added 'depth' to musical performances on record and led to a demand for improved record players.

Until the 1960s, buying music on tape was not popular, as the tape had to be fed onto a recorder by hand. In 1964 Philips launched the first tapes encased in plastic housing, which could be simply slipped into tape machines. Throughout the 1960s, a battle raged between companies that produced eight-track and four-track tapes and those that made cassettes. Cassettes won and the introduction of Dolby Noise Reduction, which removed the hiss from tapes, increased their popularity. Cassettes were more portable than records, and sales took off, especially when players began to be fitted in cars. The portable tape player, or Walkman, first marketed by Sony in 1979, created an even bigger demand for tapes.

CD and beyond

The search for better sound quality led the music industry to look at the possibilities offered by computer technology. In 1982 the compact disc or CD was launched by Sony and Philips. In the manufacturing process, recordings by musicians are changed into digital information that can be read by a computer. The quality of sound reproduction that this allowed was much better than that offered by cassettes at the time. As the price of CD players fell, they began to dominate the recorded music market. As well as new recordings, companies began to release recordings they had made in the past, known as their back-catalogues, on CD. This was seen as a brilliant marketing move, as it led many people to replace recordings they owned on vinyl with ones on CD: in other words, they bought the same recording twice.

The jukebox was invented in the 1930s. Since then, technology has developed rapidly.

A new chapter in the story of tapes began in 1987 when Sony introduced the helical scan recording technique, which had been developed for video into sound recording. The result was the digital audio tape, or DAT. Before this development, different sounds were recorded onto different tracks that ran parallel to each other on the tape. The helical scan system records sound onto tracks that cross each other diagonally, which provides better reproduction. The sound quality offered by DAT soon led to it being widely used in recording studios, although the price stopped large sales to the general public. Small digital compact cassettes with high-quality sound reproduction were launched in the 1990s.

In 1992 Sony introduced the MiniDisc, a compact disc that can be used to record in the same way as a blank cassette tape. The division between musician and listener began to break down with the introduction of the CDi format. These are music albums that, when used on a computer with a media player, allow listeners to create their own mixes of tracks.

IN PAIRS

List all the forms of musical reproduction hardware that you can. Think not only of the types of hardware, but also where they are used. Early gramophones were targeted for home use, but the jukebox opened up a new market. Where are music reproduction systems an accepted if not an essential part of the atmosphere?

Today there is a battle of the formats raging on the high street, with manufacturers trying to ensure that their type of music reproduction technique, be it disc or tape, wins out. Internet music consists of recordings that are only available via computer. David Bowie has released recordings solely on the Internet.

Music video

Video changed the face of the music industry. Seen initially as a way to advertise records, music videos have become an industry in themselves. Today it is inconceivable for a major, or even a new, band to release a recording without a video to accompany it. The complexity of videos has also increased. The first videos usually showed a band performing on stage or in a carefully chosen scene. However, their success led to increased budgets and pop music mini-epics made by cinema directors.

A major factor in the growth of the pop video was their popularity with television producers. Videos provided TV with ready-made footage that they could simply broadcast for free. They fitted easily into the format of the BBC's *Top of the Pops*, and provided the material for ITV's *Chart Show,* which showed nothing but videos.

MTV broadcasts music programmes 24 hours a day.

It was the birth of the satellite channel MTV, or Music Television, that provided the biggest platform for music videos. Launched in 1981 and broadcast all over the world, much of MTV's output is made up of pop videos, punctuated with music news bulletins. Its sister channel VH-1 relies on videos, but its focus is older 'adult' listeners. CMT is a satellite channel devoted completely to country music.

The music industry today

To begin with, recording companies were simply recording companies. Their main product was the reproduction hardware – they produced records so that people who bought their gramophones would have something to play on them. They had no real interest in music as a money-maker in itself.

Recording companies became aware, however, that they could only make so much money from selling record players. Record players have always been an expensive purchase and once people have bought one they tend to keep it for a while before replacing it. Realizing that the real money lay in the software – the records – led the recording companies to invest money in producing their own recordings by popular musicians. It was this move into the field of music production that led to the music business as we know it today. Big industrial companies now own everything from the factories that make the CD and tape players to the studios where musicians record – and even the musicians themselves. The model for this type of music multinational, RCA Victor, was created in 1929 when RCA (Record Company of America), together with General Motors, took over the Victor Talking Machine Company in a bid to exploit the new phenomenon of car radios.

The music industry has always been dominated by a small number of large companies. This happened because the recording companies bought up independent record labels in the 1930s. (They were known as labels because of the distinctive stickers bearing the company's name that were attatched to every record.) Today the industry is controlled by six major companies:
- **Philips**, which owns the Polygram, A&M Mercury and Island record labels
- **Sony**, which owns Columbia Records, S2, Epic and Higher Ground
- **Matsushita**, which owns MCA Records and Geffen
- **EMI**, which owns Capitol and Virgin
- **Time Warner**, which owns Warner Brothers and subsidiaries
- **Bertelsmann**, which owns RCA Records.

IN GROUPS

Major record companies often own a number of different record labels, known as divisions. For example, rap band Cypress Hill releases records on the Columbia label, which is owned by Sony. This gives the appearance that there are more record companies than actually exist.

Ask each member of the group to bring in a number of CDs or tapes. Look at the labels and the packaging and make a diagram showing which labels belong to which companies.

As an example of the sums of money involved in these companies, when it was split from its sister company Thorn in 1996, EMI was believed to be worth around £5.8 billion.

Singers and styles

Singing stars

Just as stars, rather than stories, sell films, so singers, rather than songs, sell records. This is something record companies learnt as they developed; their top priority is to find voices and, more importantly, faces that shift records.

The first and biggest recording star was Bing Crosby. He made his first record in 1926 when the music industry was in its infancy. In 1931 he was signed to CBS Records and became the first nationally famous recorded 'star'. During his career, Crosby recorded 1,600 hit songs, including 'White Christmas', which sold 30 million copies, making it the world's biggest selling record of all time.

The start of what is called the youth market for records is credited to Elvis Presley. Presley became famous in 1956 for singing a new form of music called rock 'n' roll. Rock 'n' roll was a mixture of blues music and country and western swing. Although the music itself was not created by record companies, they were not slow to exploit it. Known as 'The King', Presley sold 41 million albums for RCA during his career.

The biggest selling album of all time is Michael Jackson's 'Thriller', which has sold 40 million copies. Jackson is signed to Sony. Madonna is one of the biggest selling female stars in recording history. Her single 'Vogue' is one of the best selling of all time and her 'Immaculate Collection' album was only the second greatest hits album to achieve a position in the top ten of the charts. Madonna is signed to Sire Records, a subsidiary of Warner Brothers. The most successful group ever were The Beatles, who became closely identified with their record label, Apple.

Bing Crosby was the first major recording star.

Madonna is one of the biggest selling female recording artists of all time.

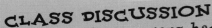

CLASS DISCUSSION

■ What qualities do pop stars have?
■ Does their fame rest on the quality of their voice, their song-writing talent, or their looks?
■ Are stars always the best singers?
■ If not, why don't good singers always become stars?

Musical styles

The history of popular music has seen the rise and fall of many musical styles. These are types of music that share certain characteristics, such as beat, speed and lyrical style. They have usually been accompanied by fashions in clothing and behaviour. They began with rock 'n' roll, which in Britain was the music associated with the Teddy Boys, who wore Edwardian-style drape suits and slicked their hair back with grease. Since then there have been Mods, Hippies, Punks and many others.

Record companies are always on the lookout for new musical styles in order to exploit them. Many people make a distinction between groups that originate a style and those who copy them. They believe the originators are 'authentic' in their musical ideals, while those that copy them are merely commercially driven.

In marketing terms, musical styles are a form of audience fragmentation (see the chapter on audience, pages 63–64). They can be used to identify types of music consumer. For example, there are general music consumers, who buy records of tunes they like. Then there are specific music buyers, who only purchase a particular type of music by certain types of bands. Record companies judge their performers in terms of their appeal to these different groups. They are particularly keen on 'cross-over' artists, who appeal to music consumers of all types. For example, Take That began life as a group targeted at young girls or teenyboppers. However, their music had an appeal for more mature listeners as well and this contributed to their huge record sales.

On your own

* How many different musical styles can you name?
* What makes them different from each other?

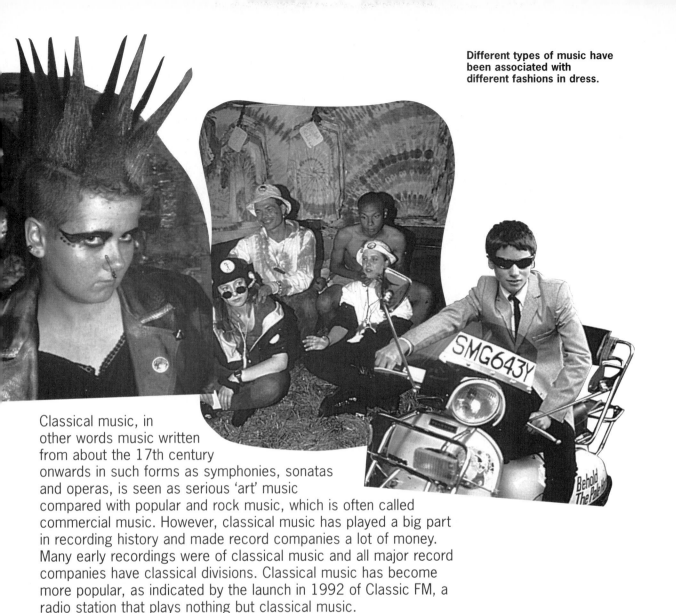

Different types of music have been associated with different fashions in dress.

Classical music, in other words music written from about the 17th century onwards in such forms as symphonies, sonatas and operas, is seen as serious 'art' music compared with popular and rock music, which is often called commercial music. However, classical music has played a big part in recording history and made record companies a lot of money. Many early recordings were of classical music and all major record companies have classical divisions. Classical music has become more popular, as indicated by the launch in 1992 of Classic FM, a radio station that plays nothing but classical music.

Getting signed

To be successful financially in the music business, it is essential for a musician or band to sign a recording contract with a major record company. Likewise, record companies are always on the lookout for new performers to sign up.

In order to attract the attention of major record companies, bands and solo artists do any number of the following:

Perform in public. Bands invite representatives of record companies to attend what are often called 'showcase' concerts or 'gigs'. In Britain, bands from the regions will often set up a gig in London to make it easier for record companies to see them.

Make a demo. This involves making a demonstration recording of their music and sending it to a record company. It is usually in the form of a tape.

Release their own record. Many bands pay to have a record released on their own label to promote themselves both to the public and to record companies.

Employ a manager or an agent. He or she promotes the band to record companies. The more experienced the manager or agent is in the music industry, the better. Some managers have become nearly as famous as the artists they represent, such as Colonel Tom Parker, who managed Elvis Presley.

Sign a publishing deal. Before the birth of recorded music, music publishers published sheet music. Songwriters and musicians give their work to a publisher who, if they like it, will agree to look after it for a fee. This means promoting the music and making sure the artist receives money whenever it is played. All musicians are supposed to receive a fee every time one of their pieces is sold on record, played live at a concert or broadcast on the radio or television. They also receive money if another artist records one of their songs. These fees are called royalties. Publishing companies are responsible for collecting royalties and subtract their fee from them before passing them on to the musician. Signing a publishing deal can help musicians, as it is in the interests of publishing companies for their artists to sign recording deals. Publishing companies actively represent artists to major record companies.

Attract attention. Unsigned bands often try everything to achieve a high profile. They will play as many concerts as possible in as many different places, produce publicity material such as posters and flyers, and badger journalists to write about them. The music press plays an important role in 'breaking' new bands by featuring them in their publications, which are read by record company representatives.

ON YOUR OWN

■ Imagine you are the manager of a band in your home town. Plan a publicity campaign that will attract attention to them. You will have to invent a band and decide on a name and style. Then think of all the ways you could promote them in your town.

Record companies do not simply sit back and wait for musicians to come to them. They go out and look for new performers and

Maker Breakers

Edited by **DAVID BENNUN**

The cream of the crop, the wheat from the chaff, the first bite of the cherry

PICK OF THE WEEK

THE ULTIMATE GAMBLE

Til Death do us part

DEATH IN VEGAS – beyond chemical beats and into the world of The King's death cult

BOMB–DIDDLY–BOMB

THE SCUD MOUNTAIN BOYS bring to mind Lou Barlow and Gram Parsons, which is not what we expected either

ALL the hopeless romantics out there will recognise the scenario immediately. You've been dumped by your dream lover, who you can't get out of your mind, so you get stoned and call them. You're fixated, you say, and friendless thanks to the intensity of your relationship, but you reckon it would be fine if you could just have sex one last time. Have a "Grudge F***", in other words.

"We don't play any happy songs," smiles Steven from American country kings The Scud Mountain Boys. "They're all just the death of it. And it's like a broken feel to the songs when you play real tiny, real slow and really quietly and

the many exhilaratingly bleak moments on SMB's new album, "Massachusetts". Singer Joe comes across like a melancholic Lou Barlow, while the band recall prime Gram Parsons.

"We used to say it wasn't a successful show unless someone hanged themselves in the bathroom," grins Steven. "We used to psych ourselves up to play a real downer of a show, just because it's fun. If I hear a sad old country song where someone paints a bleak portrait of being alive, it really lifts me up. I love that."

Me, too.
IAN WATSON

IN the big, bad world of the big, bad chemical beat only a few have managed to stand tall. The Chemical Brothers, of course, Lionrock when they're on form, and, more recently, Las Vegas' Crystal Method. Now add to that list Death In Vegas, the brain-addling brainchild of Heavenly Socialites Richard Fearless and Steve Hellier.

However, with their latest offering, "Rocco", the duo have stretched far beyond electro-imbued rock'n'roll territory – imagine Rocket From The Crypt jamming over "Soul Sonic Force" or Arthur Baker producing The Clash. Eclectro, perhaps?

"Definitely not," retorts Fearless, between frequent yawns. "Most of what is being called eclectic isn't actually eclectic – it's simply a representation of people's record collections. I think most people can see the way music is connected; whether it's rock, indie, hip hop or techno. I'm into everything from Dr John to electro stuff, so the line that binds things is obvious to me."

Indeed, Fearless has a thirst for music which verges on the obsessional. As such, he's that rare breed of musician who cares more for the actual music than the scene it belongs to.

a track before I go into the studio. 'Opium Shuffle' was going to be a house track, and look how that turned out."

"Opium Shuffle", for the uninitiated, was a downtempo classic which came out under the somewhat dubious moniker of Dead Elvis.

Dead Elvis? Death In Vegas? Is there a pattern emerging here? Or maybe it's an obsession. After all, the sleeve for "Rocco" is graced by a young Elvis in devil's horns and wings.

"I suppose I am obsessional. I collect junk like plastic toys and snow storms and, of course, records. If I want a certain track, I'll search everywhere until I get it."

And Elvis Presley?

"I'm not so much into Elvis as the cultural obsession which surrounds him," explains Fearless. "I actually love the way people still use him as a reference point to their lives. The name Dead Elvis came from a book by Greil Marcus and Death In Vegas was taken from a short film by a friend of mine which dealt with the last five minutes of Elvis' life. But you can also view Elvis' Vegas period as his creative death."

"I'm sure Elvis would be turning in his grave. If I hadn't just seen him in

---

try to sign them up before anyone else does. This is done by the company's A&R department. A&R stands for artists and repertoire and the A&R section is responsible for discovering new acts and looking after the musicians once they are signed to the label. Members of the A&R department attend concerts and listen to demos in order to spot up-and-coming talent.

If a record company is interested enough in a band, it will offer them a recording contract. The individual terms of the contract will differ from band to band, but essentially they give the company the right to release all the band's recordings. This may be for ever, but is usually for a set number of recordings, also called releases. So a band may be offered a 'three-album deal', in which they would record three albums for the company and a set number of singles. The contract will also say how much money the band will receive from the sales of their recordings.

The music press can help new bands by featuring them in their publications.

On signing a contract, a band usually receives what is called an advance. This is a sum of money given to a band in advance of any record sales and is taken out of the band's royalties once they start to sell records. Advances range in size from thousands of pounds in the case of unknown bands, to millions in the case of established stars changing labels.

Making a recording

Whether making a demo to promote themselves or producing their fortieth album, all musicians need to record their music before it can be sold. This means going into a recording studio, though this may be simply a computer and a keyboard.

A traditional recording studio is made up of two rooms. One, in which the musicians perform, is soundproofed so no other noise can be heard from outside. The other is the control room, which contains the recording equipment. The recording process is supervised by a sound engineer, a technician who ensures that the best possible recording is made. Some sound engineers grow famous for the quality and style of the recordings they supervise and become producers who are much sought-after by bands. A producer is someone brought in to oversee a recording and give it a particular 'feel'. The producer's role often merges with that of the sound engineer, as a producer has to know how a studio works in order to get the sound he or she wants.

Making a recording is a complex process.

The recording process usually involves the following steps:
Mic-up. Every instrument and singer must have their own microphone so that they can be recorded.

Setting the levels. The level at which each microphone records has to be set by the sound engineer.

Laying down the tracks. Recording studios are classified in terms of how many 'tracks' they can record onto one tape and can be four, eight, twenty-four, thirty-two track or even more. The more tracks a studio has, the more instruments or vocal tracks can be recorded. For a band consisting of drums, bass guitar, lead guitar and vocals, the tracks would normally be recorded in the following order:

• Drums and bass: this track forms the base for the rest of the instruments and vocals
• Guitars: usually laid down while listening to the drum and bass track
• Vocals: usually recorded last. Most recording sessions begin in the morning, when a singer's voice is not at it best. So recording the vocal track is left until later in the day, when the vocal cords have warmed up.

Today a lot of music is produced using electronic instruments and computers. The sounds generated are stored in the computer's memory, which does away with the need for a traditional two-room studio. It also means that one person can carry out all the functions, from playing to mixing. Recording using computers is called digital recording.

Digital recording does not require a traditional recording studio.

Mixing. Once all the instruments and vocal tracks have been recorded they are mixed to produce the version of the track that will be released. This involves combining the sounds using a recording desk. It is at this stage that 'effects' that alter the sound of instruments, such as echo and distortion, are added.
It is during mixing that the producer or sound engineer has a major creative input. They are skilled at getting a certain sound and 'feel' to a recording and mix every track to ensure it is right. A development of the 1980s was the phenomenon of remixing. This involved the separate tracks of a recording being combined in a

Sound engineers and producers mix tracks recorded in the studio.

different way to produce a different sound. Many producers are famous for this and bands approach them to do remixes of their recordings.

A technique known as sampling, in which sounds from existing recordings are used to make new ones, was also developed in the 1980s. Combined with computer-generated sounds, sampling removed the need to be able to play a musical instrument.

Formatting. Once the final mix has been decided, it is sent off to be turned into a format, such as cassettes and compact discs, that can be sold to consumers.

The work of a sound engineer

Sound engineers are the invisible people who play a major role in shaping the music that tops the charts. They supervise recordings, making sure that everything runs smoothly. Pete Darnborough, who trains sound engineers, has years of experience in helping recording artists achieve the sound they want.

❛ The sound engineer's job is to manipulate all the equipment in a studio to get the best representation of a band possible. To do this, they have to know the studio inside-out. They have to know how the mixing desk works, the best way to set up a microphone, how to balance sound levels and many other things.

❛ For example, every piece of a drum kit has a separate microphone. The sound engineer has to make sure that every mic is working and recording at the right level. They also have to ensure that the sounds don't "leak" into one another by using devices called sound gates and compressors.

> ❝ However, it is not just machinery. A recording studio is a very unnatural environment – it is two enclosed rooms with no natural light and no fresh air. If you have five or six people in a studio for a long time under pressure to produce a good recording, things can get a bit intense. Arguments can break out between members of a band, and it is the engineer's job to keep the peace and make sure the recording gets made. You have to be very diplomatic to be a sound engineer.
>
> ❝ Most important, however, is the sound engineer's feel for music. You may be highly skilled in using equipment, but if you don't care about music you will never be able to help a musician record to the best of their ability. ❞

Making money

The purpose of most recordings is to make money for those people and institutions involved in their production and sale. These include:
- The record company
- The band or performer
- Compact disc and cassette manufacturers
- Record shops.

To make money, the price of a CD or cassette has to be higher than it cost to produce. The difference between what a CD costs to produce, and what it costs to buy, is the profit margin. The profit margin is split between all those involved in the production and marketing process. The biggest percentage goes to the record company. Bands and record companies also make money from broadcasts and performances of their material. For example, in 1996 every time a recording was played on the radio, the performer received £40. When a band's recording was played on television they received £125, and £100 if their video was played on the music satellite channel MTV.

The charts
The measure of success in the music industry are the charts that show which recordings sell the most copies each week. The first music charts were published by *Billboard* magazine in America in the 1890s. They consisted of lists of the most popular sheet music. However, the charts as we recognize them today began when *Billboard* started to publish its Best Sellers in Stores listing, based on information from record shops throughout America. In 1958 the magazine launched its Hot 100 chart, which remains the main chart, in the US.

In Britain it was the *New Musical Express*'s Hit Parade, published for the first time in 1952, that pioneered music charts. It listed the 12 top selling records in the country. Today the official UK charts are compiled by the Chart Information Network (CIN). The company CIN Ltd is jointly owned by Miller Freeman plc – a UK information company that publishes *Music Week* magazine – and the British Phonographic Industry (BPI), the trade body for UK record companies. CIN makes the charts available to the music business and to broadcasters and publishers worldwide.

CIN employs Millward Brown International, a market research company, to compile the charts on its behalf from sales information supplied by members of the British Association of Record Dealers and other music retailers. Around 3,000 shops in the UK have equipment that allows them to contribute sales information to the charts. When a record or video is bought, the retailer runs a scanner over the barcode on the product. This information is stored in a file, which grows during the course of the day. After the shops close every night, the charts computers automatically telephone each shop and transfer the barcode files into a central processor. Once retrieved, the barcode information is run through a central product file. This contains details of every audio or video product sold through the panel stores. The barcodes are matched up to the product details from this file. Then the information is scanned by a security programme, which isolates any shop whose sales information does not conform to its usual pattern. The data is multiplied up to represent the full market of the 4,000 stores whose sales information is eligible for the charts. Finally, the sales figures are ranked in descending order and the charts are produced. This procedure is carried out daily and the sales totals grow through the week.

On Sunday morning, the charts are generated from sales made during the previous Sunday to Saturday. After checking, the official UK singles and albums charts are sent to the BBC and *Music Week* at 12.30 pm – less than 18 hours after the last sale was made. The BBC makes the first broadcast of the charts on Sunday at 4.00 pm. *Music Week* prints it to appear the following day.

CREATING A CLASS TOP TEN

Get a copy of the top ten singles from a newspaper or by listening to the radio or watching TV. List the titles of the singles on a form and give one to each member of the group. Each person can make three 'purchases' from the top ten list. Once they have made their choices collect in the forms and add up the 'sales'.

● Is your chart different from the official one?

● What does it tell you about the musical tastes of your classmates?

Selling performers

Marketing a performer and their recordings is the major function of record companies. Their aim is to make as much money as possible out of the acts they sign to their labels.

Crucial to the marketing of a performer is their image. This is the way they present themselves to, and the way they are seen by, their audience. It includes the style of their music, the way they dress and the things they do and say. Record companies recognize that image is especially important for performers with a mostly young audience. One image that is particularly attractive to young audiences is that of rebellion against society and the older generation. Throughout the history of pop and rock music, bad behaviour by bands has been a way of creating publicity and selling records. From the earliest days of rock 'n' roll, wearing leather, taking drugs and smashing up hotel rooms has always been good for business. Although some performers have been marketed with the opposite image, that of being safe and wholesome, these performers have always seemed to be more popular with parents than with young people.

Another technique used to market performers has been to set them in competition with rival bands and singers. This leads to fans dedicating themselves to one performer in opposition to another.

IN PAIRS
How many performers can you think of who have been marketed in competition to one another?

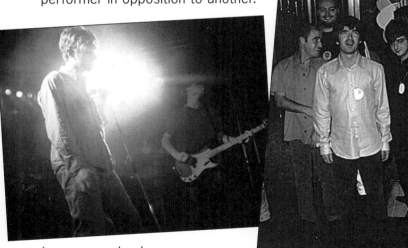

During the 1990s much publicity was given to the 'battle' for fans between Oasis and Blur.

Image can also harm a performer's success. Many acts are criticized by fans for changing their image, or 'selling out', when they sign to a major record company. A record company may insist that performers tone down or emphasize a particular element of their image in order to attract a wider audience for their music. Also, musical styles and fashion in clothes change quickly and a band that is associated with a sound or a 'look' that has gone out of fashion can find their record sales falling.

Record companies have even gone as far as to manufacture bands to cash in on a musical trend. Often these performers meet with little success, as they are seen to be 'fake'. However, in the 1960s The Monkees, an all-male band put together to milk the trend started by The Beatles, had a successful recording career and made their own TV show.

Performers and their management have also manipulated image to good effect to make successful recordings. Malcolm McClaren generated millions of pounds out of his skilful management of the Sex Pistols, who were at the head of the punk explosion of the 1970s. In the 1980s the KLF foundation wrote a book on how to make a hit record and proceeded to do so with 'Doctor in the Tardis', which went to number one in the charts.

Promotion

In order for performers and record companies to be successful they have to make as many people aware of their recordings as possible. They do this using a well-established system of promotional techniques.

Radio Having your recordings broadcast on radio is an excellent way of promoting your recording. Radio broadcasters and record companies have a close relationship, as they depend upon each other. Record companies want people to hear their recordings and radio needs something to play. A major achievement for a record company is to have its performers 'playlisted' by a big radio station such as Radio 1. A playlist is a list of records to which a radio station decides to give a lot of air-time by playing them a set number of times during a day's programming. Records that are playlisted tend to be successful simply because large numbers of people hear them. In the 1950s in America there was controversy when it was revealed that some record companies were paying radio stations to playlist their records.

DJs Disc jockeys, the people who host radio programmes, have a

DJs play an important part
in promoting records.

lot of power to promote recordings. If a disc jockey is respected for their knowledge of a particular field of music, such as rock or reggae, their approval and promotion of a record on their show can help it to sell a lot of copies. The explosion of club culture in Britain has led to the DJs who work in them becoming stars in their own right. They 'perform' at different clubs for big fees and they can promote records by playing them as part of their show. Therefore record companies, especially those that produce dance music, are keen to have their recordings backed by club DJs.

Music press The music press also plays an important part in promoting performers. There are many publications for those interested in music, each serving a particular type of consumer.

Melody Maker and *New Musical Express*, each published weekly, keep readers up to date with what is going on in the music world. They are aimed largely at young people aged between 16 and 30 and concentrate on 'alternative' bands. These are bands that are seen to be serious about music and non-commercial in their outlook. This does not prevent them from selling large numbers of records.

Smash Hits is aimed at a younger teenage readership, with features on the latest chart 'sensation' and glossy colour posters.

Q magazine is a 'heavy' music magazine for an older audience. It concentrates on famous performers and covers not only the latest releases, but also back-catalogues of older recordings.

Mojo specifically targets those interested in recording artists of the past and in re-releases of their material.

Record Collector prints how much records and CDs are worth. *Classic CD* caters for those interested in high-quality recordings of classical music.

A new development is music magazines published on CDs. These can be played on multi-media computers and contain music and video clips in their features. There are many other specialized music magazines and newspapers. Newspapers and general consumer magazines also have music sections, and record companies supply them with free copies of recordings so they can review them for their readers.

Advertising As with any other consumer product, advertising plays a crucial role in music promotion. Record companies place adverts in the press, magazines and on TV. Posters are one of the most common methods of advertising. A controversial practice – because it is often illegal – is that of fly-posting. This involves sticking posters advertising record releases on walls, fences and buildings. Sponsorship is another way of bringing in money and advertising at the same time. An example of this is Michael Jackson's contract to appear in adverts for Coca Cola.

Merchandise Merchandise is products that carry the name of a performer, for instance, T-shirts and jackets. These are a clever marketing device. Firstly, they make money for the record company and the performer. Secondly, they also advertise the performer, as other people see the product and may ask after their recordings as a result.

ON YOUR OWN

- How many different types of music merchandise have you seen?
- Can you think of a new form of merchandise for a band?

Fan clubs are a useful way of selling merchandise, as are stalls at concerts. Many bands also have mailing lists of addresses built up through pre-paid postcards included in CDs and tapes, to which they send information on new releases.

Concerts In its early days, sound recording was seen as a way of capturing live performances by musicians so those who could not attend could hear them. However, the playback quality of music produced in studios soon surpassed that of music recorded 'live'. Performers were then faced with the dilemma of trying to produce studio-quality music on stage. Today, concerts are seen largely as a way to promote recorded music. A band will tour 'on the back of' an album. That is, they make a record and use a tour to sell it. Live albums sell significantly less than studio-recorded ones.

In the shops

How people buy their products is of great concern to record companies. Early gramophone records were sold in music shops, along with instruments and sheet music. Before long, however, stores began to open that sold only recorded music. Department stores also began to incorporate record sections in their layouts. As well as general record shops, specialist shops sprang up selling recordings of particular types of music, such as jazz or classical.

Record companies, however, needed to ensure that there were enough outlets for their products and decided not to rely solely on independent shops. They began to buy up existing chains or opened their own. In doing this, the multinational music companies took control of everything from recording performers to producing the records and selling them. Today, EMI owns the HMV chain of shops, while Virgin has its own successful retail outlets.

In the 1990s, music megastores were opened. Pioneered by the Virgin group, these shops brought the selling of recorded music full circle. CDs, tapes and vinyl records are only a part of the range of products sold in these shops, which also stock videos, computer games, clothing, books and sheet music. This move from record shops to what Virgin calls 'home entertainment stores' has been followed by other music retailers.

Review The main aim of the recording industry is not to make music but to make money. Music is simply the product that the industry sells. To be successful, a record company has to present the consumer with a popular product, such as a band, in an attractive package, such as an album, recorded on an accessible format, such as CD or tape. The music you play on your CD may have been written by the performer in their bedroom, but in between it has gone through a complex industrial and marketing process as part of a multi-million pound business.

11. ADIO

HISTORY

Guglielmo Marconi sent the first wireless telegraphic message across the Channel in 1899. Two years later, he repeated the feat, but this time the message was sent across the Atlantic, from Cornwall to Newfoundland. On Christmas Eve 1906, in the United States of America, Reginald Aubrey Fessenden broadcast the first radio programme, which featured music, poetry and a talk.

It was not until 1919 that radio was successfully transmitted in the UK. In that year, a transmitter in Chelmsford, Essex, began broadcasting programmes that contained both speech and music on a daily basis. Three years later, as interest in radio grew, the BBC was born. At first it was organized around the interests of the manufacturers and broadcasters, but soon the Government stepped in and set up the BBC as a public corporation with its own board of governors and made it accountable to Parliament. Finance was generated through the licence fee. In this way, the concept of public service broadcasting was born.

Every week, nine out of ten people listen to the radio for around 21 hours. They listen to it as soon as they wake up in the morning, on their way to work, in the car or on the bus or train. They tune in while they are working, on their way home at night, while they eat their tea or do their homework. Some even fall asleep listening to the radio last thing at night.

Radio is a medium that audiences can consume while they are doing other things. Unlike television or newspapers, it doesn't

demand your whole attention; radio is an ideal medium to use while you are busy with your everyday life. Because of this, radio has some interesting functions. For many people, it provides an important source of companionship and acts as a friend who chats to them and keeps them company. It also helps people to concentrate on the tasks they have to do by shutting out the outside world. When you see someone wearing headphones listening to the radio, it is as though they are saying to other people, 'Don't try to talk to me. I can't hear you.'

Radio or some kind of background music is often played in shops and factories. It makes people feel comfortable and soothes them while they work or shop. Radio is like wallpaper, in that it is in the background, making people feel at ease with their surroundings.

ON YOUR OWN

- *Make a list of the radios that you can use.*
- *Draw up a table that shows:*
  Where they are
  What kind of radios they are
  Who uses them most.
- *If you travel in a car, who decides what station you are tuned to?*
- *If you travel abroad in a car, do you still listen to the radio?*
- *Write a short report on your family's listening habits.*

Although radio is a popular medium with audiences, especially the younger age groups, surprisingly little attention has been paid to it in Media Studies. Perhaps because it seems less glamorous then television, film and the print media, far fewer books have been written about the medium of radio.

WAVE BANDS

Most radios have both FM (Frequency Modulation) and AM (Amplitude Modulation) wavebands for receiving programmes. In general, people prefer to listen on the FM band whenever possible, because it offers better quality sound and is also capable of stereo and surround-sound reproduction. (Surround-sound amplifies sound through four or five speakers to create the effect that the sound is all around the listener. For example, an aircraft can be made to sound as though it has flown over the listener's shoulder. This technology also allows the listener to reproduce the acoustics characteristic of specific venues, for example a concert hall.)

A good way of starting to investigate the medium is to listen to it. Begin by tuning to the FM band of your radio. The frequency is measured in megahertz (a unit that measures wavelengths in cycles per second). Move slowly from the bottom of the waveband (usually 87.5 MHz) to the top (108 MHz). You may do this by turning a dial and watching a pointer, or you may have a digital tuner, where you press a button and the display changes. As you move from the bottom of the frequency range to the top, listen carefully to each station for a short time. Depending on where you live, the number of stations that you hear will vary, as will the quality of the sound. If the signal (the electronically coded message sent out from the transmitter) is not strong, the reception is often in mono. (Mono sound is amplified through a single channel and is usually heard through just one speaker. Stereo reproduction, on the other hand, splits sound into two channels and amplifies it through two speakers.)

Some digital tuners have RDS (Radio Data System), which allows them to identify the station that is playing by showing its name on the display. Analogue tuners use a pointer on a scale to show the frequency.

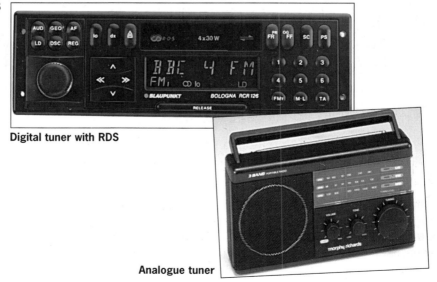

Digital tuner with RDS

Analogue tuner

Write a brief description of each station that you hear, together with its frequency. Your description should cover such information as:

■ Was the station playing music? If so, what sort of music was it?

■ Was anyone speaking on the station? What were they talking about? What did their voice sound like – did it have a regional accent, or use slang?

■ What was the presentation of the station like? Was it lively and informal, or was the tone more serious?

■ Did you like the station and want to listen to more?

■ What sort of audience do you think the station is addressing?

Of course, you need to remember that the brief sample of the stations' output that you have heard may not be typical. It is a good idea to listen again at a different time of day to see if the style and content have changed.

Each radio station aims to establish its own identity so that the audience will recognize it and want to make it the station that they tune to automatically. Different stations have different approaches to broadcasting, in terms of their style of presentation and the content of the programmes.

GROUP DISCUSSION

One way in which stations establish their identity is by using jingles. These are short pieces of music, which a presenter plays in order to let listeners know they are tuned into a particular station. What other methods are used to establish a station's identity? You might want to think about:

• How often the presenter mentions the station's name and frequency
• Slogans
• How the station is identified with the local area
• Style of presentation
• Logos
• Sponsorship of events.

Types of radio station

Radio stations can be placed in broad categories in terms of both their identity and the audience they attract.

Funding

The first division is between commercial radio and what is known as public service broadcasting (PSB).

Commercial radio stations are financed by money from advertisers. They sell advertising time between and during programmes, just like commercial TV stations.

Public service broadcasting refers to radio stations operated by the BBC, including the national stations Radios 1, 2, 3, 4 and 5 Live, as well as many local radio stations, such as BBC Radio Cleveland and BBC Radio Nottingham. Just like the BBC television channels, these stations are financed with revenue from the BBC licence fee, although you don't need a licence for a radio now.

| RADIO LICENCES |

At the outbreak of war in 1939, nine million households had a radio licence. The radio licence was abolished in 1971.

Transmission area

Radio stations can also be categorized according to their transmission area, which is the part of the country to which they broadcast.

National radio stations broadcast right across the country, although some regions may listen to them on slightly different frequencies.

Regional radio stations transmit over areas that already have local services. Scot FM, for example, broadcasts to central Scotland, which also has a number of local radio stations.

Local radio stations broadcast to smaller areas. Their transmission areas are often focused on a large city or county. For example, BBC Radio Sheffield and Hallam FM both cover the city of Sheffield and the surrounding area, including such towns as Doncaster and Rotherham. In addition, in some areas there are community radio stations that cover much smaller areas.

Material

Radio stations can also be categorized according to the type of material that they broadcast.

Music-based stations. Many stations are in essence music stations. Their main output is music, with some news and related programmes. People listen to these stations chiefly for the music content. Of course, music does not necessarily mean popular or chart music. For example, the main output of Classic FM is classical music.

Speech-based stations. Other stations are speech-based. Their output is largely people talking. For example, BBC Radio 5 Live provides a news, sport and current affairs service, whereas Talk Radio is based on the phone-in format.

Of course, most stations will have some combination of music and speech. To describe them as music- or speech-based is to focus on their main output.

RADIO STATION PROFILE

1

Draw up a profile of your favourite radio station, using the categories described above. Look at the schedules for the station, which are usually printed in a TV and radio listing magazine, or a local newspaper. Listen to the station at a variety of times.

- Does the station broadcast to different audiences at different times?
- What is the station's main audience (think about their age, sex, social class and educational background)?

2

Now try listening for a few days to a radio station you would not normally tune in to, for example, Radio 5 or Classic FM.

- How is it different from the radio station that you usually listen to?
- What is the main audience for this station?
- Write a few paragraphs comparing the two radio stations that you profiled. Mention the strengths and weaknesses of each.

NEW TALENT

Some local commercial radio stations are accused of playing only music by established bands who are already known to the audience. Critics say that this policy of 'playing safe' means that many talented new bands do not get the chance to reach a wider audience. Radio 1 argues that it has a policy of trying to give such opportunities to up-and-coming bands. It also uses presenters with a specific interest in one particular type of music such as dance, rap, indie and jungle. In this way it tries to cater for specialist tastes, rather than simply offering middle-of-the-road music that is already familiar to most of its listeners.

CLASS DISCUSSION

- *What is the music policy of your local commercial station?*
- *Is any air-time given to new bands?*
- *Do any local bands get a chance to have their music played?*
- *Are specialist music interests catered for?*

SATELLITE RADIO

A wide variety of radio programmes is available by satellite. The dish and receiver that are used to receive television programmes also pick up British and foreign radio stations. These stations transmit using the same channels as the TV programmes, but with a different sound channel, or sub-carrier. They can either be received on a normal television channel, or wired through a hi-fi system direct from the satellite receiver.

RADIO VIEW

ASTRA 19.2° E

STATION	FRQ	SUB	AU	OUTPUT
1 Live	11.052H	7.74/7.56	S	German
Antenne Bayern	11.214H	7.38/7.56	S	German language
Asda FM	11.171H	7.56	M	Supermarket music
America 1	11.538H	7.74	M	US Public Radio
BBC World Service	11.552H	7.38	M	English general
BBC1 FM	10.979V	7.38/7.56	S	English Rock & Pop
BBC Radio 2	11.552H	7.74	M	MOR music & chat
BBC Radio 3	10.979V	7.74/7.92	S	Classical & News
BBC Radio 4	11.552H	7.56	M	English Cultural
BBC Radio 5	11.552H	7.92	M	News & Sport
BRTN Nacht	10.921H	7.38	M	Music & Info
C.M.R.	11.568V	7.56	M	Country Music/Speech
CNN Radio	11.627V	7.92	M	News Reports
Deutscheland Funk	11.347V	7.38/7.56	S	News & Info
Deutscheland Funk	11.347V	7.74/7.92	S	News & Info
Deutsche Welle	11.229V	7.38/7.56	S	News/Foreign
Deutsche Welle	11.229V	7.74	M	News/Foreign
Deutsche Welle	11.229V	7.92	M	News/Foreign
Cadena DIAL	11.656V	7.38/7.56	S	Spanish
Eviva	10.803H	7.74	M	General Music
Eviva	11.332H	7.74	M	General Music
ERF1	11.038V	7.38	M	Religious, mainly German
ERF2	11.038V	7.56	M	Religious, mainly German
Irish Sat Radio	11.538V	7.92	M	Gen. Music & Info
NDR2	11.582H	7.38/7.56	S	General Music & Info
NDR4	11.582H	7.74/7.92	M	Music/News
NIEUWS Radio	10.744H	7.74/7.92	S	News etc.
N-Joy Radio	11.464V	7.38/7.56	S	Music
Radio RMF	11.420H	7.74/7.92	S	Rock & Pop
Radio Sweden	11.597V	7.74	M	Music & Speech
RNW	10.935V	7.94	M	Internation service RN
RTE Radio	11.538V	7.56	M	Irish News & Music
RTL Radio	11.391H	7.38/7.56	S	Oldies/Soft Pop (German)
RTL Radio	10.758V	7.38/7.56	S	Oldies/Soft Pop (German)
Kink FM Veronica	10.758V	7.74/7.92	S	Rock/Pop
SER	11.656V	7.74	M	Spanish
Sky Radio	11.318V	7.38/7.56	S	Soft Pop/Dutch News
Sunrise	11.479V	7.38	M	Multi Lingual
Super Gold	11.171V	7.38	M	Classical Oldies
Sputnik	11.112H	7.38/7.56	S	Rock & Pop
Switzerland (SRI)	10.802H	7.38	M	Multi-Lingual
Switzerland (SRI)	10.802H	7.56	M	English
SWF3	11.494H	7.38/7.56	S	Rock 'n' Pop
UCB	11.509V	7.56	M	Religious
Veronica Hit Radio	10.744H	7.56	M	Rock/Pop
Virgin Radio	11.377V	7.38/7.56	S	Classical Rock/New music
WDR2	11.053H	7.38/7.56	S	General Ent./Info
World Radio Network	11.538V	7.38	M	World News

EUTELSAT 2F1 13° E

STATION	FRQ	SUB	AU	OUTPUT
BBC External	10.987V	7.56	M	Info & News
BBC World Service	10.987V	7.38	M	Gen. Info & News
BBC World Service	11.265H	7.38 ---»		Feeds
BBC World Service	11.620V	7.38	M	English
BBC World Service	11.620V	7.56 ---»		Feeds
Deutsche Welle	11.163V	7.02/7.20	S	German Cultural
Deutsche Welle	11.163V	7.74 ---»	S	Language Progs.
France Info	11.321V	7.20	M	General/Music
France Inter	11.321V.	7.38	M	Info/Music
France Culture	11.321V	7.56	M	Cultural
PRT Radio 1	11.474H	7.38	M	Poland
PRT Radio 3	11.474H	7.74	M	Poland
Radio Bis	11.474H	7.92	M	Polish
Radio Canada	11.265V	7.20	M	French
Radio Exterior	11.224H	7.56	M	Spanish
Radio Finland	11.163V	8.10	M	News & Music
MBC Radio	11.554H	7.38/7.56	M	Arabic News & Music
Radio Vatican	11.554V	7.74	M	Religious
Radio Warsaw	11.474H	7.56	M	Multi-Lingual
RAI Radio 1	11.363V	7.38	M	Italian
RAI Radio 3	11.363V	7.56	M	Italian
RAI Radio 2	11.448V	7.38	M	Italian
RAI International	11.448V	7.56	M	Italian
RNE Radio 1	11.224V	7.38	M	Spanish
MBC Radio	11.554V	7.38/7.56	S	Arabic news and music
Swiss Radio Int.	11.321V	7.74	M	General + music
U.A.E. FM	11.516H	7.02	M	Arabic
Voice of America	11.163V	7.38/7.56	S	Pop & Info
WRN2	11.554V	7.74	M	News Relays

Some of the stations from all over Europe that can be received via satellite.

The radio studio

Before an audience can receive a radio station, someone has put together the words and music that they are going to listen to. This is usually done in a radio studio. Most radio studios are similar in their layout and organization, regardless of whether the station is speech- or music-based.

The nerve centre of any radio operation is the desk, or main control panel, at which the presenter sits. This consists of a series of channels, each with its own fader. Each channel controls one particular source of sound, such as a microphone, CD-player or tape-machine. Faders control the volume of a particular sound source. They can be opened or closed by sliding them up and down. The presenter can select each of the sources by opening and closing the fader to bring up or shut down the sound. At the end of a record, for example, the presenter can fade down the music and fade up their microphone to talk to the audience. One of the most valuable tools a presenter has available is the cart machine, which uses a continuous loop of audio tape so that, once it has played, it can be cued again very quickly. Using this, pre-recorded trails (which tell the audience about programmes that are to be broadcast in the near future) and jingles can be cued, so that they are ready to play immediately. Listen out for examples used by presenters on your favourite station.

A presenter has to be skilled at cueing records and tapes and fading them up or down to make the show seem professional. While one record is playing, the presenter needs to cue (or find the beginning of) the next piece of music to go on air, so that the music will be ready to play as soon as the presenter has introduced it.

Programme content

Imagine that you have been asked to work as a presenter on a local commercial radio station. What would you have to do to produce a show that would keep your audience listening? The first factor that you would need to think about is the time of day that the show went out. If your show were a drive-time show, which generally attracts a large audience, you would be broadcasting for people getting ready for, or on their way to, work or school, or who were coming home in the evening. Many would be listening in their cars, so it would be important to include information about road conditions, for example.

During the day, the audience is likely to be made up of people who are at home all day, possibly looking after children or doing housework. Evening radio shows compete with television, so this might be a good time to put out a specialist programme for a minority group.

Presenters try to keep a balance between the different elements that make up a show. Talk must be balanced with music. The music itself must be a blend of different types and different moods. Some of it should be familiar to the audience, some of it less familiar. Slow, sad ballads should be balanced with lively, upbeat, happy sounds.

IN PAIRS

Imagine that you were presenting a show that went out from midnight until 4 o'clock in the morning.
• What type of audience would be listening then?
• What sort of music would you play?

Although presenters can choose much of their own music, they have a playlist of tracks that the stations want to be played most often, which have to be built into the show. Any music used in a show has to be paid for. Such 'needle-time' is paid for via organizations that represent the interests of record companies and performers, such as Phonographic Performance Limited.
A presenter, therefore, needs to find other ways of filling up air-time if a show is to stay within its budget.

On a commercial station, advertising slots have already been allocated, so a presenter has to structure the programme around them. Such regular items as news, weather and travel updates are also built in. Additionally, the presenter may include recorded material from a reporter, who has been out collecting information to be broadcast as part of the show. This is called a package and is likely to consist of interview material and actuality (sound, recorded or broadcast, of real events or activities that are actually taking place), with the reporter's voice providing links to guide the listener through the material. The reporter gives the presenter a cue sheet, which is read out to introduce the package.

Having guests in the studio is another possible feature that a presenter might include. Most studios have three microphones (one that is used by the presenter and two extra ones), so that studio guests can contribute to the show in the form of a discussion or interview. This approach is sometimes called a 'zoo format', which means that other voices besides that of the presenter contribute to the programme. The other voices may be identified as studio guests, or they may be the anonymous voices of other people working in the studio, who chip into the discussion or bounce their comments off the presenter. This can produce lively listening, especially if the contributors are able to think up witty, off-the-cuff remarks. For the programme to keep a sense of order and shape, the presenter must be able to control the proceedings.

Phone-ins have become increasingly popular. Not only are they cheap to produce, but they also involve the audience in the show and help to keep their interest. Of course, on live radio a phone-in could cause embarrassment if a caller starts to swear, for example. Generally, callers are not allowed straight on air, but are screened by a production assistant, who tries to get some idea of what the caller wishes to contribute to the show. In some circumstances, the presenter has a delay button. This means that transmission of the 'live' show is, in fact, delayed by several seconds, so that any obscene or embarrassing remark can be covered up, with a bleep for example, before the audience can hear it. On-air competitions, where listeners try

GROUP DISCUSSION

● *Have you ever called into a radio station or had a request played?*
● *What do you think makes people want to hear themselves or their name on air?*

A roadshow is an effective way of raising a station's profile and providing lively programmes for its audience.

to answer questions asked by the presenter, are also a useful way of keeping listeners' interest in a programme, as is the playing of readers' requests and dedications.

Although a radio show may seem quite natural, with studio banter and guests dropping in, a good deal of time and effort go into its preparation. Like many other media products, it takes a lot of work to make the show seem natural and unrehearsed.

Controlling radio

Of course, there are limits to what can be broadcast, for example, material that some people would think was obscene or offensive would not be considered suitable. Also, stations cannot simply broadcast on any frequency that they choose, although there are pirate, or free radio stations, which transmit on empty frequencies.

PIRATE RADIO

Are there any pirate stations in your area?
* If so, what type of station are they?
* Are they aimed at a specific audience?
* Do they exist because this audience is not well served by mainstream

The Radio Authority was set up at the beginning of 1991 to license commercial radio stations and to regulate the material that they broadcast, including the advertising that they carry. The authority was created under the 1990 Broadcasting Act and was given three main tasks:
- To plan frequencies
- To grant licences to organizations who want to broadcast
- To regulate programming and advertising.

Planning frequencies

The job of planning frequencies is obviously an important one, with over 170 local commercial stations each transmitting a signal. The airwaves are constantly overcrowded, as stations compete with one another for both space and audiences. Part of the authority's job is to give out frequencies to stations in a way that avoids interference with other broadcasters' stations. The FM waveband, for example, is divided into sub-bands, of which three are allocated for use by independent stations, both local and national.

The FM band

In the UK this extends in frequency from 87.5 MHz to 108 MHz. FM is divided into sub-bands, used, with some exceptions, as follows:

87.6 to 88 MHz	*Restricted services*
88 to 94.6 MHz	*BBC national and regional radio*
94.6 to 96.1 MHz	*BBC local radio (and Radio 4 in places)*
96.1 to 97.6 MHz	*Independent local radio*
97.6 to 99.8 MHz	*BBC Radio 1*
99.8 to 102 MHz	*Independent national (Classic FM) and local radio*
102 to 103.5 MHz	*Independent local radio*
103.5 to 105 MHz	*BBC local radio (and Radio 4 in places)*
105 to 108 MHz	*Independent local radio*

How the FM band is divided into different types of station.

Granting licences

When the Radio Authority grants licences to organizations who wish to broadcast, it must take account of what is in the best interests of the people who live in the transmission area. Choice is the key word here. There are many stations that already broadcast a fairly predictable diet of music and news. A new station might be expected to come up with a proposal that would offer listeners something different in the way of programme content and style.

The Radio Authority has awarded three licences to national commercial stations. They are:

Classic FM, which began broadcasting classical music in September 1992.

Virgin 1215 AM nationwide and 105.8FM in London and south-east England, which went on air in April 1993, with a rock music-based playlist.

Talk Radio was launched in February 1995. It provides listener-led interactive debate 24 hours a day, plus news, weather and travel.

In addition to all the local commercial stations throughout the country, the Radio Authority also grants licences to restricted services, which broadcast over a limited area. So far it has granted 1,300 of these for temporary services that can be received by such audiences as a university or college campus, or a hospital.

The Radio Authority also grants licences to restricted services, which broadcast over a limited area.

CLASS DISCUSSION

Imagine that you had the opportunity to make a bid to put a new radio station on air in your area.

- *What sort of programmes would you broadcast?*
- *What type of presenters would you employ?*
- *Are there any sections of the community that are left out by the stations that are on air at the moment?*
- *If so, how would you meet their needs?*

Regulating content

The Radio Authority's job of regulating programming and advertising makes it an important watchdog. Stations that have been granted a licence to broadcast must provide broadcasts that are fair and decent. An important part of the Radio Authority's job is to make sure that this happens. Radio stations are required to keep a tape of all the material they broadcast for 42 days. If a listener wishes to make a complaint, they can write to the Radio Authority giving details of their complaint, including the station on which the item was broadcast, and the time and date it went out. Provided that the complaint is received within the 42-day period, the Radio Authority can ask for a copy of the broadcast to help it to investigate the complaint. Important guidelines are laid down by the Authority in the form of codes, which broadcasters are expected to follow. The codes set out what broadcasters may and may not do in terms of:

- Programming
- Advertising and sponsorship
- News and current affairs.

In the Radio Authority's advertising and sponsorship code, there are, for example, important rules about advertisements aimed at children (who are defined as being aged 15 and below).

The new Zogatron computer game can solve all your problems! Don't let the other kids at school laugh at you because you don't know how to play it. Order one now and a free cuddly Zogatron could be yours. Don't leave the Zogatron to be destroyed by the evil Vortix starfighters. Tell your Mum and Dad – at just £32.99, it's a snip!

ON YOUR OWN

Look carefully at the radio advert above. How does it break the Radio Authority's advertising and sponsorship code covering advertising and children (see opposite page)? Write a letter complaining about the advert to the Radio Authority, explaining why you think it breaks the code. Don't forget to mention the time and the date that you heard the advert, and the name of the radio station on which it was broadcast.

These are the rules that advertisers must observe
when they target radio adverts at young people.

Advertising and Children

Rule 1 Misleadingness
Advertisements addressed to the child listener must not exaggerate or mislead about the size, qualities or capabilities of products or about the sounds they might produce.

Rule 2 Prices
Prices of products advertised to children must not be minimized by words such as 'only' or 'just'.

Rule 3 Immaturity and credulity
Advertisements must not take advantage of the immaturity or natural credulity of children.

Rule 4 Appeals to loyalty
Advertisements must not take advantage of the sense of loyalty of children or suggest that unless children buy or encourage others to buy a product or service they will be failing in some duty or lacking in loyalty.

Rule 5 Inferiority
Advertisements must not lead children to believe that unless they have or use the product advertised they will be inferior in some way to other children or liable to be held in contempt or ridicule.

Rule 6 Direct exhortation
Advertisements must not directly urge children to buy products or to ask adults to buy products for them. For example, children must not be directly invited to 'ask Mum' or 'ask Dad' to buy them an advertiser's product.

Rule 7 Direct response
Advertisements must not invite children to purchase products by mail or telephone.

Rule 8 Competitions
(a) References to competitions for children are acceptable provided that any skill required is appropriate to the age of likely participants and the values of the prizes and the chances of winning are not exaggerated.
(b) The published rules must be submitted in advance to the licensee and the principal conditions of the competition must be included in the advertisement.

Rule 9 Free gifts
References to 'free' gifts for children in advertisements must include all qualifying conditions, e.g. any time limit, how many products need to be bought, how many wrappers need to be collected, etc.

Rule 10 Health and hygiene
(a) Advertisements must not encourage children to eat frequently throughout the day.
(b) Advertisements must not encourage children to consume food or drink near bedtime.
(c) Advertisements for confectionery and snack foods must not suggest that such products may be substituted for balanced meals.

Rule 11 Children as presenters
(a) The participation of children in radio commercials is acceptable, subject to all relevant legal requirements.
(b) If children are employed in commercials, they must not be used to present products or services which they could not be expected to buy themselves. They must not make significant comments on characteristics of products and services about which they could not be expected to have direct knowledge.

Rule 12 Testimonials
Children must not personally testify about products and services. They may, however, give spontaneous comments on matters in which they would have an obvious natural interest.

This extract from the Radio Authority's programme code shows how hard it is to say exactly what bad taste is.

TASTE AND DECENCY AND THE PORTRAYAL OF VIOLENCE

■ LANGUAGE

The gratuitous use of offensive language including blasphemy must be avoided. Bad language and blasphemy must not be used in programmes specially designed for children or broadcast in circumstances such that children might be expected to be listening.

There is no absolute ban on the use of bad language but its use must be defensible in terms of context and authenticity. It is one thing, for example, when such language occurs in a documentary programme, and quite another when introduced for its own sake in, for example, a music-based entertainment programme. Many people who would not be unduly shocked by swearing are offended when it is used to excess and without justification.

■ SEX

The portrayal of, or allusion to, sexual behaviour must be defensible in context and presented with tact and discretion. Smut, titillation, crudity and sexual stereotyping must be avoided.

No portrayal or description of sexual activity between humans and animals or between adults and children may be transmitted and it can be referred to in programmes only after consultation at senior radio station management level.

The same considerations apply here as to bad language. Popular entertainment and comedy have often relied to some extent on sexual innuendo: but this does not justify smut, titillation, mere crudity, the portrayal of perversion, sexism, or the degradation of either sex. Much of the world's great drama, music and fiction has been concerned with love and passion, and it would be quite wrong

(if not impossible) to require writers or lyricists to renounce all intention to shock or disturb: but the aim should be to move, not offend.

■ BAD TASTE IN HUMOUR

(a) Licensees must avoid humour which offends against good taste or decency. There is a danger of offence in the use of humour based on particular characteristics like race, gender or disability.

Even where no malice is present, jokes can all too easily, and plausibly, exploit or humiliate for the purpose of entertainment. This not only hurts those most directly concerned but can repel many listeners.

(b) *Recorded items*

Items not used immediately must be checked before transmission to ensure that jokes or scenarios are not rendered tasteless by intervening events, such as death, injury or other misfortune.

■ CHILDREN AND YOUNG PERSONS

The Radio Authority believes that adult radio listeners have the right to enjoy material which would not be thought suitable for children. However, Licence Holders must be aware of circumstances such that large numbers of children and young persons might be expected to be listening. Adult material must not be broadcast at times when a Licence Holder regularly directs his programmes at children and young persons by the inclusion of music, stories, or speech items acknowledged to be specifically attractive to children and young people below the age of 18.

Adult programmes include drama where strong language or violent scenarios might occur, discussion or 'phone-in' programmes which cover explicit violent or sexual topics in a frank manner and musical items with violent or sexually explicit lyrics, unless the programmes have educational aims.

CLASS
DISCUSSION

What are your views on the
Radio Authority's
programme code? Do you
think that it is right to
control what can be
broadcast in this way? Or
do you think that the
audience is less easily
shocked and upset than the
Radio Authority thinks?

The programme code covers a range of issues, such as religion, good taste and decency and the portrayal of violence. The news and current affairs code concerns itself very much with impartiality, bias and the reporting of politics. It insists, for example, that all news broadcasts should be accurate and impartial. When dealing with controversial subjects, the station should broadcast a range of views from people within its bulletins. Equally, the host of a discussion or phone-in programme should make sure that everyone has a chance to express their views.

As well as sticking to these codes, broadcasters are expected to broadcast the type of material that they outlined when they applied for their licence. A description of this material is contained in each station's licence, under the heading 'A promise of performance'.

In considering a listener's complaint, the Radio Authority must decide if any of its codes or the promise of performance have been broken. If it decides that they have, the Radio Authority has a number of options open to it:
• It can tell off the station
• It can ask it for an apology or correction to be broadcast
• In serious cases, it can fine the station, and shorten or even take away its licence.

The Authority publishes a list of all the complaints it has followed up. It also gives its response, details of whether the complaint was upheld or not and what action, if any, it decided was necessary.

Review

Radio is often given a low priority by Media Studies students, just because it is easy to take it for granted. Radio is a medium that is often on in the background. People can listen to it without concentrating totally on it. They often listen while they are doing something else, such as homework or cooking dinner.

In this chapter, you have learned that radio is in fact a complex medium, which is just as interesting and worthwhile studying as television and film. So next time you find yourself listening to the radio, think about what you have learned about the medium and ask yourself some important questions about what you are listening to:
• What station am I tuned in to?
• What is the station's identity and how is it established?
• How is it financed?
• What sort of audience does it cater for?
• To what sort of geographical area does it broadcast?
• What rules must it stick to in order to carry on broadcasting?
• What do I like about the station?
• How could it be improved?

12. ADVERTISING

Advertising is the presentation of goods or services in such a way as to encourage people to buy or use them. Each section of the media uses its technology to make advertising presentations. Money paid to media institutions by advertisers funds much of their activity and without it many television programmes would not get made, newspapers and magazines published, or records played. Most media, therefore, depend on advertising revenue for their survival. In fact, some people say the main function of the media is not to inform or entertain audiences, but to deliver audiences to advertisers.

In the UK there is a publicly funded television organization, the BBC. It does not rely on advertising as it gets its money from the sale of TV licences, which viewers must have if they are to watch its programmes without breaking the law.
However, it is worth noting that even the BBC carries adverts for its own products, such as videos, tapes and books associated with its programmes.

On your own

List the occasions when you come into contact with advertising. You will be surprised how often this happens.

Forms of advertising

Television commercials

Advertising on television usually takes the form of short films broadcast between and during programmes in what are called commercial breaks (although it could be argued that the programmes are merely made to be shown between the adverts). These commercial breaks are called slots and TV companies sell them to advertisers. The cost of a particular slot depends on the popularity of the programme broadcast around it. Currently the most expensive slot on ITV is during *News at Ten*. A 20-second advert in this slot costs the same as an advert lasting around 12 minutes broadcast at 4 am.

Advertising costs have grown and grown. On its first night of broadcasting in May 1956, Granada TV charged £14,215 in total for commercial break air-time. On Granada in 1996 it cost around £600,000 for a 40-second commercial during *Coronation Street*. Television advertisements in the 1990s cost an average of £400,000 to make.

Advertising slots on TV tend to be sold to advertisers in packages. This means that they buy a set number of slots in commercial breaks throughout the day, some at peak time during the evening, others at less popular times in the morning and afternoon and late at night. Most television commercials are made by commercial production companies on behalf of advertisers.

The first advert broadcast on TV in Britain was for Gibbs SR toothpaste 1955.

You've just missed a short programme on oral hygiene

Radio adverts

Adverts are played during most programmes on commercial radio stations. Radio commercials are less expensive to produce than those for television and the cost of air-time is also significantly lower. This means that more companies can afford to advertise, especially small local ones.

Radio commercials usually take the form of a short presentation using music and speech. Most use a catchy piece of music with simple lyrics called a jingle to get listeners to remember the advert. A large majority of radio adverts are made by local radio stations that have their own production units. Others, especially those that are broadcast nationally, are made by commercial companies.

In Groups

Using a tape recorder produce a radio advert for a new product of your choice. To do this, you will have to write a script and choose appropriate music. Remember that most radio adverts use a catchy jingle. It may be helpful to tape some examples of adverts from the radio and study them before you begin.

Press advertising

A large proportion of newspapers and magazines is taken up by advertising. In fact, some papers are made up of nothing more than adverts. Publishers design their products around what are called 'advertising ratios'. This means how much of a magazine or newspaper will be made up of adverts and how much will be taken up by stories and pictures (editorial). The percentage of adverts in newspapers depends to a large extent on their circulation figures. National daily newspapers tend to have the smallest amount of space devoted to adverts, while small local papers usually have the largest percentage of adverts.

IN PAIRS

Using a calculator work out the advertising ratios of the following:
- *A national Sunday paper*
- *A national daily paper*
- *Your local evening paper.*

This will give you an idea of how much space in newspapers is sold to advertisers.

Advertising in newspapers and magazines falls into three types:

Display adverts: these use visual images in the form of photographs or graphics to attract the attention of the reader, and are generally placed by commercial advertisers. They can range from adverts for small local firms, containing a simple company logo in black and white, to full-page, full-colour adverts for internationally famous products.

Display advertising.

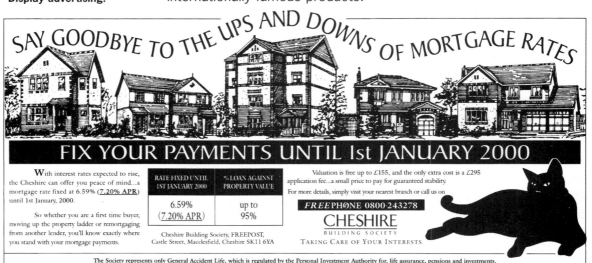

SAY GOODBYE TO THE UPS AND DOWNS OF MORTGAGE RATES

FIX YOUR PAYMENTS UNTIL 1st JANUARY 2000

With interest rates expected to rise, the Cheshire can offer you peace of mind...a mortgage rate fixed at 6.59% (**7.20% APR**) until 1st January, 2000.

So whether you are a first time buyer, moving up the property ladder or remortgaging from another lender, you'll know exactly where you stand with your mortgage payments.

RATE FIXED UNTIL 1ST JANUARY 2000	% LOAN AGAINST PROPERTY VALUE
6.59% (7.20% APR)	up to 95%

Cheshire Building Society, FREEPOST, Castle Street, Macclesfield, Cheshire SK11 6YA

Valuation is free up to £155, and the only extra cost is a £295 application fee...a small price to pay for guaranteed stability.

For more details, simply visit your nearest branch or call us on

FREEPHONE 0800-243278

CHESHIRE
BUILDING SOCIETY
TAKING CARE OF YOUR INTERESTS

The Society represents only General Accident Life, which is regulated by the Personal Investment Authority for, life assurance, pensions and investments. Any financial advice given will relate only to the products and services of the Society and General Accident Life.

The Fixed Rate mortgage is not available in conjunction with the Society's Discount, Capital Release, or Cash for Homebuyers schemes. Shared ownership and commercial mortgages are also excluded, as are further advances. The Fixed Rate is subject to an Application Fee of £295 of which £100 non-refundable is required on application with the balance charged at completion. The Fixed Rate is subject to taking the Society's buildings insurance for at least the duration of the fixed rate. The minimum advance is £25,000. The maximum advance is £150,000. In the event of the mortgage being repaid, in full or in part, during the first five years of the mortgage a penalty will be incurred. Details are available on request. Typical Example: The APR calculation based on a fixed rate mortgage to 31st January 2000. Assumptions:- Repayment loan of £50,000 over 25 year term ,towards the purchase of a property priced at £75,000. Building insurance valuation £80,000 throughout the Fixed Rate period. The APR has been calculated on the assumption that the variable rate throughout the term will be the same as the Fixed Rate. In practice at the end of the Fixed Rate period the Society's variable rate then applicable will be charged and this may differ from the Fixed Rate.The Society's current variable rate is 6.74%. The total amount payable is £104,664 which includes the initial amount borrowed, an Application fee of £295, charges and expenses incurred in arranging the loan and buildings insurance premiums throughout the Fixed Rate period and all monthly repayments. Remortgages from other lenders are available up to 80% of the value of the property and must have completion dates after 31st December 1996. Further details and written quotations are available on request. All mortgages are subject to status, valuation and financial appraisal.

YOUR HOME IS AT RISK IF YOU DO NOT KEEP UP REPAYMENTS ON A MORTGAGE OR OTHER LOAN SECURED ON IT.

Classified adverts: these as a rule do not use visual images and consist almost completely of words. They are generally arranged in columns towards the back of the publications and are often known as the 'small ads'. They include things such as births, marriages and deaths, job adverts and adverts placed by members of the public.

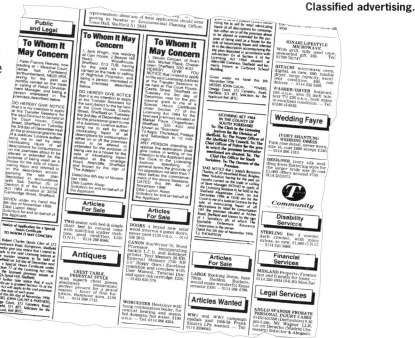

Classified advertising.

Advertorials: these are pieces of writing about companies, describing and promoting their products. They can be accompanied by photographs. By law, such pieces of writing must have the words 'advertising feature' printed next to them so that people do not confuse them with news stories.

Advertising feature: bright ideas to help you in your preparations for Christmas

For once - sit back and relax

CHRISTMAS comes just once a year and with it comes cooking, cleaning, washing up and frantic shopping expeditions. So this year, for once, sit back, relax and let someone else do the worrying.

England has all the answers when it comes to relaxation and enjoyment this Yuletide with a whole range of Christmas breaks, days out or original gift ideas.

Christmas away from home means all the fun but none of the washing up and the chance to make new friends into the bargain.

There are a multitude of hotels open over the Christmas period that offer all the festive favourites

such as carol singers, mulled wine awaiting your return from church, board games, competitions and treasure hunts. Plus all your favourites to eat.

And kids, don't panic. Santa will be aware that you're away for Christmas and will call on everyone as usual.

All the major hotel groups such as Forte, Hilton, Best Western have brochures in travel agents, as do coach operators and self catering cottages agencies.

The Sheffield Newspapers Holiday Service also has a range of breaks at home and abroad.

If it's just impossible to get away from family commitments

then don't despair. Why not treat yourselves to a couple of days out instead. Although most theatres are shut on Christmas Eve and Christmas Day they open again for Boxing Day and New Year's Day.

Apart from the traditional pantomime, there are also craft fairs, carol concerts, steam train rides and exhibitions.

On December 14-15 there is a Victorian Christmas Party at Buxton Museum in Derbyshire or if you fancy a little shopping, Lincoln's German-style Christmas street market has 200 stalls and seasonal entertainment (December 5-8).

Now, if you want to treat someone special to a Christmas present with a difference, then look no further than England's tourist attractions.

A trip of a lifetime is offered by Heart of England Balloons. Scenic flights are currently from the village of Wallcote, near Stratford-upon-Avon or from Honington near Shipston-on-Stour. Call 01789-488219.

Membership of the National Trust would help someone appreciate the beauty of Britain for Christmas for just £26 or family membership at £48. Call 0181-3151111 for details of how to give a gift that lasts all year.

An advertorial.

Prices for advertising in print publications depend on how much space the adverts take up on a page, and are charged by the column centimetre. Publishers provide firms who are interested in advertising with a rate card that tells them how much an ad of a particular size will cost (see page 200). Where the advertisement appears in the paper or magazine also affects how much it will cost. An advert at the top of a page close to the front of the publication will cost more than one at the bottom of the page towards the back.

A newspaper advertising rate card.

Rates & Mechanical Data

Classified Advertising Rates 1995

	STAR	All Editions	All Editions + Telegraph
Recruitment			
Linage	£3.10	£4.15	£5.25
Semi Display	£17.35	£19.60	£22.35
Full Display	£19.95	£22.85	£26.10
Public and Legal Notices			
Linage	£3.00	£4.05	£5.15
Semi Display	£16.80	£19.05	£21.55
Full Display	£19.45	£22.45	£26.95
Trade			
Linage	£2.50	£2.90	£3.90
Semi Display	£12.80	£14.35	£16.85
Full Display	£15.00	£17.10	£21.60
Death Notices			
Linage	£2.05	N/A	N/A
Full Display	£9.00	£10.50*	£10.50

*plus Telegraph at no additional charge

Column Width

1 col - 31mm
2 col - 65mm
3 col - 99mm
4 col - 133mm
5 col - 167mm
6 col - 201mm
7 col - 234mm
8 col - 268mm

Page Dimensions

Full Page	340mm x 268mm
Half Page	170mm x 268mm
Qtr Page	170mm x 133mm

ON YOUR OWN

Design a display advert for a new product of your choice. Think who would buy the product and what sort of advertising image would appeal to them.

Sponsorship

Another popular form of advertising that uses the power of the media is sponsorship. This involves an advertiser paying for the right to have their name associated with a media event. Examples of this are sporting events, when the advertiser's name forms part of the event's title, such as the Milk Race cycling competition or the Coca Cola Cup in football. Other advertisers sponsor teams and have their names and logos printed on players' shirts, or have posters put on hoardings around sports grounds. The idea behind this is that large numbers of viewers will see the names when matches or tournaments are broadcast on television. This is one way firms can actually get advertising courtesy of the BBC, even though it does not carry paid-for advertisements.

The sponsorship of actual programmes on commercial TV stations is increasingly popular. Advertisers pay to have their name shown or read out at the beginning and end of the programme and either side of the commercial breaks. So a police drama series may be produced in association with an insurance company, or a première film with a soft drinks manufacturer.

Product placement is a new form of advertising that is gaining popularity. It involves advertisers paying the producers of films to have characters use their products. For example, the main character in a film may wear a certain brand of jeans or drive a certain type of car. The jeans or car will be provided by the company that makes them and they will pay for them to be used.

Product placement is becoming more and more popular.

How are adverts produced?

All commercial television, radio and publishing companies have departments dedicated to selling advertising space. Companies that wish to place advertisements contact people working in these departments, known as advertising sales representatives. Representatives also approach businesses and try to persuade them to place advertisements with their publication, radio or TV station.

If a business wants to advertise, the next step is to produce the advert. For television commercials, advertisers approach a production company to make the advert for them. This involves a team of scriptwriters coming up with an idea for the commercial. Once an idea is agreed upon a storyboard is drawn up. This is a series of drawings showing how the action in the advert will develop. A production team, including camera operators, sound recordists, actors and a director then goes into a studio or out on location and films the advert. The finished product is delivered to the TV company ready to be broadcast in the agreed advertising slots.

In the cases of radio, newspapers and magazines, the sales representatives usually contact their own in-house production department. For radio, a script is written for the advert by a copywriter and then recorded in a studio by engineers and presenters. In newspapers and magazines, copywriters work with artists, known as graphic designers, who come up with the images to be used. Once the designs have been approved by the advertiser, they are positioned in the page design of the publication.

Advertising agencies

Instead of looking after their own advertising, many big firms use professional advertising agencies to ensure they get the best from the opportunities offered by the media. Advertising agencies specialize in handling all aspects of advertising, from designing the commercials to buying the air-time or page space. They are particularly good at conducting advertising campaigns that use all forms of the media. A typical campaign would involve the following steps:

- Client contacts agency to develop a publicity campaign for its product. The client gives the agency an idea of how much it wishes to spend. The contract to carry out advertising for a company is known as an account.
- The agency carries out research to discover who would be interested in buying the product.
- Adverts are designed to appeal to the people whom the agency thinks will be attracted to the product.
- All options for advertising are considered, for example, TV, radio and press. A decision is made about which type of advertising is best for the product: this may include one or all three of the different media.
- If a television commercial is needed, the agency contracts a production company to make it. Press and magazine adverts and scripts for radio commercials are developed by creative teams at the agency.
- Agency buyers purchase at the lowest price possible the best spots for the adverts on TV and radio and in the press.
- Research is carried out following the campaign to see how successful it was in generating sales of the product.

IN GROUPS

Design your own advertising campaign. Each group acts as an advertising agency for an imaginary product chosen by the class leader. Each group should work out how to advertise the product.
- Think of all the different forms of advertising available and decide which would be best for your product.

- If possible, work out the cost of your campaign by checking advertising price rates with media producers.
- Remember that advertising agencies have to work to tight budgets given to them by their clients.

The class can vote on which campaign they think would be most successful.

The NCH Action For Children advertising campaign

The National Children's Home was founded in 1869 by Methodist minister Thomas Bowman Stephenson to provide accommodation for young people in need. It is now known as NCH Action For Children and its work has grown to include family centres, services for children with disabilities and schemes for young people leaving local authority care.

When NCH Action For Children celebrated its 125th anniversary, it launched a fund-raising drive to help it continue its good work. To publicize the anniversary it needed an advertising campaign.

Aims and research

The charity had two main aims it wished to achieve through its advertising campaign. These were:
- To launch and communicate its new name and logo
- To heighten awareness of its work and campaigns in order to raise funds.

Five leading advertising agencies were invited by NCH Action For Children to come up with ideas for the campaign. The contract was awarded to Mustoe Merriman Herring and Levy, based in Covent Garden in London. The agency started their research by interviewing NCH Action For Children project leaders, voluntary fund-raisers, members of the public and other charities. It identified a target audience for the campaign made up of current and possible donors that included churches, businesses, consumers (donations and legacies from people the charity had helped) and the general public. The agency also carried out research into the effectiveness of press advertising and billboard and poster advertising.

The campaign

Adverts were designed showing photographs of orphans cared for by the original National Children's Home and modern-day children in need; they were divided by a picture of a collecting tin. The slogan 'We've been carrying the can for 125 years' was chosen as the campaign's theme and used in all adverts.

Advert designed for the NCH Action For Children 125th anniversary campaign.

We've been carrying the can for 125 years.

Founded in 1869, NCH Action For Children is now Britain's second largest children's charity.

We work with, among others, children with disabilities, sexually abused children, homeless young people and families in crisis.

Through our two hundred projects nationwide, we give practical support, counselling and specialist treatment.

Above all, we give 16,000 children a year the hope of a better future.

Please support us in our anniversary year: NCH Action For Children 071 354 9530.

Adverts were placed in national newspapers and posters were put on 1,200 billboard sites throughout the country. The campaign also generated a lot of interest from journalists and many papers carried stories on it. *The Times,* for instance, carried a half-page article next to a half-page paid-for advert.

The overall cost of the NCH Action for Children 125th anniversary campaign was around £200,000. While it is difficult to say exactly how many donations to the charity resulted from the advertising campaign, £14 million was raised during the NCH Action for Children's anniversary year, compared with £9.7 million in the year before and £10 million in the year following the campaign. Research done by the advertising agency after the campaign showed that public awareness of the work of the NCH Action For Children had risen from less than 1% to around 10%. The charity thought that the campaign had been a success.

CLASS DISCUSSION

Look at the NCH Action For Children adverts.
- How effective do you think they are?
- Could they have been done differently?
- Can you suggest alternative images or slogans?

The power of advertising

Money talks

The relationship of advertising to the content of media products has been the subject of much debate. Critics say that because of the amount of money advertisers pay to the media, they can, if they wish, influence what is shown or printed. They also argue that TV programmes, newspapers and magazines will not broadcast or publish material that is harmful to their advertisers. So, they say, a story about defects in a particular product may not be published by a newspaper if the company that makes it advertises with it. They also say that the line between news and advertising may become blurred when the subject of the story is linked with a major advertiser. For example, a new product may become the subject of an editorial feature if there is the promise of a lucrative advertising contract.

Although rare, there have been incidences of advertisers putting direct pressure on media producers. However, these have largely been in the form of advertisers using their financial muscle to protest against particular stories or features in the media, rather than blatant attempts to avoid bad or achieve favourable publicity. In 1993 the *Daily Mirror* printed pictures of Princess Diana working out in a gym and many large companies withdrew adverts from the paper in protest. In 1996 watch manufacturers Omega stopped advertising with *Vogue* to protest against what it saw as the promotion of the skinny 'waif' look through the magazine's use of very thin models.

However, the real that power advertisers have over the media works in a more subtle fashion. The majority of the media in Britain exist to make a profit. To do this, they must attract as many advertisers as they can and charge them as much as possible. Advertisers are interested in media products because they reach large numbers of potential customers. To charge high advertising rates, a programme or newspaper must prove it reaches a big audience through viewing figures or sales. This leads to the media producing products not on the basis of their ability to inform or entertain, but to attract large audiences. So if a television station has a choice between showing a documentary about an issue of importance that will attract an audience of hundreds of thousands, or showing a game show that will attract an audience of millions, the game show will be chosen.

A similar process can be seen to operate in the planning and marketing of new media products. The decision to launch a new magazine usually boils down to the existence of an audience ready to buy it. If the publishers can sell a magazine to a lot of new readers, they can convince advertisers it is worth paying to promote their products in its pages. The birth of 'lifestyle' magazines for men grew out of the recognition that men would buy publications dedicated to male interests in the same way that female readers had been buying 'women's' magazines for years. In turn, advertisers used the pages of these new magazines to promote products for men, such as skin care products and high fashion, traditionally aimed at women.

Advertisers threatened to stop advertising with some magazines in protest at the use of extremely thin models, which they said could encourage eating disorders.

Advertisements from male lifestyle magazines. Such magazines offer advertisers a platform to sell men products they hadn't considered buying before.

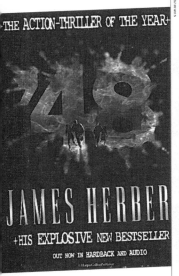

On your own

List the types of manufacturers who would be likely to advertise in a new magazine for middle-aged people. Do you think such a magazine could be successful, based on your list of potential advertisers?

How seriously do we take adverts?

How justified are fears about the supposed grip that advertising has on the media? Although advertisers may try to use the media in as many ways as possible to promote their products, how do audiences use advertising? As we saw in the chapter on audience, many people believe that viewers, listeners and readers are not brainwashed by the media (pages 65–67). In fact, the reverse is true: audiences use the media for their own ends and have a healthy scepticism of what it produces. Points that should be taken into account when looking at the power of advertising include:

- Just because an advert is good does not necessarily mean it is effective in selling more products. Viewers may watch or look at it purely because it is funny or entertaining and never have any intention to go out and buy the product.
- People tend to be highly suspicious of claims made in adverts and take most with a pinch of salt.
- Adverts may be 'invisible'. That is, people may switch channels in commercial breaks or go and make a cup of tea in order to avoid watching advertisements. They may also skip past adverts in newspapers and magazines, concentrating only on stories they are interested in.

Class Discussion

■ What are your favourite adverts?
■ Why do you like them?
■ Are they for products you would buy?
■ If so, do the adverts have an effect on you – do you go out and buy because you have seen the ad?

The Advertising Standards Authority

The Advertising Standards Authority (ASA) was set up in 1962 as an organization independent of both the advertising industry and the government, to make sure that all advertisements that appear in the UK are legal, decent, honest and truthful. (It does not regulate advertisements that appear on TV and radio: these are regulated by the Independent Television Commission and the Radio Authority respectively. For radio advertising, see pages 192–195.

The ASA is funded from the money spent on display advertising (advertising in newspapers, magazines and on posters) and on direct mail advertising (advertising material sent through the post). Advertisers pay a levy of one pound for every thousand pounds they spend on display or direct mail advertising. The money is collected by the Advertising Standards Board of Finance, a body that is independent of the ASA.

Around 30 million adverts are published in the UK every year and the ASA ensures that those producing them follow the British Codes of Advertising and Sales Promotion.

The British Codes of Advertising and Sales Promotion

These codes say what is and what is not acceptable in advertisements. They were drawn up by the advertising industry itself and have two main aims:
• To make advertisers take responsibility for backing up the claims they make for their products in their advertisements
• To avoid causing offence.

The codes are monitored by the Committee of Advertising Practice, which works alongside the ASA. The codes are in addition to the 120 laws passed by successive governments that apply directly or indirectly to advertising.

The codes include a set of general rules that apply to all published adverts. These rules are based on the following principles:
• All advertisements should be legal, decent, honest and truthful.
• All advertisements should be prepared with a sense of responsibility to consumers and to society.
• All advertisements should respect the principle of fair competition generally accepted in business.
• No advertisement should bring advertising into disrepute.
• Advertisements must conform with the advertising codes. Primary responsibility for observing the codes falls on advertisers. Others involved in preparing and publishing advertisements, such as agencies, publishers and other service suppliers, also have to abide by the codes.
• The codes should be applied in the spirit as well as the letter of the law.

Issues such as decency, truthfulness, safety, the depiction of violence, privacy, guarantees and political bias are all covered in the general rules.

The codes also contain a number of rules relating to specific categories of advertisements. These include adverts for alcoholic drinks, cars, medicines and slimming products. They also cover advertising relating to children and adverts making environmental claims. A separate code applies to adverts for cigarettes.

Monitoring advertisements

Only cigarette adverts have to be cleared before they can be published. However, thousands of advertisers, agencies and publishers seek advice and guidance from the ASA on the content of their adverts.

The ASA deals with around 10,000 complaints about adverts from the public and industry each year. Around a quarter of these complaints are upheld, or supported, and action is taken against the advertiser (see below). The ASA carries out its own regular surveys of adverts in the press, on posters and on adverts sent through the post. In addition, the ASA's research department keeps a watch on adverts in areas of particular concern such as medicines and slimming products.

Around 30 million adverts are published in the UK every year.

The government and the European Union consult the ASA whenever they are drawing up policies referring to advertising.

If the ASA decides an advertisement is unacceptable because it is misleading or likely to cause offence, the advertisers are told to remove it. Failure to do this can lead to the following:
- Bad publicity generated by the report that the ASA sends round of its judgements
- Suspension or withdrawal of trading privileges or financial incentives, or the refusal of publishers to sell space to the advertisers
- A court appearance, if the advertisers are referred to the Office of Fair Trading by the ASA for refusing to abide by the codes.

Review

Advertising is the foundation on which most of the media is built, and so deserves close investigation. We have seen in this chapter that media producers get money from two main sources:
- Audiences who pay for their products
- Businesses who pay to advertise in their products.

The money paid by audiences is usually not enough both to support the production of films, programmes and publications, and to allow them to make a profit as well. Because of this, advertising plays a major role in financing media production. In fact, without funds from advertising, most media products would not get made. This has led to major problems about the influence advertisers have had over what the media produces and what we see, hear and read.

13. PRACTICAL PRODUCTION AND ASSIGNMENTS

The coursework component of the exam (SEG Paper 1) is worth 50% of the total marks. It consists of one major piece of practical production and three assignments.

THE PRACTICAL PRODUCTION

> **'Candidates will be expected to submit a practical media production, either individually or as part of a group, and an individual supporting account which includes evaluation of the process and practice involved in working on a production, and an awareness of target audience.'**

This is Section B of the SEG coursework paper, which is worth 25% of the total marks available for the exam. Many Media Studies courses include some similar coursework.

Production work is an important part of your GCSE. Many students find that it is what they enjoy the most about their course. However, for others it can be a source of great frustration. You must, therefore, be prepared to put some thought into the early stages if you are to avoid the pitfalls that may lie ahead.

Remember, too, that all the work you put into planning, sometimes called pre-production, can gain you marks. If you want to do well, you must do this thoroughly and be sure you include it as part of the work you want to have marked.

Getting started

Before you can start work on your production, it makes sense to think about a number of issues.

Resources

The first and most obvious thing to consider is what equipment is there for you to use. It is quite natural at this stage to want to get your hands on sophisticated technical equipment, such as a video editing suite or recording studio. Not only is it fun to play with, but potentially it can give you a better quality finish and hence make your production look good.

Remember, though, that you have to be able to operate such equipment properly if you are to get the results that you hope for. Simply using the equipment is in itself no guarantee of success. On the contrary, you may end up with something worse than if you had settled for more basic equipment that you were more familiar with.

Make a list of equipment that it might be possible to use. Remember that if your teacher agrees, you may be able to use equipment from sources other than your school or college. For example, you may be able to get hold of a video camera for a weekend. You must, however, make clear any help that you have been given by people outside.

Now make a list of your current skills that you think might prove useful in working on your production. Then make another list of skills that you might need to learn to help you complete your work. For example, maybe you already know how to use a word processor, but you may feel it would be useful to learn a software package such as Pagemaker to help you do page layouts for a magazine.

An appropriate medium

Once you have established what is available, the next step is to decide on the most appropriate medium for your idea. Suppose, for example, you decide to base your idea on providing a news service for your school or college. Obviously there are several media you might choose for this:

- **Video:** recording your own locally based lunchtime news programme
- **Radio:** a similar approach using recording or broadcast equipment
- **Print:** a newspaper or magazine for distribution to your fellow students and staff.

Each of these approaches will have its own advantages and disadvantages, so you obviously need to think hard about which is going to be best for what you want to do.

IMPORTANT TIP

Start making a note of all of your ideas and the decisions you have reached at this point. It is important information that you need to put in your supporting account (see pages 225–232).

The audience

What is the audience for your production? There is no point in producing a magazine that no one wants to read or a video that no one wants to watch. Don't assume that if a topic interests you, then everyone will want to know about it. Remember, getting the attention of your audience is hard and keeping it is even harder.

DISCUSSION POINT
• What makes some media texts more interesting than others?
• What is special about your idea? Why will people want to see, read or hear it?

Before you launch into your production, it helps to know who your audience will be and how they would like to see the information presented. The best way to do this is by undertaking some audience research, which means asking people the right questions. You can do this in a number of ways. Perhaps

Viz started as a magazine produced by a few friends: it now has a national circulation.

you will decide to design a detailed questionnaire for people to complete. Alternatively you may find it as effective to do a survey of your potential audience by simply asking for their views informally. Either way you need to undertake some form of market research to find out about your audience and their interests and needs.

For example, you might want to produce a new football magazine. Start off by finding out what your potential audience reads now and what they like about it. What improvements would they like to see? Many successful publishing ventures have begun with people finding a gap in the market and producing a magazine to fill it.

You may be tempted to choose to produce material for an audience similar to yourself (in other words, your peers). This has the advantage that you will know quite a lot about the needs of this group. There is, though, a disadvantage in that you can easily confuse your own personal interests, tastes and attitudes with those of your proposed audience.

Often it helps to target a group of people with whom you are less familiar. This way you will be forced to pay close attention to their likes and dislikes. Groups of people you might not have considered as a possible audience can include:
• Retired people
• Members of a minority
• People with a disability such as hearing impairment.
Ask yourself what special needs are these groups likely to have? How will your production satisfy these needs?

Should I work in a group?

Media production is often a team effort. Look at the list of credits at the end of any film or TV programme to see how many people helped to make it. You may decide to work as part of a team to make your product. However, there are a number of points you need to bear in mind before embarking on a group project:

- Don't try to form a team with too many people in it. Four or five is an absolute maximum
- Remember, each group member must produce an individual supporting account
- Agree before you start how decisions will be made.
- Establish individual roles
- Agree a timetable
- Make sure you stick to what you have agreed!

A key factor in how well your group works is how you make decisions. You might decide to ask one person to act as the leader in the same way that a director or editor takes responsibility for a film or newspaper. All members of the group will then have to accept his or her decisions. Another approach is to be democratic. This way all members of the group have an equal say and vote on key decisions. Some alternative and community magazines are run like this. Whichever approach you choose, it is important that you all keep to this way of working. Otherwise your production may suffer because of squabbling within the group.

So who does what?

If you decide that a group production is what you want to do, there is another important issue to consider. When your work is assessed, it needs to be clear who did what, so that marks can be awarded according to each person's contribution to the piece.

Roles and responsibilities need to be sorted out from the start and written down, so that everyone is clear what they are expected to do. You probably already know that a big problem in group work is caused by people not doing their job. Bear in mind that this can be for a number of reasons: lack of confidence, for example. Be prepared to make allowances and always be sure you have a plan to cover for people who may let you down. At a simple level, this may mean sharing out the extra work. At worst, it could mean rearranging a whole day's work.

You may find it useful to make a list of the different roles that people play in some aspect of media production: all the jobs that appear at the end a TV programme, for example, or the list of people at the front of a magazine. Now decide what the important jobs on your production will be.

The inside cover of a magazine will show you all the different jobs that make up the team who produces it.

- Find out what resources are available.
- Choose an appropriate medium.
- Find out about your audience.
- Decide whether to work in a group or by yourself.
- If you are in a group, make sure you are clear about roles and responsibilities.

Remember, you need to do all this for your supporting account.

All you need now is an idea to work on! Obviously, you will have thought about this already. It is likely, though, that you may have changed your original idea in response to some of the issues raised above.

Don't be too ambitious. It is important that you are realistic about what you can achieve. A half-hour soap opera or a 100-page magazine is a daunting task, even with several people working on it. Don't be afraid to scale it down. Maybe produce the opening five minutes of your soap, or the front cover and some key pages of the magazine. This way you will do a much better job and show what you would be capable of, given more time and resources.

Hello, Prime Minister, I wonder if you can help me with my GCSE Media Studies Project.

Working on your idea

One useful way to begin your production is to research how your topic is treated by existing mass media. This will give you the chance to look at the forms and conventions used to address the audience by media institutions.

For example, the market is often full of magazines aimed at a specific readership. Take the case of magazines that producers want young girls to buy. If you are thinking of producing a magazine aimed at a similar market, then look closely at some of the material already on sale. You might like to think about:

- **Content:** what themes do you find most often?
- **Layout:** how is the magazine organized? Is the front cover similar each week? Are some items more important than others?
- **Illustration:** what sort of photographs and graphics are used? How do these relate to the text?
- **Style:** how does the magazine talk to its readers? Does it tell them how to live their lives? Does it suggest role models who they might look up to? Does it feature minority groups, such as young girls with disability?

The next important bit of research will be about the subject matter itself. Whether you want to make a video, write an article or produce a radio package, you need to find out about your topic. To do this may involve you in a number of activities:

- You may need to telephone people to ask if you can interview them or to get permission to film

- You may need to prepare to interview someone
- You may need to find information from existing sources such as libraries or local archives.

Don't forget that the best media production is about people. Even if you are dealing with quite a technical subject, such as a local archaeological dig, tell the story from the viewpoint of the people involved.

IMPORTANT REMINDER

Make sure you keep all this research – you need to incorporate it into your supporting account.

Writing a script

A lot of what the media produces tries to look spontaneous, as though it has happened with very little planning or scripting. If you try to work like this, you'll soon discover how much careful preparation goes into quite a straightforward production. Documentaries, which often seem simply to record what is happening, need a good deal of careful planning and organization.

An example of a basic storyboard. More information can be added if necessary, for example the duration of each shot, the type of shot and details of any special effects. You could also get actors to pose for photographs, and use these instead of drawings.

Blind Date

Rachel: I hope the boys will wait for us. I promised we'd be there for 7.30.

Paul: I told you they wouldn't turn up. They're just having a joke on us.

Fiona: Come this way. I know a short cut through the park. We'll be there on time.

Mike: Let's go. They're already ten minutes late. It's all a laugh to them. They'll be telling all their mates tomorrow.

Leader of gang: Come on. Hand over your money and your cigs.
Rachel: Let us go. We're already late. Get out of the way.

Mike: Come on, let's go down the chippie. I'm starving. Those two aren't going to turn up.

So you need to do some writing before you can even begin to think about using equipment. For video or radio work, this involves producing a script. For a magazine, you need a rough draft of your articles and features before you plan the layout. Remember the work you did on narrative in the chapter on media language. Think about how you will make your narrative work.

Suppose you wanted to produce a short piece of TV drama, an extract from a new soap, for example. There are a number of ways to produce a script. One method is to use a storyboard. This is particularly effective for short sequences where you need to focus on the visual elements, such as camera movement.

Notice in the example on page 215 how the sound is linked closely to the visuals. Look at how the visuals vary between different types of shot (for example, CU, LS) and different camera angles to produce a visual narrative. Being skilled at drawing is less important than having ideas about how to make a video sequence interesting visually. A good storyboard is an opportunity to try out ideas to help you save time when you start using the equipment.

Another approach to scripting for film or TV is shown below.

A straightforward script showing how the sound and visual images of a film or TV programme are matched. Again, more detail can be added, such as timings and the type of edit that will link the visuals (cut, dissolve, etc). This is often a much quicker way of working than a storyboard, as it enables you to get ideas down quickly.

AFRAID OF THE DARK
Script for the opening sequence of a short television film.

Visuals	Sound/dialogue
Establishing shot of a small town viewed from the distance in daylight. Montage of shots of people shopping, going into and out of offices, catching buses, driving cars. Parents collecting small children from school.	Narrator: By day, Weatherfield was just an ordinary town, somewhere in the north of England. People went about their daily business, in the office, at the shops, on their way home from school.
Streets at dusk. Streetlamps coming on. People hurrying to catch a bus or hail a taxi. Empty streets – night time.	But then darkness must fall ... Suddenly the streets are empty. (Eerie music played softly in background.) Nothing stirs. (Music fades.)
Shot of family at home watching TV.	Everyone is safe at home, huddled around the television.
Old man walking through dark and empty streets.	Except for one unfortunate soul who has ventured into the night.

Here the convention is to write the dialogue on the right and to explain the visuals on the left. This format can work well for programmes where words are important, such as the voice-over for a documentary or the dialogue spoken by actors. You can develop this kind of script to include information about camera movement, sound effects and music. If you are using actors, they can have a copy to learn their lines.

USEFUL TIP

If you want to write dialogue for a piece of fiction, then listen to people talking, on buses, in shops or at school. Try to make your own writing natural, as though it were spoken by people you have listened to.

Does the dialogue on TV soaps sound natural? Or does it sound as though it has been written for actors to deliver?

Now you have made a start on the pre-production work, it is time to look at how to go about the production itself.

NOTE TO TEACHERS

It is a good idea at this stage to get students to fill in a production registration sheet. An example of one that can be readily modified for individual centres is given in SEG's own Syllabus Support Material booklet. This has the benefit of focusing students on precisely what they intend to do for the production and how they intend to work. In addition, it provides an opportunity to raise some of the broader issues that will need to be dealt with in the supporting account.

Production skills

It would be impossible in this section to explain to you how to use every piece of equipment available. Not only is there such a wide variety of equipment around, but technology changes so rapidly that the information would be rapidly out-of-date. Instead, here are some general rules and advice on the different bits of technology you might want to use.

Video

Most video cameras have similar features and controls, even though tape formats may be different. One way to learn how to use the equipment is to take out a camera and see what it can do.

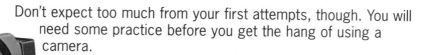

Don't expect too much from your first attempts, though. You will need some practice before you get the hang of using a camera.

First, make sure you are familiar with the basic controls. You will need to know how to:
- Switch the camera on
- Load a tape
- Set the camera to record
- Use the pause button.

It's also a good idea to know how to check that the batteries are OK and that there is enough light for you to film in. Check in the manual or ask someone who has used the equipment before.

Recording Be sure you can tell when the camera is recording. It is very frustrating to set up and film a scene only to discover the camera was not running.

If you want to make your efforts look professional, then you need to try to avoid some of the pitfalls students often fall into when they first try to make films. A very common mistake is to move the camera too much. This may take the form of using the zoom (moving in and out on the subject), panning (moving horizontally to follow the action) and/or moving vertically. Another temptation is to hold the camera by hand and move around after the action.

All of these techniques have their place. Hand-held camera can be very effective in chase sequences, for example. But often the best shot is to hold the camera steady on a tripod and let the action take place within the frame. Watch how professionals use a film or movie camera. You will notice how little movement there actually is.

It is also important to try to get variety into the way you frame your images. In the chapter on language (pages 14–17), we saw how visual narratives are composed of different shots. Here is your chance to look at how you can use different angles and sizes of shot to make your film interesting.

How can you include sound on your film? Video cameras have an integral microphone that will record sound synchronized with the pictures. Sound quality is radically improved, however, if an external microphone is used, especially a directional one. This will allow you to get in close when someone is speaking, cutting out any unnecessary background noise. Don't forget, though:
- Keep the microphone out of shot
- No unnecessary talking when recording is taking place.

If you are intending to edit your video (see pages 219–221), you should also take care to ensure plenty of run-in time before each shot. This means letting the tape in your camera run for, say, ten seconds before any action takes place. This way, when you come to edit, vital action should not be lost. For example, if you want to film someone entering a room, keep the camera running focused on the door for ten seconds before your character walks through it. If you intend to use a professional edit suite, ensuring enough run-in time is essential.

If you are going to be able to edit your work, then you don't have to shoot the film in the sequence in which it will finally appear. Your shooting script, which sets out the order in which scenes are recorded, must be based on the locations you are going to use and the availability of actors and props.

It's always a good idea for one member of the crew to log the scenes you shoot so you know in what order sequences appear on the tape. If one of you has a video recorder that shows timings in minutes and seconds, this can be done when the tape is replayed at home.

The single camera interview. The interviewer must ask their questions twice so that the interview can be edited to look 'natural'.

(a) The 'establishing two shot', which shows the interviewer and interviewee together in a single frame.

(b) Close-up of an interviewee answering a question. Camera is looking over interviewer's shoulder.

(c) The interviewer asks a question or nods in agreement. Camera is now looking over the shoulder of the interviewee.

IN PAIRS

Imagine you want to conduct a short interview on location, for example, outside your school or college. Devise a storyboard showing how you would go about this, bearing in mind you can only use one camera. How will you get shots of the interviewer asking the question? Do you need any shots other than those of the two people involved in the interview?

Editing The editing equipment available to you may vary between a professional edit suite and nothing at all. If the latter is the case, you will need to plan your film very carefully and edit 'in camera'.

EDITING IN CAMERA

Editing in camera needs a lot of careful preparation and planning. You need to storyboard your film precisely and shoot all your scenes in the exact order in which they will appear in the finished film. After that, it is a question of using the pause control on the camera to get a clean cut between each section of the film. Remember, it is possible to tape over the bits you got wrong, but you need to take great care not to erase the bits you got right. The camera's own playback facility is very useful here to show you exactly what you have recorded on to the tape. A pair of headphones will let you hear the sound too.

Even if you can't get your hands on proper editing equipment, it is always possible to link together two standard VHS machines, such as you may have at home, and use the pause facilities to 'crash edit' your footage together (see diagram). Some machines also have an audio dub facility that allows you to replace the existing soundtrack with a voice-over or music. ('Dubbing' is copying from one tape to another.) Some cameras also link to a domestic video recorder to allow editing of tapes.

Editing film by linking two domestic video machines with a scart connector. The signal from the left-hand machine is fed to the second machine, which is used to record, via a scart connector. When putting in an edit, both machines should have the videotape laced up ready over the heads. This way there will be no tear in the picture as the edit 'crashes in' when the pause button on the recording machine is released at the right moment. The instruction manuals of most recorders explain in detail how this arrangement can be set up for their particular model. They also give useful information about audio dubbing and linking up a video camera.

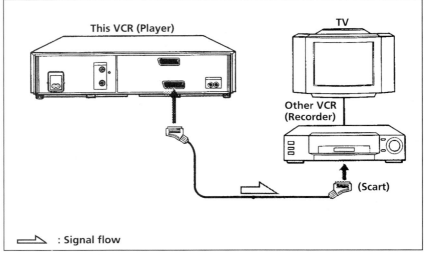

This VCR (Player) — TV — Other VCR (Recorder) — (Scart)

⟶ : Signal flow

A more recent development is the arrival of non-linear technology. Now widely used in the television industry, this technology is becoming increasingly available in homes and educational establishments. A video recorder can be interfaced with a personal computer that is loaded with a special software programme. This then allows a tape to be edited on the computer.

Titles and end credits can help make your video look professional. Some video cameras have a capacity for generating basic titles. It is also possible to link a computer to your editing suite to create titles. If no such technology is available, then you can always make your own captions, either using copy printed from a computer, or simply by writing on a whiteboard and using a camera to record them. If your camera has a switch to create negative images, this can be particularly effective.

Whilst you will want to get the best finish you can for your video, always remember it's the ideas that are important. You will be judged more on your ability to work within the limitations imposed on you by the technology available, than on the professional quality of the end product.

Don't forget that once you have finished editing your video, remove the plastic safety tab to prevent your work from being accidentally wiped. It's also a good idea to have your tape cued at the start of your film, ready to show it.

Radio/sound

You can easily forget radio as a possible medium for a production. It doesn't have the glamour of video. Yet it is a very popular medium, especially with young people, and you don't necessarily need a lot of equipment to make a quality programme. If you are lucky to have a recording or broadcasting studio, then you will be able to produce high-quality work, either as a package, where you record and edit information, or perhaps a live show, using a combination of music and talk to create an interesting piece of radio. Even if you can't get access to a sophisticated studio, it is still possible to create imaginative and lively radio work.

Obviously, you need some means of recording. A basic tape recorder with either an in-built microphone or, better, an external mike, will get you started.

The technology of radio is changing. Traditionally radio journalists have recorded on open reel tape on portable machines and then spliced the tape, literally by cutting out the bits they don't want with a razor blade and sticking the tape together with adhesive tape. More recently, DAT technology (see page 162) has taken over and tapes are edited electronically. This kind of technology is obviously expensive, so most of you will be working with rather less sophisticated equipment.

You can, however, achieve a similar effect by using a twin cassette deck or by hooking up two cassette decks together. By using the pause control on each machine you can transfer the bits you want from one tape to another. If the tape deck is a good one, there will be little loss of quality in the process of dubbing sound from one deck to another.

One problem with sound recording is getting the levels right. This means making sure that the bits you record and join together are all about the same volume. It may be possible on your equipment to monitor the volume through a meter and adjust it accordingly, but you will have to be well organized.

If you can get hold of a mixing desk, this can be really useful. Recording studios use this equipment for making records. What it allows you to do is to put together several different sound sources and to fade up and down the level of each. If you want to put together your own radio show, then a mixer can be used to fade in and out music and speech to give a professional effect.

However you decide to make your radio production, don't forget your audience. Think about what music they might want to hear or what sort of studio guest they might want to listen to. Equally, consider what news and information is important to them. A good radio programme is more than just playing your favourite music.

A simple four-channel mixing desk. The sliders on the desk can be used to control the sound levels going through to the recorder. A radio broadcasting studio is a more complex example of this type of set-up.

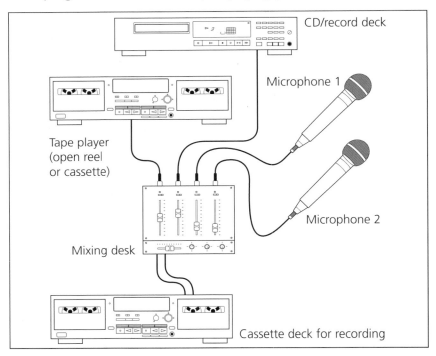

CD/record deck

Microphone 1

Tape player (open reel or cassette)

Microphone 2

Mixing desk

Cassette deck for recording

Newspapers and magazines

Producing a magazine or newspaper allows you to work independently outside class time without having to use technical equipment. Of course, many of you will want to use computer technology to make your finished product, but in the early stages a lot of work can be done without a computer.

Some students get poor marks for this type of work because they simply copy, or even cut and paste, articles and features from existing sources. Inevitably, some of your ideas may link in with items previously published, but if you are to do well you must generate your own ideas to capture the interest of your audience.

of topics, but alternate the size of the images.
The best magazines are likely to challenge some of the
assumptions most frequently made in popular publications. Think,
for example, of some of the issues raised in the chapter on
representation (pages 28–37) and see how you might look for new
ways of presenting ideas and addressing your audience.

If you are able to use a computer for your work, then it is worth
trying to do your layout and design work using software for on-
screen page make up. If you can't do all of the layout on screen, it
may be possible to produce some of the work using a computer
and to complete your page design by more traditional methods.

One way in which you can add originality to your work is to take
your own photographs. Unless you have a darkroom, this is likely
to mean taking photographs with a 35 mm camera and getting
prints done at the local processing shop. You might decide to
organize a fashion shoot, using friends as models, or perhaps take
photographs to illustrate a story or feature article.

Once you have got your prints, you can either cut and paste them
directly onto your page or scan them for use in a page make-up
programme on your computer. Either way, you will probably have to
crop and scale the images. Cropping means selecting the area of
the print you want to use; scaling means deciding the size that will
fit best into your layout.

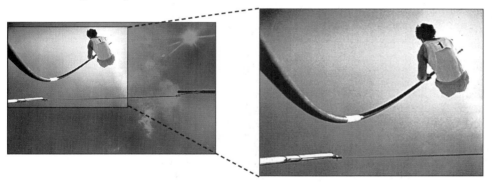

A photo cropped
and scaled up.

Remember, too, the importance of a caption to anchor the
meaning you want to give to your image. Look to see how captions
are used in publications aimed at a similar market.

There are a few simple tips worth keeping in mind if you want to
produce a newspaper or magazine that will be attractive to your
audience:
• Remember that your front page is like a shop window. Be sure
  your best stories are in it. You have less than 20 seconds to
  persuade the average browser to buy it.
• Try to get a mixture of stories – some long, some short, some
  happy, some sad.
• Create variety with your pictures too. Don't just look for a variety

STEADY HANDS

Standing in the right way can stop your hands shaking and ruining the photo. Stand with your feet shoulder-width apart. Keep your elbows close to your sides. Steady the camera by holding it right up to your eye.

COMPOSITION

Put your subject in the middle of the photo or arrange a symmetrical scene. Use the border markers in the viewfinder to make sure that your subject will be in the picture.

ANGLE

The most common camera angle is eye-level. Try crouching down or standing on a chair to get a new angle on a scene. When taking pictures of animals and children, try getting down to their level.

LIGHT

Make sure there is plenty of light. Try to get the light behind you. If it isn't, you may need to use a flash.

SCENERY

Don't just shoot whatever you see. Try including a branch or some leaves or flowers in the foreground to add perspective. Or use a window, door or gate to frame a view.

TRICK PHOTOS

Use your imagination, props and scenery!

PEOPLE

Expressions Expressions make a portrait. Chat with your subject as you shoot, to help them to relax. Ask them to turn their back for a moment, then tell them to face the camera. This will help you to get a natural, unposed look. Keep the background simple. Think about the direction of your subject's movement or gaze, as these create a feeling of depth and movement in a photograph.

Action photos To take action photographs, try to press the shutter just before the highest point of the movement.

Position Where is your subject in the photo? If the girls running in the photo were to the right of the picture, they would seem to be running out of space, whereas showing them to the left makes it seem as if there is lots of room.

- Don't put too much detail in photographs – make sure they are clear. Be sure to have the people in them doing things, not just standing in a line.
- Use features like crosswords, puzzles and comic strips to break up the blocks of text.
- Organize your publication so that people can easily find their way around. Use headlines and pictures as 'signposts' to help them.
- Most important of all – know who your audience is and what they are interested in. Never take them for granted!

Other technologies

We have looked at three popular ways of doing the practical production. The syllabus says that you can use any media format. Such areas as computer games, comics, animation or interactive computer technology are all open to exploration, if you have the relevant skills and interest. Do remember, though, that you are looking at mass media and the codes and conventions under which it operates. That has important implications for the type of production you undertake, particularly in relation to how you define the audience for your product. If you are uncertain, then be sure to check with your teacher that your idea is acceptable and falls within the syllabus. It would be a shame to do a lot of work and then discover that you wouldn't get any marks for it.

The supporting account

You must submit a supporting account along with your practical production. Even if you have worked as part of a team on the production, the account has to be your own individual effort.

Many students think that once they have completed work on their production, it is time to have a rest. Sadly, this is not true. What you write about your production is just as important as the production itself, and in some cases more important.

Writing the account

Basically a supporting account is a written commentary, linked to the work you did on your practical production. It should show some of the thinking behind your practical production. Therefore, it should help to explain how you arrived at your decisions and why the finished product looks or sounds like it does.

The syllabus recommends a length of about 1,000 words and says that in your account you should relate the work on your practical production to the key concepts. To put this another way, you are being asked to show what you have learned about the media from doing your own practical work. This can best be achieved by

I chose Media Studies because I didn't think I would have to write very much!

making connections between your production and the work on the key concepts that you have done in other parts of the course. This is an important skill you need to develop at any level of media education. You are asked specifically to look at the context, audience and purpose of your product.

The syllabus also talks about 'evaluating both the finished product and the chosen medium'. You will often hear the word evaluation used in the context of the supporting account. One thing it means is that you should take the opportunity to stand back and look at what your finished product has achieved. Your job is to decide how far your work is effective for the purpose you intended it. In fact, you are being asked to judge your own work in the way that you have learned to evaluate other mass media products.

You are also asked to evaluate the chosen medium. This means deciding whether the medium you chose, for instance, radio, was right for what you decided to do, or whether it would have been better to have chosen a different medium.

Think what other people might say about what you have produced. In the end, your audience are the people who must decide whether what you have produced is a success or a failure.

> Before starting filming, we looked at some documentaries that had been shown on television earlier in the month. We were particularly interested to see how they captured the viewers' attention in the opening sequence.

> By placing the camera in front of Jason and zooming in, I made it look as though the stranger was much closer to him than he actually was.

Remember that when we were looking at your practical production work, you were asked to make notes on any important research you undertook and decisions you made. You may like to approach this by keeping a diary or log. In this, you would record what you have done at each stage of the process, and, in some cases, evaluate these activities as you do them. This approach is fine as the basis for your supporting account, especially if you are going to use it as a reminder of what you did. It is probably not a good idea, though, to make this the actual account you submit. The danger of this approach is that it simply becomes a description of what you did, or, in many cases, didn't do.

We evaluate media products all the time.

> Today we planned to film the sequences where the students get in to trouble with the teacher. Unfortunately Rachel and Mike were off sick so we couldn't film it.

> Today we had hoped to do the layout work for the article on boys' fashion, but John forgot to bring in the computer disk.

> We did a really good interview with a local shopkeeper about her attitude to the parking ban, but unfortunately the tape broke when we tried to take it out of the recorder.

These three extracts from students' diaries tell us a lot about the students and the others in the group but very little about how media theory related to their production.

The best way to produce a good supporting account may be to organize it under a series of headings, like those used from here to page 231.

Context Where do you think your product belongs? If it is a TV programme, what channel would it go on, and what time of night would it be shown? If you have produced a magazine, who might want to publish it? Is it something that you would find on the shelves of your newsagent's, or is it likely to be sold in a different way, by subscription or on the streets, like *The Big Issue*?

> We had some important decisions to make about how we were going to approach the topic of the shortage of decent recreational facilities in our local town. We considered making an item for the regional news programme which is shown after the national news each evening. We decided, though, that it was not really sufficiently newsworthy for a programme covering such a large area. The local newspaper seemed a better idea.

Some media products have a fairly narrow or local market. A fanzine about up-and-coming bands in your area is a good example. It is still important that you look at the context of the product. How will it be distributed? How will you ensure that your audience gets to see it?

You also need to talk about context even if you have chosen to do just a sequence from or a part of a larger product. For example, trails for films at the cinema or radio advertisements are consumed by audiences within specific contexts.

The work you did in the chapter on media language on codes and conventions (pages 13–14) is important here. Look at your own production and compare it to professional productions that might occupy a similar context. How does it compare? Have you adopted the same conventions or have you chosen a different approach?

Audience You have learned about audiences and why they are important in an earlier chapter (pages 58–75). In your supporting account, audiences are also a key element, especially from the viewpoint of identifying who they are. In this section write about what you found when you did some market research (see page 212).

> I needed to find out if there would be people interested in a fanzine about local bands. A good place to start was the local record shop, where I asked the manager if any of the customers ever asked for a local gig guide or something similar.

What is your audience? Remember that there are often several audiences for a media product. A women's magazine may well have an important secondary audience of male readers. Remember also to think about your audience in terms of gender, age and social and educational background. What assumptions did you make about their expectations?

A women's magazine may well have an important secondary audience of male readers.

How will you reach your audience? Obviously you will need to relate this section to what you have written about the context. Should your audience be offered any additional or follow-up materials, such as a telephone helpline or an information pack? You can mention this, even though you may not have prepared one as part of your product.

Purpose What is your product for? What is its function? You may argue that it has more than one function. If so, then explain what these are. Is it there to entertain, to inform, to provoke debate?

> I was worried that the purpose of the radio programme was not clear. I wanted to get a message across to people about the dangers of drinking and driving, but at the same time I wanted to produce an entertaining show with plenty of music.

Very often the success of your production will depend on a clear sense of its purpose. It may be, however, that the purpose has changed during the production process. What started out as a light-hearted piece, the purpose of which was to entertain, may have turned into something controversial and thought-provoking. You need to explain how this came about. What factors and decisions along the way made it change?

Evaluation In this section you need to look at your production and decide how successful you have been in fulfilling your original intention – how effective your product has been.

It may be that you have market-tested your product. This would have involved showing or playing it to a sample of your audience and getting their reactions. Don't just write, 'Our audience thought it was really good' (even if they did), but try to get some constructive criticism from them by way of specific responses. Was it interesting? Were there bits that went on for too long? All this information should then be included in your supporting account.

> All in all, I think our production was successful. People who saw it, including parents and teachers, found it entertaining and informative. I still feel it is too long, though, but that is perhaps because I have grown bored after seeing it so many times.

You might also like to think how you would improve it. Imagine you have the chance to start again. How would you try to make the end-product different or better?

Self-assessment Another important area you need to look at is yourself. You probably learned a lot about yourself while working on your production. For some of you, it may have sparked off ideas about your career, getting a job or choosing what course you will do next. As part of your account, you may find it useful to answer the following questions:

- Am I good at managing my time? Do I meet deadlines that I set myself or have been set by other people?
- Do I work well unsupervised or do I need someone to tell me what to do and urge me on?
- Am I a good member of a team? Do I contribute well or do I have to be forced to work? Am I good at sharing ideas with other people? Do I get on with other people?
- Do I have to get my own way all the time or am I prepared to compromise?

You might also like to write about the roles you played within the group. For example, if you worked with video, did you like to be in front of the camera? Did you enjoy the technical aspects of the production, such as editing or graphics?

> Our group worked well together. Rebecca wrote down everything we agreed and the names of people who would do things and the date when they should have it finished. This way, if someone didn't pull their weight, everybody knew.

What skills have you learned? These need not just be technical skills, such as using a word processor, but more general skills, such as making appointments over the telephone. Do you feel more confident as a result of doing the production?

However you decide to organize your personal account – and there is no right way or wrong way to do it – remember that it is your opportunity to show what you have learned in the process of your production work. Even if you are not very pleased with the end product and feel your production has been a failure, a good supporting account, looking at what went wrong and how it might be improved next time, can gain you valuable marks in this part of the exam. This is especially true if you have got some good planning materials, such as scripts and bits of research, that you can include with the practical production.

Presenting the account

There is no set format for presenting your supporting account, so you obviously have some freedom to choose a style that is best for you. What is important is that you present it in such a way that it is both attractive and easy to read. If you can use a word processor, then that will help, but writing the account by hand is also acceptable.

To make it easier to read, consider using a series of headings. These will help the reader navigate through the text. You may like to consider some of the headings used above (pages 228–231) as a means of organizing your account.

You can also include diagrams and tables, or even photographs and drawings where these are appropriate, to illustrate a point. For example, you may have made some rough sketches or photographs to show the camera positions for a scene you filmed. These could be included as a part of the explanation of the thinking behind the shot.

Some design work by way of a front cover will also enhance the appearance of the account and provide those of you with a flair for design with the chance to show off your skills.

GCSE Media Studies
Southern Examining Group
Name: Alan Trewartha
Centre: Ryton Comprehensive School

Date: 15th May 1997

Title: A fanzine for local bands
The supporting account

THE ASSIGNMENTS

❛ Candidates are required to submit *three* assignments of equal weighting, up to the equivalent of approximately 3,000 words (in total). ❜

This is Section A of the coursework paper (Paper 1), which is worth 25% of the total marks available for the exam.

This means that your teacher will choose the best three assignments that you have produced in the course of your Media Studies programme. Your teacher will make sure that the three assignments chosen cover all the three assessment objectives (knowledge, analysis and production skills), show knowledge of the four key concepts of language, representation, institutions and audience, and cover at least two different media. The assignments must avoid the topic of the controlled test (see pages 238–246).

The syllabus says *'up to the equivalent* of 3,000 words' because many of the assignments include visual work such as storyboards, or even practical work such as video recordings. Even though these may not include words, the amount of time you have spent producing them will be taken into account and given an equivalent value in terms of word length.

The type of assignment you are given to do will obviously depend on your teacher. Most probably, you will be provided with a sheet of instructions with a list of tasks to be completed, very like the sample assignment shown here. On some occasions, however, it may be more appropriate for your teacher to give you the instructions verbally. Either way, it is important that you make certain that you understand exactly what you are being asked to do. If you are not sure, it is better to ask now, rather than find out when you have already done a lot of work that may be irrelevant.

You will find that much of the work you do for an assignment will allow you to respond in your own individual way. Although you will have to show some knowledge and offer some information, most of the time it is your ability to show your understanding and to think critically that is being tested. In many assignments, you will also need to show that you can be creative and come up with ideas. Your coursework may well provide you with several opportunities to develop your own responses and ideas.

ASSIGNMENT: LOOKING AT NEWSPAPERS

You have been given the front pages of a broadsheet and a tabloid newspaper published on the same day. Look at them and attempt the following tasks:

Task 1

Identify which is the main story on each front page. If both lead with the same story, write a comparison of the two versions, in terms of the content and style of each. If each title has a different lead story, look at each story individually and analyse the difference in content and style between the presentation of the two.

Task 2

Look in detail at the remainder of each page and answer the following questions:
1. What other information is given on these pages?
2. How is it presented in terms of layout?
3. What information is given about the institution that produced the title?
4. What assumptions about the audience does each newspaper make?

Task 3

Write your own story. Possible sources for this might be:
• TV or radio news
• A story in a local newspaper
• An event within the community, school or college
• Teletext news.

Your story must be written in the style of a new tabloid paper aimed at the audience that normally reads the broadsheet.

Now produce a mock-up of the front page of the paper, including a title and other appropriate detail, with your story as the lead.

Working on your assignments

Exactly how you work on an assignment will depend on your teacher. It may be that you will have to complete all of the work in class, perhaps with a time limit for doing it. On other occasions, it may be possible to have a go at some of the tasks in the assignment as homework.

Whatever the circumstances for completing the assignment, you should bear in mind some important principles. Firstly, before you do anything, be sure you have all the essential information you need to undertake the assignment:

- What have you been asked to do?
- How and where are you to do it?
- When must it be finished and handed in?

Secondly, try to get an overview of the tasks to be completed. Decide in which order it is best to do them. Make a note of any information you need to collect or materials you need to find for the work. Make arrangements to get access to any special equipment you need, for example, a camera or tape recorder.

Thirdly, take care in presenting your assignment. Try to organize your material so that you are showing off what you know and what you can do. If you are asked to write down information, that does not mean that you have to write it as an essay. This may not be the best format to adopt if you want to get information across clearly and concisely. Think about how using headings to prioritize the information might help. Try bullet points (as in the list above) or numbers to separate out important points you wish to make.

Where appropriate, you should use coloured pens or pencils and drawing instruments for sketches, diagrams and layouts. Don't forget some of the important skills that you have learned in doing your production work. There are marks to be gained for using these in many of the assignments you will be doing. Make sure that you lay out scripts and storyboards properly, and do design work such as posters and layouts on plain paper.

Remember, though, that the ideas that you are putting forward are the most important things. Drawing skills are less crucial than getting across the ideas you want to communicate. If possible, use a format that allows you to display the skills you feel most confident about. If you like writing, then a script might be more manageable for you than a storyboard, for example.

If your work is clean, neat and presented in such a way that it is easy to follow, you are likely to get a much better mark than if you hand in messy scraps of paper that make little sense. Once you have completed the work, make sure you look after it properly. Don't get it creased and dirty and, above all, don't lose it.

Bear in mind that there are special marks given for spelling, punctuation and grammar as part of the three assignments. So not only will your work look better if you have taken care with this, it will also earn you extra marks.

Finally, before you hand in your work, check it thoroughly. Imagine for a moment that it is your job to mark it (along with a pile of others). Ask yourself if it is easy to read and understand. Are the tasks you have completed clearly separated from one another and labelled? Does it give a good impression of your attitude to your work and the care you have taken? If you can answer yes to all these questions then your work should at least do justice to the effort you have put into it.

Imagine for a moment that it is your job to mark all the assignments...

On your own

Have a look at the assignment on page 234 in which you are asked to work in the medium of newspapers. Think how some of the points mentioned would apply to this assignment if you were asked to do it. For example, how might you use headings in Tasks 1 and 2 to present the information you want to get across? What is the best way to approach Task 3? What resources would you need for this task? It may be helpful to look at the section on the practical production to help you with this (pages 210–225).

When you have completed all your assignment coursework, your teacher will give a total mark out of 75 for the three pieces that are to be submitted for your exam. Remember, this represents a quarter of the marks that are available for the whole exam.

MAKING THE GRADE

Once all your coursework has been marked by your teacher, you will have some idea of how well you have done on Paper 1. However, you need to bear in mind that the mark awarded by your teacher may not be the final mark that you will receive from the exam board.

Each centre (in other words, school or college) has to send off a sample of the work marked by its teachers, to ensure that all centres are marking to exactly the same standard throughout the country. Marks for any candidate may go up or down, therefore, if the exam board feels that an adjustment is necessary.

Your final grade will be a combination of your coursework mark, with any adjustment made by the board, and your mark for the controlled test, which is marked by examiners employed by the board. You will get to know your final grade towards the end of August, along with all your other GCSE results.

14. THE CONTROLLED TEST

> 6 The controlled test ... will take a case study approach based on a topic area set in advance. 9

The controlled test (SEG Paper 2) is worth 50% of the total marks available for the exam. Preparing for it properly and trying your best at the test is obviously important if you want to do well.

What will the test be like? Well, it won't be like a traditional exam where you have to memorize information and sit writing essays or solving mathematical problems for two hours. Instead, the test takes place over a period of time, decided by your teacher, and you will work on it for a number of sessions until you have completed a total of four hours on the test. Many of you will work on the test during normal lessons. You will, however, be working under exam conditions. That means you will have to work in silence, by yourself and not disturb other people taking the test. Nor will you be allowed to take any notes into the room with you. Between each period when you work on the test, your teacher will lock away the work you are doing, which means that you can't do anything to your paper outside of the special times when the test takes place.

NOTE TO TEACHERS

Candidates will be issued with their own copy of the controlled test by the centre at the beginning of May. Arrangements for taking the test vary from centre to centre, but many candidates will find that they will sit the test, for a total of four hours, during normal lesson times in the month of May.

What makes the test most different from a traditional exam, though, is that you will have the chance to see the paper before you actually start taking the test. The paper will be given to you on or soon after 1st May. You can then spend the time before the first test period doing research and preparing for it. Of course, you can also work on ideas for the test in between the times when you are actually sitting it. There is nothing to stop you improving part of the test you have already done, next time you work on it. It therefore makes sense for you to use this time to make sure that you find out as much appropriate information as you can and to work on the ideas and issues that come up in the test.

The topic area for the controlled test is published in the syllabus over two years before the test itself. Each year it is different. Your teacher will obviously do some work on the topic area to prepare you for the test, but you won't be allowed to submit any assignment coursework that covers that particular topic.

The controlled test will, of course, be concerned with the same key concepts that you have read about earlier in this book – the same ones that you have been working on as part of your course, including your coursework assignments. You can take an educated guess, therefore, that the test is likely to cover at least some of the following areas:
• Analysis of texts
• Promotion/marketing
• Institutional background
• Audience
• Media language – forms and conventions
• Representation.

You will also be tested on the 'assessment objectives', which cover:
• Knowledge and understanding
• Analysis and interpretation
• Production skills.

So what does this mean in practice? Well, to some extent it determines the kind of task that you will be given. For example, one possible approach is the 'simulation'. In this you will be asked to play a role, or possibly a number of roles, in order to complete the tasks set. This might involve you undertaking work in a production company, submitting script ideas for a situation comedy, identifying the main elements of the sitcom, suggesting possible settings/characters, designing trailers and presenting ideas for promoting the show. Obviously a wide range of skills is called for here.

It is unlikely that you would be expected to take on the role of a Hollywood film director.

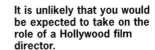

Examiners like to make the roles that you are asked to play realistic, by choosing something that you might reasonably be asked to do at some point early in a career in media production. On some occasions, therefore, a simulation would be inappropriate; the test might then ask direct questions, such as 'What characteristics do you expect to find in the majority of Westerns?'

Preparing for the test

To help you prepare for the controlled test, here is an example.

SOUTHERN EXAMINING GROUP
General Certificate of Secondary Education

MEDIA STUDIES   3380/3PM
(3380)

Higher Tier
Sample Paper 3 (Controlled Test)

Time allowed: 4 hours

The question paper is given to candidates at any time on or after 1 May, before the supervised time during which the answers will be written. Another copy of the questions is provided for use in the Test.

Instructions

Candidates are advised to read all the Tasks before attempting any.

In the 4-hour time test period you will have to attempt all **four** tasks.

Use the Special Answer Booklet provided for your answers.

You may **not** take any of your work into the test.

Information

The topic area examined in this paper is **Action Films**.

The maximum mark for this paper is 105. Mark allocations are shown in brackets.

You will be awarded up to 5 marks for accurate spelling, punctuation and grammar.

Advice

You are recommended to do the Tasks in the order given.

Complete ALL tasks, but read through them all first.

Task 1

(i)   Using examples from films that you have seen, identify what you consider to be the key elements that audiences expect to see in action films.

(ii)   To what extent does a film's commercial success depend on its fulfilling these expectations?
(35 marks)

Task 2

Imagine you have the opportunity to develop your own ideas for a new action film. Produce a short outline of your film to include a title, plot summary and information about the setting and the characters. Explain briefly why your film would appeal to audiences.
(20 marks)

Task 3

(i)   An important element in determining a film's success is how it is marketed. What do you consider to be the most effective methods a film company can use to promote an action film?

Give reasons for your choices.

(ii)   For the film you have outlined in Task 2, produce **one** of the following:

either (a)   The script for an advertisement to be broadcast on local commercial radio stations.

or   (b)   A storyboard for a trailer to be shown at the cinema prior to the film's release.

or   (c)   A full page magazine advertisement.
(25 marks)

Task 4

Several letters have appeared in your local newspaper suggesting that action films encourage violent behaviour in young people. The editor of the paper has asked you to write an article in not more than 800 words covering **two** main areas:

(i)   A simple explanation of how the viewing of films on video and television, and at the cinema, is currently regulated.

(ii)   Your own views of the appropriateness of this system.
(20 marks)

NOTE TO TEACHERS

The current intention is that the test papers from 1999 onwards will be offered in two tiers, foundation and higher. The example shown is from the higher tier. Copies of the foundation level test and marking scheme are available from the Southern Examining Group. Also available is a sample controlled test, complete with marking scheme, on game shows. Copies of the first live test, on the topic of soap operas, are available from the autumn of 1997.

The first thing you should do when you get any exam or test paper is to read it all the way through. This will give you an overview of the paper, so that you can see how the tasks relate to each other, and so that you can work out how you are going to divide up the four hours between the tasks.

An important clue in deciding how much time to spend on each task is the mark scheme. Note in the example that the tasks break down as follows:

Task 1 35 marks
Task 2 20 marks
Task 3 25 marks
Task 4 20 marks.

Rather than simply spending an hour on each question it would obviously make sense to spend more time on the first task, which is worth more than any of the other questions. In fact it is worth 35% of the total mark. As this is just over a third, you should aim to spend about a third of the time available – an hour and 20 minutes – working on this task.

Don't forget that there are an additional five marks for spelling, punctuation and grammar, so do take care over these details.

You will have some time between seeing the test paper and the first session when you start work on it. Use this time intelligently to do some preparatory work. It is a good idea to make some fairly detailed notes: even though you aren't allowed to take notes into the exam room, they are a useful way of helping you both to remember your ideas and to revise between exam sessions.

Planning: firstly, you need to plan how you are going to approach the test. Assuming you have already planned how long to spend on each task, you must now decide in what order to have a go at the tasks. It will probably make a lot of sense to tackle them in the order they appear on the paper. The reason for this is that the tasks may well be related in such a way that you will find it easier to tackle some tasks after you have completed others. For example, in the paper we are looking at, you can see that it would be helpful to have worked through the first task to give you some ideas as a basis for the second and third tasks.

Research: secondly, you need to do some research to help you complete the tasks. Some of the marks are given for knowledge – information that you have learned or found that you use to complete the tasks. In the example, you would need to do some research into action films to help you with the first part. This would include work on genre, narrative, visual style, audience and representation, as they all relate to cinema, video and feature films shown on television. Much of this will be work you have already covered as part of your course. To complete part two of the first task, some information about the production and distribution of films would be useful.

Notice that the last question would involve you in finding out about how films are regulated – how the viewing of them is controlled in the various different viewing contexts, such as the cinema, on video and on TV, both terrestrial and satellite.

Production skills also play an important part in the tasks you are likely to be set in the controlled test. These are worth nearly a third of the total marks available. (Production skills are discussed in more detail on pages 217–225.) Tasks two and three show the sort of work that you are likely to undertake to cover this assessment objective. Developing your skills in writing scripts, drawing storyboards and laying out advertisements and posters are all skills that you need to work on to prepare for the controlled test.

Your drawing skills don't need to be especially good to score marks on the more graphics-based tasks – it is your ideas that are important. A storyboard that shows a good variety of shots, an ability to construct narratives and a capacity for linking visual images to soundtracks is fine, even if you can only use drawings of matchstick people.

When you come to take the test, you will be given a special answer booklet by the examining board. In addition to the standard lined and unlined paper, there will also be special stationery suited to the tasks that you are asked to do. It is a good idea to think in advance how you might make the best use of these.

You will have to hand your work in for the last time after the final session of the test. Before you do so, check it thoroughly for spelling, punctuation and grammar, and make sure that it is logical and clearly signposted, so that when it is marked the examiner will be able to work out easily what you have done and in which order.

Practising the test

It would be a good idea to practise a controlled test before you come to sit the real one – rather like a mock exam. Here are some suggestions for how you might approach the sample test printed on page 240. Why not have a go at working though it now?

Before you begin work, bear in mind that it doesn't matter in which viewing context you have seen or studied action films, whether at the cinema, at home or in the classroom. Be sure you have a clear idea which films can be classified as action films – movies where action, such as car chases, shoot outs, and so on, are an important way of moving the narrative forward. Remember too that you are not limited to contemporary films (ones that are now being shown in the cinema). You may like to use examples of earlier films, such as the Rambo movies of the 1980s.

A — Instruction page

EXEMPLAR COVER of SPECIAL ANSWER BOOKLET for MEDIA STUDIES

Candidate Name

Subject

Component Code

Centre Number	Candidate Number

**Special Answer Booklet for
MEDIA STUDIES**

20 Pages

INSTRUCTIONS TO CANDIDATES

Insert the information required in the spaces above.

Use both sides of the paper.

Do all rough work in this Answer booklet and cross it through without making it illegible. No part of this booklet is to be torn out.

Check that you have inserted the correct information in any Supplementary Sheets which you use.

When you begin a new Task, start on a new page.

INFORMATION

This Special Answer booklet contains four types of page:

pages 2-5:   Storyboard Sheets;
pages 6-9:   Production Sheets;
pages 10-12: Plain Sheets;
pages 13-20: Ruled pages, for specified Tasks and for any rough working.

For each Task, use the type of page which best suits your response.

Task Number	For Examiner's use
1	
2	
3	
4	
SPaG	
Examiner's Initials	

64

SOUTHERN EXAMINING GROUP

A

B — Storyboard sheet

Task number

Page 2

Do not write in this margin

STORYBOARD SHEET
Directions, dialogue, camera, music, special effects (sfx)

B

C — Production sheet

Task number

PRODUCTION SHEET

MEDIA: FILM, TELEVISION OR RADIO

Do not write in this margin

Special instructions: Vision	Special instructions: Sound	Dialogue	Other information: Setting, interior, exterior, action	Timing

Page 7

C

Three pages from the SEG answer booklet:
A The instruction page
B One of the storyboard sheets
C One of the production sheets.
These relate to the specific tasks that you are asked to complete in the controlled test shown on page 240.

Task 1

This is a chance to show off your knowledge and understanding of the genre. You will obviously want to refer to the idea of thrills and adventure, but don't forget the importance of characterization, for example, the way in which male and female characters are represented, and how good and evil traits are often given to characters according to their race and background. You also need to think about the narrative structures, especially their final outcomes, that are common to many films of this type. Setting and historical context also are key elements in action films. Choose examples carefully so that they illustrate the points you are making.

The second part of the question obviously links to some extent with the work you have done on audience. You need to think about the hype that surrounds films when they are released, especially at the cinema, but also when released on video or premiered on TV. This hype often plays on such elements as genre, by comparing the new release to other films of its type. But does it guarantee success? Do audiences want a film that works to a formula, or do they demand something more than that? Does a film have to have original elements to make it successful? Do many sequels succeed, for example?

Task 2

This is an opportunity for you to show off your creative skills. You can respond to it in a number of different ways. You may decide to produce an outline that will be a traditional Hollywood product, with a tough guy hero. You may decide to reverse some of the typical Hollywood stereotypes and create a female lead who is tough and uncompromising in the action sequences. You may look at other possible settings – maybe even the town where you live – to produce your own home-grown British action movie. You may even decide to parody the genre and produce an outline that pokes fun at the conventions of this type of film.

Notice that the question also asks you to explain the attraction of your film to audiences, so it is important that you think about your audience before you start work on the outline. For example, would a film with a strong female character only appeal to female audiences? Would men be put off going to see it?

Task 3

Notice that this task has an either/or section, so don't make the mistake of tackling all parts of it – you won't get any extra marks!

The first part asks you about marketing an action film and invites you to identify the most effective methods of promoting it. Certain obvious possibilities will immediately spring to mind. Don't forget

Genre is used as a marketing ploy in this publicity poster.

some of the less obvious ones, though – stars appearing on chat shows, stories in newspapers, production reports on TV film shows and in movie magazines, and so on. Don't forget, too, that you are expected to give reasons for your choices: you must explain why you think your chosen methods would be the most successful.

The second part of the question gives you chance to do some practical work. You are invited to choose between a script for a radio commercial, a storyboard for a trailer or a magazine advertisement. Your choice may be affected by what you feel you're best at doing, but don't forget that it is the ideas that are important, rather than any special drawing skills you may have.

You can look back to the relevant sections of this book, where we talked about magazine ads, storyboards and writing scripts, for some help with this. It is also worth reminding yourself of how the professionals do it, by looking at trailers at the cinema or on TV, adverts in magazines and radio ads for newly released films.

Task 4

You will need to do some research for this one. You may be able to find out about regulation in books like this one. Other sources of information may be your local cinema and video shop. Magazines listing TV programmes are likely to have some information on how the viewing of films is regulated.

PRODUCTION SHEET

Radio advert for an action film

Special instructions: Vision	Special instructions: Sound	Dialogue	Other information: Setting, interior, exterior, action	Timing
	Tyres squealing and engine noise. Two cars involved in a chase.		Played loudly	
		Voice-over Are you ready for the action film of the year?	Deep male voice, as used in cinema trailers.	10 seconds
	Car chase fades down. The sound of a gun battle fades up.			
		Male actor through megaphone Come out, Walker, you can't escape this time.	Urban siege taking place.	
	Gunfire continues in the background.			25 seconds
		Voice-over No way would he be taken alive unless he could prove his innocence. The story of one man's fight against the odds. A man at war with society.		
	Film soundtrack plays theme tune.			

One way of producing a script of a radio advert for an action film.

You are asked to use all this information to produce an article for your local newspaper. It's a good idea, therefore, to look at the newspaper to see how articles are written, especially in terms of the style of language used and the mode of address adopted. Remember, too, that the article should include your own ideas on the system – is it fair, is it too complicated, does it need changing?

Before you finish

Now it is time to check your work through:
- Have you had a go at all the tasks?
- Is it easy to work out which answer belongs with which task?
- Does it all make sense?
- Is the spelling, punctuation and grammar as accurate as you can get it?

Once you are satisfied that everything is in order, you are ready to hand in your script.

All you can do now is wait, and hope that your result is as good as you expect – or maybe even better!

CONTACTS AND RESOURCES

A number of organizations have built up resources that can be used by teachers as part of the coursework to a syllabus of this type. The **British Film Institute** (21 Stephen Street, London W1P 2LN, tel. 0171 255 1444) produces an extensive range of books, teaching packs and allied resources. **Film Education** (41–2 Berners Street, London W1P 3AA, tel. 0171 637 9932) also organizes events for teachers and students, as well as producing useful study guides and occasional video trailers of films on general release. The **English and Media Centre** (136 Chalton Street, London NW1 1RX, tel. 0171 383 0488) organizes INSET support for teachers and produces stimulating materials for use in class. The **Northern Ireland Media Education Association** (NIMEA, Belvoir Primary School, Belvoir Drive, Belfast BT8 4DL, tel. 01232 491801) offers support to teachers.

Some trade organizations and bodies produce materials that can be used for particular class activities. The **Radio Authority** (Holbrook House, 14 Great Queen Street, London WC2B 5DG, tel. 0171 430 2724) publishes its codes of practice and a quarterly report on complaints it has dealt with. Similarly, the **Press Complaints Commission** (1 Salisbury Square, London EC4Y 8AE, tel. 0171 353 1248) has materials on making a complaint and details of past adjudications. The **British Board of Film Classification** (3 Soho Square, London W1V 6HD, tel. 0171 439 7961) produces a students' guide to film classification. The **Northern Ireland Film Council** (21 Ormeau Avenue, Belfast BT2 8HD, tel 01232 232444) has an education department. The **Newspaper Society** (Bloomsbury House, 74–7 Great Russell Street, London WC1B 3D, tel. 0171 636 7014) is an excellent source of information on all aspects of the industry.

For teachers and students a visit to a media organization can be worth hours of classroom study. There are a number of organizations that welcome pre-booked visits by students, and provide an opportunity for them to undertake structured learning programmes on site. The **Granada Studios Tour** (Water Street, Manchester M60 9EA, tel. 0161 832 9090) offers a tour of the site, including a visit to Coronation Street. The **Museum of the Moving Image** (South Bank, London SE1 8XT, tel. 0171 815 1337) and the **National Museum of Photography**, **Film and Television** (Pictureville, Bradford BD1 1NQ, tel. 01274 727 488) both offer an opportunity for students to explore an interesting range of media-related exhibits and activities.

A number of useful publications are available from the **SEG** (Ewert House, Ewert Place, Oxford OX2 7BR, tel. 01865 554291; from autumn 1997: Stag Hill House, Guildford, Surrey GU2 5XJ, tel. 01483 506506): the syllabus; specimen controlled tests, complete with marking schemes; the Syllabus Support Materials book, containing useful advice, suggestions and coursework exemplars; reading lists; and copies of past papers for the controlled test, complete with marking scheme.

One excellent but under-used resource is the **Teletext** service, which contains a wealth of information not only about TV itself, such as previews, programme guides and viewing figures, but also film information and details of newspaper stories. A guide for teachers on using the service is given in the education section of Teletext on Channel 4.

The **Internet** offers a vast range of resources that can be accessed and used for study. There are scores of web sites that are useful to media students and teachers. One way of finding sites is by using a search engine, such as Alta Vista, Yahoo or Excite. This is a software package that comes up with a list of web sites when you type in a keyword such as 'film' or 'newspapers'. Here are a few sites to get you started (these addresses may change):

The Times: http://the-times.co.uk
PA News: http://pa.press.net/
BBC: http://bbc.co.uk/
Eastenders: http://vnet/users/emmett/ee.html
Coronation Street: http://coronation street.co.uk/
The Archers: http://news:uk.media.radio.archers
MTV: http://mtv.com/main.html
Internet movies database: http://cscf.ac.uk/Movies
Time Out: http://timeout.co.uk

GLOSSARY

Italic text indicates that the word is defined elsewhere in the glossary.

> **KEY**
> F   Film
> M   Music
> P   Print (newspapers and magazines)
> R   Radio
> TV Television and video

Academy ratio [F] The standard frame *Aspect ratio* adopted by Hollywood of 4:3, or 1.33:1, width to height.

Actuality [R] Sound, recorded or transmitted, of real events that are taking place outside the studio, such as an interview.

Advertising ratio [P] The proportion of a newspaper or magazine taken up by adverts, as opposed to stories and pictures.

Advertorial [P] An advertising feature about products, written like a news story and usually accompanied by pictures.

AM (Amplitude modulation) [R] Long and medium wave frequencies on which radio stations are received.

Anamorphic lens [F] A projection lens used to produce *Widescreen* images at the cinema.

Anchor [TV] The presenter of a programme, so-called because he or she holds the show together.

Anchorage [P TV] The use of words in a caption or commentary to hold or limit the meaning of an image.

Animation [F] Method of making drawings or models move on screen, by shooting still images a few frames at a time.

A&R (Artists and repertoire) [M] The department of a music company responsible for discovering new acts and looking after the musicians.

Aspect ratio [F TV] The relationship between the width and height of a film or TV image. See *Academy ratio* and *Widescreen*.

Astra [TV] The satellite positioned at 19.2 degrees east that carries all the Sky channels.

Audience fragmentation [F M P R TV] The identification and splitting off of particular audiences by media producers.

Audience participation [F M P R TV] Getting the audience involved in the media.

Audience positioning [F M P R TV] The relationship between the audience and the media product. How the media tries to determine the response of an audience to its products.

Audio [F M R TV] Sound, either as part of a *Broadcast* or as a *Soundtrack*.

Auteur [F] The author of a film. The person who gives a film its special identity or style.

Autocue [TV] A screen that displays what the presenter has to say during the broadcast.

Back announcement [R] Information about an item given by a presenter after it has been broadcast.

Backlighting [F TV] Lighting placed behind a subject to create a silhouette.

BARB (Broadcasters' Audience Research Board) [TV] The organization that collects and publishes weekly audience figures or ratings.

Best boy [F] The assistant to the *Gaffer*.

Big close-up (BCU) [F TV] A shot that shows the face filling the frame, good for expressing strong emotions.

Bollywood [F] The nickname of the Indian film industry (a mixture of 'Bombay' and 'Hollywood').

Boom [F R TV] A long pole on which a microphone is placed in order to pick up sound.

British Board of Film Classification (BBFC) [F] The organization that issues certificates to films and videos, stating whether they are suitable for children or young people to watch.

Broadcasting Standards Commission [R TV] The organization set up by Parliament to investigate complaints about taste and decency on TV, video and radio.

Broadsheet [P] A newspaper printed on sheets of paper 116.83 x 81.28 cm (46 x 32 inches). See also *Tabloid*.

Bulletin controller [R TV] The person responsible for the film reports and still photographs needed for the broadcast.

Bulletin producer [R TV] The person who makes sure that the bulletins run exactly to time.

Bulletin script [TV] A typed script of the words that appear on the *Autocue*, along with other information about the bulletin.

By-line [P] Information giving the name of the person who wrote an article.

Camera script [F TV] A script on which camera angles and shots have been planned.

Cardioid [F R TV] A radio that picks up sound from directly in front and to the sides.

Cart machine [R] A machine that records and plays short sound recordings such as *Jingles* and *Trails*.

Cassette tape [R] A tape system in which the tape is enclosed in a plastic cover and played on a cassette player.

Catch-line [P R] A word used to identify a story.

Cathode ray tube [TV] A tube in a TV set that produces the picture on screen.

CB radio (Citizen's band radio) [R] System used by amateurs to communicate with each other.

CD (Compact disc) [M R TV] Musical or video recording in digital form impressed onto a plastic disc.

CD-ROM (Compact Disc-Read Only Memory) Information in the form of video, sound or text, stored on a CD that is read by a computer using a laser.

Censorship [F M P R TV] The control of what the media reproduces by governments or other agencies, on either moral or political grounds.

Channel [TV] A fixed band of frequencies on which transmission can be made.

Chief sub-editor [P] A senior journalist with design and layout skills. He or she decides which stories will go on each *Page scheme*.

Chroma key [TV] A device that allows an image to be filmed in front of a background that has been produced elsewhere.

CinemaScope [F] A *Widescreen* film image.

Cinerama [F] A *Widescreen* process using three projectors to produce an image on a curved screen.

Circulation [P] The number of copies that a newspaper or magazine sells.

Clapperboard [F TV] A board on which details of each *Take* are given, and which is clapped in order to synchronize sound and vision.

Classified adverts [P] Small adverts in columns, arranged into categories, e.g. Situations Vacant, usually placed in newspapers by individuals.

Cliff-hanger [P R TV] A situation that keeps the audience guessing what will happen in the next episode of a programme or story.

Close-up (CU) [F TV] A shot in which only a subject's head and shoulders are shown.

Colour separation [P] A printing process where pages are printed using only four colours: black, yellow, red (or magenta) and blue (or cyan). All the colours needed to produce a full-colour photograph are made by mixing different sized dots of these four basic colours.

Code [F M P R TV] An element or convention through which the media communicates meaning to us because we have learned how to read it.

Community radio [R] A station serving a small community, e.g. a university campus.

Connotation [F P R TV] The secondary, associated or additional meaning that a *Sign* carries in addition to its everyday meaning. See also *Denotation*.

Context [F M P R TV] Where we consume media products.

Continuity [F TV] Ensuring that each shot in a film or TV programme has details that match.

Convention [F M P R TV] The accepted, or apparently natural, way of constructing a media text, which familiarity will have made an audience come to expect.

Copy [P] 1. A story written by a journalist. 2. Words written by an advertising agency to sell a product.

Crane [F TV] A shot from above, using a device of the same name.

Crash edit [TV] Editing video footage on domestic VHS machines by using the pause facilities.

Credits [F M R TV] Details of the people involved in the making of the media product.

Crop [P] To cut down a photographic image, usually to get rid of unwanted detail.

Crosshead [P] A word used to separate paragraphs in a newspaper or magazine story.

Cross-over artist [M] An artist who appeals to music consumers of several different types.

Cue [R TV] To find the beginning of a piece of music, film or tape and prepare it for transmission.

Cue sheet [R] An introduction to a *Package*, which is written by the reporter for the presenter of a radio programme to read out.

Cut 1. [F TV] An edit in which two segments are joined together by simply switching from one to the other. 2. [F] The edited version of a film. 3. [P] To reduce the length of a story.

Cut-away [F TV] A shot inserted into a scene that shows action taking place somewhere else.

DAT (Digital audio tape) [M R] Tape used to store *Digital recordings* of a high quality.

Deep focus [F] A cinematic technique whereby objects are kept in focus in both foreground and background.

Delay system [R] A system to prevent obscenities being broadcast on live radio, by delaying transmission by several seconds.

Denotation [F M P R TV] The everyday or commonsense meaning of a *Sign*. See also *Connotation*.

Depth of field [F TV] The distance in an image over which images remain in sharp focus.

Desk-top publishing (DTP) [P] Software packages that enable print publications of a professional quality to be designed on a personal computer.

Digital broadcasting [R TV] A technique of transmitting signals digitally to produce better reception and to allow greater use of capacity by transmitters.

Digital recording [M] A form of recording that changes sound into a signal of on and off electrical impulses. It produces better sound quality than traditional recording techniques.

Direct inputting [P] Using a computer terminal to key in *Copy* ready for subbing and typesetting.

Director [F TV] The person responsible for the artistic interpretation of a film or programme.

Display advert [P] An advert for a product, with

photographs and graphics, that is placed in a newspaper or magazine by a business.

Dissolve [F TV] An editing technique in which one image or scene fades into another.

Dolby [F M R TV] A technique in sound recording that helps cut out background noise and distortion.

Dolby Surround [F R TV] A type of *Surround sound*.

Dolly [F TV] A wheel on which a camera can be mounted to allow it to move around a set.

Double heading [R TV] The use of two presenters on a programme such as a news bulletin.

Dual keying [P] A system in which *Copy* was first typed by a journalist and then typed again into a linotype machine by a compositor.

Dub [R TV] To copy from one tape to another.

Editor 1. [P R TV] The person ultimately responsible for the content of a newspaper, magazine or news programme. 2. [F TV] The person who puts together a film or TV programme from the footage shot.

Elaboration [P] The paragraphs that follow the *Intro* of a story, which tell readers more about it.

E.N.G. (Electronic news gathering) [TV] A report from the scene on video.

Establishing shot [F TV] A shot that shows the characters in a location, to let the audience know where they are and how they are situated.

Establishing two shot See *Two shot*.

Event movie [F] A *Blockbuster* film that is accompanied by a large amount of *Hype*.

Exciter lamp [F] A light in a projector that enables the optical soundtrack to be read.

Exposure [F TV] The amount of light allowed to enter by a camera.

Fade [F TV] An editing technique in which an image disappears gradually, leaving the screen blank.

Fader [R] A slider on a radio desk that alters the volume of a microphone or other sound source.

Fading up [F TV] A technique in which an image slowly appears from a blank screen.

Fanzine [P] A low-budget publication produced by enthusiasts about their particular area of interest, such as a band or a football team.

Feature [P] An article that takes an in-depth look at a topic or issue.

Feature film [F] A full-length film, often the main film, usually fictional.

Feed [R TV] Transmission of a programme or information, usually to or from headquarters.

Feedback 1. [M R TV] A high-pitched sound created by placing a mike too close to a speaker. 2. [P R TV] Responses from an audience about an issue or programme.

Fibre optic [R TV] Transmission of a *Signal* down a thin cable by means of light beams.

Fill [P] A story of no more than one or two paragraphs, used to fill a gap on a page.

Film gauge [F] The size or width of film, e.g. 35 mm or 16 mm.

Final cut [F] The last version of an edited film prior to release. See *Cut*.

First run [F] The first showing of a film, usually in selected London cinemas.

Flashback [F TV] A narrative device in which a character thinks back to a previous event, which is shown on screen.

Flat plan [P] A plan of a magazine that shows every page and what will appear on it.

Floppy disc [P R TV] A means by which information from a computer can be stored in a portable form.

FM (Frequency modulation) [R] A system of transmitting high frequency signals to give good quality sound reproduction.

Focus [F P TV] To make sure that the important images are sharp.

Focus puller [F] An assistant camera operator, part of whose job is to operate the focus on the camera.

Footage [F TV] Film or video tape that has been shot.

Footprint [R TV] The area over which a satellite transmission can be received.

Format [R TV] The way in which a programme is put together or constructed, e.g. as a studio discussion.

Fps (Frames per second) [F] The unit of measurement of the speed at which a film is projected or shot.

Fragmentation [F M P R TV] See *Market fragmentation* and *Audience fragmentation*.

Frame [F TV] The way the camera is used to place an image within its field of view.

Freeze-frame [F TV] Stopping the action and creating a still image, e.g. when athletes cross the winning line.

Frequency [R] The position on the dial of a radio station on a scale that uses units called hertz to measure the cycles per second at which the station is broadcast.

Gaffer [F] The person in charge of the electrics and lighting on a film set.

Gap in the market [F M P R TV] An area that is not catered for by any products. See also *Market saturation*.

Gate [F] The part of a camera or projector in front of the lens, through which the film passes.

Gauge [F] The size or width of celluloid on which a film is shot, e.g. 35 mm.

General release [F] The *Exhibition* of a film that is shown in cinemas across the country.

Generation [TV] The number of times a tape has been copied.

Genre [F M P R TV] The type or category of a film, programme or other media text. See *Sub-genre*.

Gold (Classic gold) [R TV] A type of broadcast in which music or programmes from a previous era are featured.

Grip [F] Stagehand. See also *Key grip*.

Gross [F] The total revenue of a film from *Box office* and *Spin-offs*.

Hammocking [TV] Placing a new or less appealing programme between two successful shows in order to attract an audience.

Hand-held [F TV] Using a camera without a tripod.

Hard news [P R TV] News that is important and needs to be reported immediately.

High angle [F TV] A shot taken from above a subject.

Highlight [R TV] Part of an event or programme considered worthy of special attention, e.g. highlights of a football match.

Home pages Documents containing information on the Internet.

Hot-metal printing [P] A kind of printing that was used until the 1960s. Ink was placed onto movable metal type and newsprint was then run over the top of the plates.

Hypodermic model [F M P R TV] The idea that the media injects its consumers with the messages and meanings it chooses and that the audience has no real power to resist.

Ideal viewer/reader [F M P R TV] Someone who is typical of the audience for a particular product.

Ident [R] The identity of a radio station, established, for example, by the use of *Jingles*.

Image [TV P] A visual representation of something.

Image analysis [F M P TV] The study of how images are put together, and how the audience takes meaning from them.

Index [F M P R TV] A sign that works by having a link with the concept it represents, e.g. a thermometer is often shown to imply extreme heat or cold.

Industry [F M P R TV] The organization that produces media products, e.g. a Hollywood studio or a newspaper proprietor.

Insert [F TV] A shot that is put into a sequence to give a more complete view of what is going on, e.g. someone's reaction to an event or comment.

Institution [F M P R TV] An organization that produces media products. It has a system of values, usually apparent in the way in which texts are produced.

Intercut (Cross cut) [F R TV] To present action from two different scenes by shifting from one to the other, to suggest they are happening simultaneously.

Internet A world-wide system of communication between individuals through the use of personal computers.

Intro [P] The first paragraph of a story.

Iris [F TV] A device on a camera that determines how much light passes through the lens.

Item [R TV] A single news story in a bulletin.

Jump cut [F TV] An edit in which action appears to jump in an illogical way.

Key grip [F] Person in charge of the *Grips*.

Key light [F TV] The main light used to illuminate a scene.

Laserdisc [F TV] A high-quality means of reproducing a film on a TV screen, whereby video and sound signals are encoded on reflective discs and read by a laser.

Leader 1. [R] The beginning of a piece of recording tape. 2. [P] The main editorial in a broadsheet newspaper.

Letterbox [TV] A technique whereby *Widescreen* films are shown on TV, leaving black spaces at the top and bottom of the screen.

Libel [F P R TV] A law aimed at preventing false and damaging statements about people being published in a permanent form in print and broadcast products.

Library shot [TV] Footage shot by a TV crew, which is then stored in a library to be used as illustration for a news or current affairs story.

Linotype [P] A machine used for composing blocks of text in newspapers, magazines and books.

Lip mike [R TV] A microphone that is held close to the lips to cut out most of the background noise, e.g. at a football match.

Lip sync [F TV] Keeping the sound and the movement of the actors' lips in time with one another.

Live action [F TV] Film or television that involves people as opposed to *Animation*.

Long shot [F TV] A shot that shows the characters in the distance, with details of their surroundings, before they are seen in *Close-up*.

Macro lens [F TV] A lens that allows very close-up detail.

Market fragmentation [F M P R TV] The breaking down of the market for media products into small units.

Market saturation [F M P R TV] When a particular part of the market is seen to be completely catered for by products. See also *Gap in the market*.

Masthead [P] The title of a newspaper on the front page.

Media language [F M P R TV] The means by which the media communicates to us and the forms and conventions by which it does so.

Media text [F M P R TV] Any product of the media designed to be consumed by an audience.

Mediation [F P R TV] The process by which the media represents an event or issue, by intervening and selecting information for the audience.

Medium shot (MS) [F TV] A shot between *Close-up* and *Long shot* that gives the character and the surrounding roughly equal amounts of the frame.

Megahertz [R] A measurement of wavelength that stands for one million cycles per second.

Minority audience [F M P R TV] A small audience with an interest in a subject not regarded as popular or widespread.

Mix [F M R TV] To put together sound or images from different sources, e.g. the visuals on a TV programme or the sounds on a record. See also *Remixing*.

Monitor [F TV] A TV that allows someone to watch action that is being recorded on screen, to ensure that it looks as it should.

Mono (Monaural, monophonic) [R TV] Sound that is produced through just one channel or speaker. See also *Stereo*.

Montage [F P TV] The putting together of visual images to form a sequence.

Multi-media Computer technology that allows text, sound, graphic and video images to be combined into one programme.

Multiplex [F] A cinema with several screens.

Nag (News at a glance) [P] A short summary that gives the main points of the news.

Nagra [F] A sound recording machine used in film-making.

Narrative [F M P R TV] The telling of a story or unfolding of a plot that is common to most media texts.

Narrative code [F P R TV] A way of describing the conventions or elements that the audience has come to expect to be included in a story.

Narrowcast [P R TV] Sending a message or information to a small and defined audience, as opposed to broadcasting to a mass audience.

Needle-time [M R] The time used in playing records that a radio station must pay for.

Negative [F P] An image that has been shot on to film from which a *Print* or *Positive* is taken.

News agency [P R TV] A private company that sells stories to the news media. See *Wire Service*.

News agenda [P R TV] A list, made by the *News editor*, of stories that should be followed up.

News bulletin [R TV] A short summary of the current main news stories.

News editor [P R TV] Person who assesses the value of news coming in and gives it to reporters.

News list [P R TV] A list with information on events and stories.

News sense [P R TV] A word used by journalists to describe a gut feeling about what makes a good story that will interest readers.

News values [P R TV] Factors that influence whether a story will be selected for coverage.

Nib (News in brief) [P] A one- or two-paragraph story that gives only the basic facts.

NICAM stereo (Near-Instantaneous Companding System) [TV] A technique that allows TVs to broadcast programmes in *Stereo* sound.

Nine-o'clock watershed [TV] An agreement not to show explicit sex or violence before 9.00 pm, so that parents will know that it is safe to allow their children to watch TV before this time.

OB (Outside broadcast) [R TV] A broadcast from outside the studio, usually of an important news or sporting event.

Offset [P] A system of printing in which the image is transferred to a roller before being printed on to the newsprint itself.

Optical soundtrack [F] A way of putting sound on to a film print so that it can be read by a photoelectric cell.

Out-take [F TV] A scene that is unusable because of technical problems or errors in it.

Overexpose [F] To allow too much light on to a film, spoiling the image.

Package [R TV] A pre-recorded news item or feature provided by a reporter for a programme.

Page lead [P] The main story on a newspaper page, usually the longest story with the biggest headline.

Page scheme [P] A plan of the news pages, drawn up by the advertising department to show where the adverts that have been sold on the page are placed.

Pan and scan [F TV] Technique of selecting part of a *Widescreen* image to make it fit onto a standard TV screen.

Pan shot [F TV] A shot in which the camera moves horizontally, either following a piece of action or shifting across from one image to another, as though making a survey of a scene.

Parallel action [F TV] A technique in which the action is edited to show two separate events taking place at the same time.

Pay-per-view [TV] A system used by subscription channels in which the audience pays to see specific programmes, such as films or sport.

Phototypesetting [P] A technique in which stories are typed on computers and then printed onto bromide paper. This paper is then cut to size and pasted onto page plans, which are photographed.

Pirate radio (Free radio) [R] Stations that are not licensed.

Playlist [M R] A list of records that the radio station is committed to playing.

Point-of-view shot [F TV] A shot that shows the audience exactly what a particular character sees.

Positive [F P] Photographic image or film that has the colours and tones of the original.

Post-production [F TV] The editing of a film or TV programme.

Pre-production [F TV] The planning stage of a film or TV programme.

Press Association (PA) [P R TV] An agency that supplies news to organizations such as newspapers.

Prime time [TV] Peak viewing time, usually the evening.

Print [F] A *Positive* copy of a film.

Producer 1. [F TV] The person responsible for initiating, organizing and financing a venture. 2. [R] The person responsible for the production of a radio programme. 3. [M] Someone who oversees a recording in the recording studio and gives it a particular 'feel'.

Product placement [F TV] A form of *Sponsorship* in which advertisers pay the producers of films to have characters use their products.

Profit margin [F M P R TV] The difference between what a media product costs to produce and what it costs to buy.

PRS (Performing Rights Society) [M] Organization that looks after the interests of musicians and artists and collects royalties for work that is broadcast.

Public service broadcasting (PSB) [R TV] Broadcasting that is funded by the taxpayer, as opposed to commercial broadcasting, which relies on advertising revenue.

Qualitative data [F M P R TV] Information on people's opinions about media products, e.g. whether they like them and why.

Quantitative data [F M P R TV] Information in the form of numbers, such as how many people watched a particular programme or read a specific magazine.

Quintrophonic sound [F] Sound system amplified through five speakers, three in front of the audience and two behind them.

Rate card [P] A list of the advertising fees charged by the publication.

Ratings [R TV] The number of viewers or listeners that a programme attracts.

RDS (Radio Data System) [R] A tuning system that allows the station that is playing on a radio to be identified by showing its name on a digital display.

Reaction shot [F TV] An image showing a character's response to a piece of action or dialogue.

Reader [F M P R TV] A member of the audience, especially someone who is actively responding to the *Media text*.

Rear projection [F] A technique of filming an image projected behind another image to suggest that action is happening on location.

Reel-to-reel [R] An open-reel tape recorder/player, as opposed to a cassette player.

Remixing [M] Combining the separate tracks of a recording in a different way to produce a different sound to the original *Mix*.

Representation [F M P R TV] The act of communicating by using symbols to stand for things.

Rolling news station [TV] A channel that broadcasts nothing but news 24 hours a day.

Rotary press [P] A means of printing newspapers and magazines by using a cylindrical drum.

Royalties [M] Fees paid to an artist if one of their songs is broadcast or recorded by another artist.

Running order [R TV] A sheet that lists each news item in the order in which it will appear in the *Broadcast*.

Run-of-paper advertising [P] An advert in a newspaper, whose position is left up to the newspaper.

Rushes [F] The film shot in one day.

Sampling [M] A technique in which sounds from existing recordings are used to make new ones.

Satellite broadcasting [TV] The use of satellites to bounce a signal back to earth to be received by a dish.

Scale [P] To reduce the size of an image without cutting out any detail.

Scan [P] To make an electronic copy of an image.

Screenplay [F] The script for a film.

Serial drama [TV] The technical name for *Soap opera*.

Sexism [F M P R TV] Prejudice against a person based on their gender.

SFX [F TV] Special effects or devices used to create particular visual illusions, e.g. battles in space or animated characters talking to actors.

Short 1. [F] A film of less than feature length. 2. [P] A story usually between three and eight paragraphs in length.

Shot [TV] A single image taken by a camera. See also *Long shot*, *Medium shot*, *Close-up*, *Big close-up*, *Point-of-view shot*, *Pan shot* and *Zoom*.

Showcase concert [M] A gig intended to show record companies the quality of a band.

Shutter [F TV] A mechanism that opens and closes as film moves behind the camera's lens.

Sign [F M P R TV] A word or image that is used to represent an object or idea.

Signal [R TV] An electronically coded message that is sent out from a source, such as a radio transmitter, to be picked up by a receiver, such as a radio.

Sitcom [TV] A *Genre* of programme that relies for its comedy on a particular situation, e.g. students living together in a flat.

Slide [TV] A still photograph of a person, symbol or scene.

Slot [R TV] A time period on a TV or radio schedule.

Soap opera [R TV] A *Serial drama* that is broadcast in frequent episodes.

Soft focus [F TV] The device of shooting the subject a little out of focus to create a specific effect, usually to do with nostalgia, an attractive female star or dreams.

Soundbite [R TV] A phrase that is memorable and can be easily absorbed into a news report. Much favoured by politicians.

Sound effects [F R TV] Additional sounds other than dialogue or music, designed to add atmosphere and realism to a piece.

Sound engineer [M] A technician who sets up and operates the recording studio.

Soundtrack [F TV] The *Audio*, as opposed to the visual, element of a film or programme, which is usually a mix of dialogue, music and effects.

Splash [P] The main story on the front page of a

newspaper or magazine.

Splice [F R] To join two pieces of film or tape.

Split screen [F TV] A technique in which two or more images are shown at once on the screen.

Sponsorship [F M P R TV] A form of advertising in which advertisers pay to have their name shown or read in association with a media product.

Staff writer [P] A journalist who is employed to work on one particular newspaper or magazine.

Steadicam [F TV] A device that allows a camera operator to move with the camera without jolting or shaking it.

Stereo (Stereophonic) [F R TV] Sound reproduction simultaneously through two separate channels. See also *Mono*.

Stereotyping [F P R TV] Representation of people or groups of people by a few characteristics.

Still [F TV] A static image.

Storyboard [F TV] A mock-up of how a sequence will look when it has been filmed.

Style mag [P] A magazine dealing with fashion in things such as dress, interior design or motoring.

Sub-editor [P] A person responsible for checking a journalist's copy, deciding its position in a newspaper or magazine and designing the page on which it is to appear.

Sub-genre [F M P R TV] A *Genre* within a genre.

Support [P] Usually the second longest story on a newspaper page, 'supporting' the main story.

Surround sound [F R TV] A technique using a number of speakers to improve the sound quality of films and radio and TV programmes.

Sync [F TV] When sound and image are linked properly together in time.

Tabloid [P] A newspaper half the size of a *Broadsheet*, with pages measuring 58.42 x 40.64 cm (23 x 16 inches).

Tail [R] The end of a piece of tape.

Take [F TV] A single recording or filming of a scene. Several takes may be needed to get the scene right.

Talkback [R TV] A system of communication used off-air between the studio and the production team.

Talking head [TV] A shot of a person talking to the camera.

Technical code [F M P R TV] The conventions of producing a media text that are determined by the equipment used and what it is capable of doing, e.g. different camera angles or zooms.

Teletext [TV] A film and information service broadcast as a separate signal on TV channels, which can be received by a TV set with a special decoder.

Terrestrial television [TV] Television stations whose signals are transmitted and received without the use of satellite technology.

Tilt [F TV] Camera movement in a vertical direction.

Time lapse [F TV] A technique of filming single frames of action at delayed intervals and replaying them at normal speed, to speed up dramatically an action or event.

Track [F TV] To move the camera alongside a piece of action.

Trail/trailer [F R TV] An edited version of a film or programme designed to interest an audience in the text itself.

Transmission area [R] The part of the country to which a radio station broadcasts.

Transponder [R TV] An individual channel of communication from a satellite.

Travelogue [R TV] A programme about travel.

Treatment [F TV] A preliminary script showing how a film or programme might be put together.

Two shot/Establishing two shot [TV] A shot in which two people are shown in the frame together, often used as an *Establishing shot* at the opening of an interview or some dialogue.

Typography [P] 1. The design of lettering in printing. 2. The process of setting type.

Underground [F P] An alternative publication or film, which often attacks or ridicules the mainstream.

Unidirectional [F R TV] A microphone that picks up sound from the direction in which it is pointed.

Uses and gratifications approach [F M P R TV] The study of how people use media products and what they get out of them.

VCR [TV] Video cassette recorder.

VHS (Video home system) [TV] The standard system used for domestic video recording.

Viewfinder [F TV] The part of a camera in which the operator can see and frame an image.

Vision mixer [TV] Equipment for linking together two camera images on the screen.

Voice-over [F TV] Off-screen voice that usually tells the story, explains the action, or comments on it .

VOX pop [R TV] A collection of comments from members of the public.

Web site A publication on the *Internet*, named after the World Wide Web, which organizes the information.

Whip pan [F] A very fast movement of the camera along a horizontal plane.

Widescreen [F TV] An *Aspect ratio* in which the width of the image is much greater than its height.

Wildtrack [F R TV] A recording of background or atmospheric noise that can be used at the editing stage.

Wipe [F TV] An edit in which one image moves across the screen to replace another by apparently wiping it off.

Wire service [P R TV] A *News agency* that provides national and international news to a media organization.

Zoo format [R] A radio programme that includes other voices besides that of the presenter.

Zoom [F TV] 1. Device on a camera that allows movement towards or away from an image or piece of action. 2. A shot in which the camera zooms in from a *Long shot* to a *Big close-up*.